The Landed Gentry & Aristocracy

of

Kilkenny

Volume 1

Art Kavanagh

2004

The Landed Gentry & Aristocracy

of

Kilkenny

Published by Irish Family Names
11 Emerald Cottages, Grand Canal St., Dublin 4
and Market Square, Bunclody, Co. Wexford, Ireland.

Copyright © Art Kavanagh 2004

All rights reserved. No part of this publication may be reproduced, stored in a retrieval system, or transmitted in any form or by any means, electronic, mechanical, photocopying, recording or otherwise, without the prior permission of the copyright holder.

ISBN 0 9538485 6 6

Coat of Arms by Tomas O'Baoill, Heraldic Artist, The Tower IDA Centre.
Set in Times New Roman 11 pt.

Author's Acknowledgements

The Author is deeply grateful to the following –The Dean and staff of St. Canice's especially Mr. Noel Copley, the staff of Rothe House, the staff of Kilkenny Co. Library, Fiachra Kavanagh for his help with photographs, the various authors mentioned whose works have been acknowledged in the book and the staff of The National Library for their courtesy and patience.

The author would like to thank the following people who have contributed to this book in various ways.
Pat Hegarty and Mount Juliet
Peter Smithwick
Lady Blunden
Lady Langrishe
Sir Philip Blunden
Dermot S. L. Butler
Bru Bellew
Julia Crampton
Simon Loftus
Richard St. George
Mrs. Wright
Mary Moran
Anthony Malcomson
Seamus Costelloe
Michael Dwyer
Kieran White
Turtle Bunbury
John Kirwan
Guy Loftus
Melo Lenox Conyngham

The Main Entrance Gate at Bessborough
(courtesy College Books)

A St. George Residence – possibly Kilrush

Contents

Preface	vi
Illustrations	vii
Agar of Gowran	1
Blunden of Castle Blunden	15
Bryan of Jenkinstown	25
Butler (Lords Carrick)	38
Butler of Maidenhall	50
Butler (Lords Mountgarret)	60
Butler (Earls of Ormonde)	75
Cuffe (Lords Desart)	93
De Montmorency	115
Flood of Farmley	126
Langrishe of Knocktopher	134
Loftus of Mount Loftus	146
McCalmont of Mount Juliet	163
Ponsonby (Earls of Bessborough)	168
Power of Kilfane	183
Smithwick of Kilcreene	193
St. George of Freshford	202
Wandesforde of Castlecomer	216
Index	229

Preface

> What matter that at different times
> Our fathers won the sod
> What matter if at different shrines
> We pray to the one God
> In fortune and in fame we're bound
> By links as strong as steel
> And neither shall be safe or sound
> But in the other's weal
> (*Thomas Davis*)

The story of Kilkenny is inextricably linked to the history of the Butlers, a family that stamped its mark not alone on Kilkenny but on the entire south east of Ireland. Today Kilkenny Castle stands as a monument to this remarkable family and Kilkenny city owes its existence to them. What was probably one of the most extraordinary facets of the Butlers was the fact that they were most prolific and their many sub branches included the Butlers of Mountgarret, the Butlers of Dunboyne, the Butlers of Carrick and numerous less well known branches such as the Butlers of Maidenhall. The fact that they managed to survive the Cromwellian carve up of Catholic lands is a tribute to their tenacity and intelligence.

The various Cromwellian families that settled in Kilkenny did so at the expense of families that were less powerful such as the Shees, the Rothes and the Shortalls and the remnants of the Gaelic families such as the FitzPatricks. Many of these new families such as the Agars of Gowran, the Ponsonbys of Pilltown and the Wandesfordes of Castlecomer left indelible marks in their areas and many fine golf courses and parks exist today because of their industry. The legacy of beautiful houses and well maintained demesnes has all but been lost. Fortunately enough remain to ensure the continuity of settlement so vital to our understanding of history.

Other families to emerge such as the Smithwicks, the Bryans, the Powers, the Floods and the St. Georges gave Kilkenny many distinguished and talented men and women who contributed to the advancement of mankind not alone in Ireland but in other far flung lands.

List of Illustrations

Gowran Castle	5
Kilmurry	8
Lake at Castle Blunden	16
Castle Blunden	18
The Ice House at Castle Blunden	20
George Bryan	26
Jenkinstown House	29
Naughty Margaret	33
Bryan Hunting Party	35
Lismolin Castle	39
Mount Juliet	43
Maidenhall	51
Hubert Butler	53
Sir Tyrone Guthrie	58
Tyrone Guthrie Centre	58
Mountgarret Castle	62
Ballyragget Castle	69
Nidd Hall	73
Kilkenny Castle	76
Ormonde Effigy	80
Black Tom Butler	83
The Marquess of Ormonde	92
Desart Court	95
Desart Court rear view	98
Stairs at Desart	101
Drawing Room at Desart	106
Ceiling detail at Desart	110
Captin Otway Cuffe	112
Viscount Frankfort	119
Castle Morres	121
Venerable W. de Montmorency	123
Shooting Party at Burnchurch	124
Knocktopher Abbey	136

Hunt at Knocktopher	140
Rev. Sir Hercules Langrishe	141
Pingo in uniform	144
Lady Langrishe	145
Adam Loftus	148
The Hon. Sir Nicholas Loftus	152
Sir Edward Loftus	153
Sir Nicholas Loftus	155
Edward Loftus	157
Mary Murphy (nee Loftus)	158
Mount Loftus	161
Lady Helen McCalmont	166
The McCalmont Rolls Royce	167
Bessborough House	173
Lady Elizabeth Conyngham	175
Lady Caroline Lamb	177
The Club House Hotel	187
The Residency at Lucknow	189
Sir John Power	190
Kilcreene Lodge	194
Smithwick Gravestone	196
Kilcreene House	199
Hatley St. George	204
Richard St. George	207
Woodsgift	209
Mrs. St. George	213
Castlecomer House	220
The Hunt at Castlecomer	226

Agars (Lords Clifden) of Gowran

When James Agar chose to challenge Henry Flood, the famous Kilkenny politician to a duel, little did he know he was signing his own death warrant.

James was the second son of James Agar (d.1733) of Gowran Castle (grandfather of the 1st Viscount Clifden, another James Agar, elevated to that creation in 1781).

The Agars were ambitious people and when the Callan property of the Cuffes, Earls of Desart, with its rights and privileges, came on the market in 1765 James Agar promptly bought it up[1]. One of the reasons for the purchase was to get the parliamentary representation which normally belonged to the Lord of the Manor. As the purchaser of the rights of the Ormondes (via the Cuffes) James Agar junior became the de facto Lord of the Manor. His father James senior had represented

---

[1] He paid over £17,000 for the estate, most of which was borrowed. - Malcomson – *Archbishop Charles Agar*

Agar of Gowran

Callan from 1715-1727. At this stage the Flood family had come upon the scene. They settled near Callan and acquired the seat by the manipulative methods usual at the time – bribery, blackmail and coercion. This led to animosity between the families of Agar and Flood. Another bone of contention was the rejection of Ellis Agar by Warden Flood in 1725, in favour of a love match with a London lady. Prompted by his sister, the jilted Ellis, now Countess Brandon, James Agar decided to concentrate his energies on winning control of Callan.

But unfortunately for James his opponent was the young Henry Flood, an energetic and able politician who succeeded his father, Warden Flood, as the M.P. for Callan in 1762.

James Agar, now a man in his mid fifties, worked assiduously to gain control over the borough, which at the time had a Corporation. By 1768 he had managed to win over half of the voters.[2] Henry Flood controlled the other half. Whoever controlled the borough controlled the election of the Sovereign and that election was due to happen in October, so it was vital for both men to gain control.

The crucial time arrived and the date set for the election of the sovereign of Callan was to take place on the 29th of that month.

Disastrously for Agar, as it transpired, fate seemed to gift him with a winning hand. A man called Knapp, a tenant of the Floods at Burnchurch, sent his wife to see Agar at the Red Lion Inn, in Kilkenny the day before the election. As a member of the Corporation he had a vote and he offered to cast his vote in favour of Agar in return for being given money and a farm on the Agar estate. In addition Knapp requested James Agar to go to Burnchurch and give him his personal guarantee. Agar, who was not in good health and who felt that he was being set up, declined but sent the landlord of the Red Lion back to Burnchurch with Mrs. Knapp to give the assurance. They travelled in Agar's coach and the landlord, Keogh, also brought Agar's pistols with him in case of any trouble arising.

The sight of Agar's coach immediately alerted Flood's supporters to the fact that something was afoot. When it arrived in Burnchurch the coach was attacked. Keogh fired the pistols in the air and fled, leaving the weapons behind. Mrs. Knapp ran for the safety of her home. The coach was destroyed, the young driver assaulted and the pistols stolen.

When the election was held the next day Knapp voted for Flood's nominee and so the control of the borough was secured for Flood. Agar accused Flood and his supporters of trying to entice him to go to Burnchurch with the intention of murdering him there. He also wrote to Flood demanding the return of his pistols.

---

[2] James started a weaving industry in Callan shortly after his purchase of the lands there and thereby improved his popularity ratings. Some at least of the workers there were Huguenots.

Flood asserted that he knew nothing of the pistols. Agar persisted over the course of the next number of months but to no avail. Eventually on the 22nd August 1769 he sent Richard Rothe of Mountroth with a message to return the pistols or 'meet him'. Flood continued to deny his involvement in the loss of the pistols and it was then arranged that they would meet at the Triangle Field in Dunmore.

They met in the afternoon of the 25th August. Rothe acted as Agar's second and Gervase Parker Bushe acted for Flood. Bushe measured the twelve paces and both men took their stance. When the order was given to fire Agar shot first but missed his target. Flood had delayed his shot as he was in the act of taking a pinch of snuff. Agar took his second pistol and then shouted at Flood to fire. The shot was fatal and Agar fell mortally wounded. It was said that Flood was distraught when he stood over the dying man. He then rode off to get medical assistance but Agar died a short time later[3].

Flood was arrested and tried for murder, but as in most cases of that kind at the time, he was acquitted.

The origins of the Agar family according to Malcomson in his book about Archbishop Charles Agar were somewhat obscure. The first of the family in Ireland was a Charles Agar from Yorkshire[4]. He came over to Ireland during the early years of the Cromwellian government and later settled at Gowran.[5] He married Ellis the daughter of the dispossessed Peter Blanchville and claimed the ownership of the Blachville estates in Co. Kilkenny centred on Rathgarvan[6]. However he did not get ownership to those lands but some of them were later purchased by the Agars in succeeding generations. Charles did lease the castle and some lands in the Gowran area from the 2nd Duke of Ormonde.[7] James Agar, his son, made substantial purchases of lands in the first decade of the 18th century, including Rathgarvan.

Charles and Ellis had four children, two sons and two daughters. Elizabeth, the eldest married a Samuel Bradstreet and her daughter Charlotte Bradstreet married the 10th Viscount Mountgarret and that event was significant for the Agars, as the Butlers of Mountgarret were a very high profile family in the county. In the very dangerous times in the 1689-1690 period Charles managed to support the Jacobites

---

[3] *An Affair of Honour* – Michael Barry
[4] It is just possible that the Agars were in Ireland much earlier. Anthony Colclough of Tintern (d. 1584) was married to Clare Agere, daughter of Thomas Agere esq.
[5] Most authorities including Burtchaell agree that Charles Agar was the first of the family to settle in Kilkenny. Burtchaell implied that he was a trooper in Cromwell's army and had very little when he settled in Gowran. Despite this he was able to send both his sons to school in Kilkenny College, so his wife may have provided an ample dowry.
[6] Near Gowran
[7] Malcomson in *Archbishop Charles Agar*

initially and then as the tide turned he was seen as favouring the Williamites[8]. At a meeting of the Corporation of Gowran held in October 1690 the following resolution was passed "It is unanimously agreed upon that King William having honoured this Corporation of Gowran with his presence, riding through the same after the rout of the Boyne, and delivering the rod and mace of said Corporation to Charles Agar, one of our ancient Burgesses, that therefore we elect the said Charles Agar to be our Portrieve in the ensuing year".[9] Charles held other official posts and was sufficiently in funds in 1695 to be able to loan £150 to Kilkenny Corporation to enable them to build the Tholsel.[10] He died the following year.

The very first of the Agar lands were leased and as time progressed and as their finances improved they bought lands eventually building up a profitable estate. Malcomson suggests that it was James Agar, the eldest son who was the acquisitive one. The parcels of land he acquired included some of the Ormonde lands in and around Gowran and a large estate in the Fassadinin area (near Castlecomer) totalling more than 3,800 statute acres[11]. Prior to that he was noted as being the biggest purchaser of forfeited estates in the county. He bought most of the lands of the Butler Viscount Galmoy[12] who had been attainted after the Williamite wars. These lands included the Abbey lands of Graiguenamanagh and totalled over 11,000 acres. This huge purchase left Agar short of ready cash and he had to sell over 800 acres of the estate to Captain Ralph Gore of Barrowmount, Goresbridge. In 1709 James was again ready to buy lands and he bought over 3000 acres from the Hollow Blades Company. These lands were in the Thomastown and Graiguenamanagh areas.[13] He paid over the very large sum of £2,228 for that purchase[14]. Some of the lands in and around Gowran had been in the ownership of James II and as such were forfeited. They were bought by the Hollow Blades Company who sold them on to a Dublin merchant Lewis Chaigneau[15]. He rented some of the lands to a Joseph Bayly and then later sold the lands with Bayly still in situ to James Agar for the huge sum of over £4,000. The amount of land in question was just over 1300 acres. The Agars

---

[8] *The Agars of Gowran* – Mary Moran in Duchas Tullaheerin Journal 1990
[9] Burtchaell
[10] Mary Moran – *The Agars of Gowran*
[11] Ibid.
[12] This was Piers Butler the 3rd Viscount Galmoy who was a Jacobite general.
[13] The Hollow Blades Company was a London based company that speculated in land. They bought over a quarter of a million acres in Ireland from the trustees of forfeited estates in many counties, including Kilkenny and Wexford.
[14] Malcomson quoting a conveyance deed of 23 June 1709.
[15] Chaigneau represented Gowran in Parliament as an M.P. from 1715-53. (Power in *Kilkenny History & Society*) In doing so he was actually acting on behalf of the Agar family.

and Baylys had several disagreements in the ensuing decades over rights of way. Chaigneau sold Gowran Castle and lands (about 1700 acres) to James Agar, who was already the tenant.

Gowran Castle

The Agars eventually gained full control in area. James's final large purchase was the Rower in south east Kilkenny which he bought in 1718. It had formerly been in the possession of Thomas Crawford of New Ross who died in 1707. It included the income from ferry operations across the Barrow at Mountgarret, near New Ross. Other smaller purchases gave him properties in Kilkenny and Waterford cities.[16]

James was also politically active and represented Old Leighlin, Gowran, Callan and St. Canice in turn from 1703 until his death in 1733[17]. By any standards he was an amazing man, blessed with intelligence, foresight and vigour. In his own lifetime he established an estate of some 20,000 acres and launched his family as a de facto gentry family in Co. Kilkenny. In 1715 he was elected Mayor of Kilkenny.

The Castle he purchased had been battered by Cromwellian artillery and was all but a ruin. It had been built at the close of the 14th century by the then Earl

---

[16] Malcomson – *Archbishop Charles Agar*
[17] *The Agars of Gowran* – Moran in Duchas Tullaheerin Journal 1990

of Ormonde. James Agar carried out much repair work and extended the edifice to make it habitable and prestigious, following a fire there in 1713. He altered the castle by casing the walls with stone and building a front two storeys high with nine windows at both levels.

Despite his obvious ambition James was known to be a charitable man. Sometime before his death in 1733 he set in motion his plans to build an Alms House in Gowran. It was situated near the gate of the demesne. Four widows and their children were installed in the Alms House and Agar paid £21 per annum for their upkeep and for the upkeep of the House. A garden at the back provided the women with potatoes – three ridges each. James Agar made provision in his will for the £21 to be paid in perpetuity. The Alms House went through many transformations over the centuries and was used as a Barracks, a Post Office and a Court House at various times and is now a private residence.[18]

James Agar's second wife was Mary Wemyss the eldest daughter of Sir Henry Wemyss of Danesfort (Bennetsbridge). He had two sons and two daughters by Mary. The eldest daughter, Ellis, actually became a peeress in her own right as Countess of Brandon. She was married twice and her first husband was the 7th Viscount Mayo. He died in 1742 and in 1745 Ellis married the 21st Lord Athenry. Ellis had no children and her title died with her in 1789[19]. The second daughter Mary married James Smyth of Tinny Park, Delgany, Co. Wicklow[20]. Her daughter's marriages were significant too for the family of Agar. One of them married Francis Mathew, the 1st Earl of Llandaff[21] and the other married John Preston from Co. Meath, who later became Lord Tara. Marrying off daughters to titled husbands was

---

[18] Mary Moran – *The Agars of Gowran*

[19] The countess was a formidable lady and settled in Gaelic speaking Galway with her husband Lord Mayo. It took three companies of foot and the building of a permanent barracks in the 1750s before Lord Mayo's cousins the O'Flahertys could be reduced to order. She was painted twice by the Irish portrait painter Philip Hussey. The second portrait now hangs in Glin Castle where she is described by the locals as 'the hatchet faced countess'. Why she was created a Duchess is still a mystery. Malcomson suggested that she may have been a mistress of George II. She left a legacy to her nephew in Gowran on condition that he would build a monument in her memory in St. Mary's Church in Gowran. She stipulated that £300 was the sum to be spent. Her wishes were adhered to and the monument was created by Edward Smyth. Duchas is currently restoring the church interior and the monument– Malcomson in *Archbishop Charles Agar*.

[20] He was the son of the Bishop of Down and Connor whose 2nd wife was a daughter of Viscount Massareene.

[21] See *The Tipperary Gentry Vol.1* by Art Kavanagh and Wm. Hayes for the details about the Mathew Family.

expensive and it is estimated that it cost the Agars in the region of £16,000 to purchase husbands for Ellis and Mary.

It is highly likely that many of the land and property purchases were made with borrowed money and despite a healthy rent roll the mortgages had to be paid.

In his will James Agar left the Rower and his Kilkenny and Waterford properties to his second son James. This new estate now became known as the Ringwood estate. All other properties went to his elder son Henry. He also left legacies (despite the financial constraints) to his son James of Ringwood (£3000) and to his daughter-in-law Anne[22], Henry's wife (£1500).[23] Henry's wife was Anne Ellis the daughter of the Bishop of Meath. This family was very wealthy and owned much property in Dublin which later passed to the Agars. Henry's son, who became the 1st Lord Clifden, had a residence at Arran Quay adjacent to the Ellis properties on lands by the Liffey stretching from Arran Quay to the Phoenix Park, some of which came to be known as Ellis Quay.

As we have seen in the early part of this chapter, James of Ringwood went on to buy a large estate at Callan that cost him his life. His eldest surviving son, George who was created Lord Callan[24] eventually won control of the borough in 1776. Flood made one final effort to win it back in 1783 but was unsuccessful.

---

[22] This was Anne Ellis, daughter of the Bishop of Meath, in whose family there was a tradition of 'Divines'. Malcomson attributes this as a major influence on Charles Agar who later became the Archbishop of Cashel and Earl of Normanton. This marriage was most important to the Agars as Anne's brother Welbore Ellis was one of the most powerful men in England in his day. Educated in England at Westminster and Oxford he went on to become a very important government official and occupied such posts as Lord of the Admiralty from 1774-55, Joint Vice Treasurer for Ireland intermittently from 1756-77, Secretary at war from 1762-65 and Secretary of State for America and the Colonies in 1782. He was created Lord Mendip in 1794 and died in 1802. After his death his property and wealth passed to the Agars. From that date onwards they had a town house in Dublin at Ellis Quay (called after Bishop Ellis).

[23] Malcomson – *Archbishop Charles Agar*

[24] George was the first and last Baron Callan. He had a brother Charles, who became the Archdeacon of Emly, and a sister Mary, who married Philip Savage. Neither George nor Charles had legitimate families and so the legitimate line of James of Ringwood died out in 1815 when George died. George was very active politically and represented Callan from 1777-90 when he was created Baron. During the heady days of the Volunteer movement he established a regiment at Callan and was Colonel. He enthusiastically supported the demands of the Volunteers. When he died he left sixteen illegitimate children by two London mistresses – one an actress. He provided for the children in his will leaving money for their education and lump sums of £1000 each when they married or came of age. He was sixty one when he died. – Malcomson.

George, who was only eighteen at the time of his father's death never afterwards resided at Ringwood, but rented Kilmurry from the Bushe family. Kilmurry, near Thomastown was about halfway between the Callan and Rower estates. After his elevation to the peerage he leased Westcourt castle in Callan from the Ormondes and in 1794 he bought it outright. He pulled down the castle and built a mansion there, calling it Westcourt House[25]. After his death in 1815, Callan and the Rower passed under the terms of his will to Lord Clifden, his cousin.

Kilmurry near Thomastown

The Agar family, now highly prestigious, stumbled along from one minor financial crisis to the next. Younger sons had to be paid off and older members of the family, especially the dowagers[26] had to be given annuities. This still did not deter the incumbents from buying properties that arrived on the market and they continued to be represented in Parliament by brothers, cousins and other nominees becoming a very powerful Parliamentary force by the end of the 18th century.

Two of the most famous members of the Agar family were brothers. They were two younger sons of Henry Agar of Gowran (married to Anne Ellis), who had succeeded the ambitious and acquisitive James. They were Archbishop Charles

---

[25] Demolished in the 20th century.
[26] One of the dowagers, Mary Wemyss, lived to be 106.

Agar and Welbore[27] Agar. Welbore or 'Welby' as he was affectionately known went on to become very wealthy in England and at the end of his life was the owner of one of the most valuable and prestigious collections of paintings in private hands. His collection included works by Van Dyck and Rubens and eight paintings by Claude[28]. He also left two illegitimate sons. It would seem that he had some kind of relationship with a lady after his wife's death. In his will he left them £100,000 – a fantastic sum by modern standards.

The Archbishop was a controversial figure in his time. In his magnificent work entitled *Archbishop Charles Agar*, A.P.W. Malcomson has explored the background and life of this complex man and has rescued his reputation which had reduced him to the ranks of the less than mediocre. After his death the Archbishop was vilified by writers with ulterior motives, particularly Watty Cox (a former United Irishman) who specialised in attempting to undermine the 'establishment'[29]. The fact that the Archbishop managed to accumulate considerable wealth during his lifetime and was honoured with the title Earl of Normanton was only grist to Cox's mill. Now, fortunately, the damage of centuries has been undone and the Archbishop's invaluable contribution to the Church of Ireland and to the fabric of the state, in the many fine buildings he encouraged, has been finally given due recognition.[30]

The eldest son, James Agar, called after his grandfather, was very politically involved and was an M.P. for Gowran from 1753-60 and for the county from 1761-76[31]. He held an important and lucrative post as a revenue commissioner from 1771-85. In 1776 he was created Baron Clifden and took his seat in the House of Lords. In 1781 he was elevated further as the 1st Viscount Clifden. He died at the comparatively young age of 54 and was buried at Gowran. His wife was Lucia

---

[27] Called after his grandfather the Rt. Revd. Bishop Welbore Ellis
[28] Ibid.
[29] The fact that the Archbishop was opposed to granting relief to Catholics did not endear him to the supporters of such measures, but in his defence it should be pointed out that he saw such moves as most threatening to the status quo of the Church of Ireland. Also the Agar family seems to have been, if anything, most sympathetic to the plight of Catholics as exemplified in their acting as trustees for the Catholic family of Knaresborough and thereby saving their estate.
[30] The house of Normanton has continued down to the present day. Many of the members of the family followed careers in the Defence Forces and some lost their lives in such far flung places as Sebastopol in the Crimea and the North West Frontier in India. The present Earl is Shaun James Christian Welbore Ellis Agar the 6th Earl of Normanton. King Edward VII was baptismal sponsor for his father Edward John the 5th Earl.
[31] One of his defeated opponents was Henry Flood.

Martin of Dublin, the daughter of a Colonel. She was a young widow when she married James Agar[32].

The remaining son of the four[33] was Henry who became the bane of the Archbishop's life. He appears to have been a most unsavoury character, who, although a clergyman, led a life of dissipation and scandalised not alone his embarrassed family but his flock as well. The Archbishop came to the conclusion he was mad and had him withdrawn from active work in his parish where the day to day administration was delegated to the curate. Henry was married and had two sons, Charles and Henry. Charles although less than mentally competent, entered the Church. He also had a daughter Mary, who was raised in the Archbishop's house[34]. In his will the Archbishop made provision for the unfortunate Charles. Henry's uncle Welbore Ellis, Lord Mendip, in his will stipulated that Henry be excluded from sharing his fortune.

James the 1st Viscount Clifden[35] succeeded to the estate in 1746, at the age of thirteen. He was fortunate in having such an uncle as Welbore Ellis, who not alone looked after his affairs and his political inheritance, but actually lived with the Agars for a time at Gowran. James and his wife, Lucy, whom he married in 1760, had three sons and a daughter, Anne who died unmarried. James and Lucy's marriage seemed to founder a bit in the later stages and in some letters to the Archbishop (the 1st Viscount's uncle), Lucy implied that her husband had a mistress. She also continually complained about straitened finances.

In 1779, James, in common with his peers all over the county founded a battalion of four companies of the Volunteers in Gowran, which was used to quell any local disturbances arising from Whiteboy activities[36]. The members of these

---

[32] Her first husband was the Hon. Henry Boyle Walsingham the 2nd son of the 1st Earl of Shannon.

[33] In addition to the four sons Henry Agar also had a daughter Diana who died unmarried, but who was quite influential in the family. She was particularly close to the Archbishop – (Malcomson in *Archbishop Charles Agar*).

[34] Mary's descendants named Finley live in Newcastle on Tyne.

[35] He took the name Clifden as this was the new name the family had placed on the old Rathgarvan.

[36] Whiteboy activity in Kilkenny was only sporadic and was not as violent as in neighbouring Co. Tipperary. The Whiteboys were disgruntled tenants who opposed land enclosure, potato tithes and evictions. They generally assembled at night dressed in white sheets and threatened land agents, immigrant workers, would be occupiers of lands where evictions had occurred and tithe proctors. There is no record of Agar having arrested any of the Whiteboys but his nightly patrols, which were begun in the early 1770s, may well have helped deter them. The best remembered Whiteboy incident in Kilkenny occurred in Ballyragget and was known as the Battle of Ballyragget, where three Whiteboys were shot by people defending

companies were the tenants or the sons of tenants. James proclaimed himself their commander or Colonel. There definitely was some Whiteboy activity in the general area particularly Callan, Thomastown and the Rower that may have arisen because of the Enclosure Acts. Earlier in 1770 James Agar offered a reward for information leading to the arrest of those who had forced a Thomas Rourke to take an oath. He also issued a statement to his tenants as follows – 'I hope that all the tenants on my estate will be particularly careful that none of their sons or servants are anyways concerned with these meetings and outrages'.[37]

James also contributed to the building of roads and bridges and to the erection of the county infirmary.[38] He extended the family holding further in 1773 when he purchased the Knaresborough interest in Dunbell and Maddoxtown. It was to the credit of the Agars that they had sheltered the Catholic Knaresboroughs during the worst of the Penal times by acting as the Protestant trustees of the estate. James was also noted as a sportsman and kept a pack of hounds. A report in Finn's Leinster Journal gave a description of a hunt that took place in 1768 noting that Mr. Agar's pack of hounds from Gowran, were used. The fox ran all over the county taking the weary dogs and huntsmen on a 37 mile trek before surrendering.[39]

The Viscount's three sons were Henry Welbore, John Ellis and Charles Bagenal. Henry Welbore the eldest son and heir became the 2nd Viscount. John Ellis followed in the footsteps of his illustrious grand uncle Archbishop Agar and entered the Church. Although married to Lady Harriet Ashbrook he had no family and he died at the very young age of 33 the year before the 1798 rebellion. Charles Bagenal was a most interesting man who, like his grand uncle Welby became a barrister and practised in England. His marriage to Anna Maria Hunt who was the heir of her great uncle Henry Robartes, the 3rd Earl of Radnor, meant that he became a very wealthy man. His son, Thomas assumed the name Robartes and was created the 1st Lord Robartes in 1869. His son Thomas Charles eventually became the 2nd Lord Robartes and the 6th Viscount Clifden.

Henry Welbore, the 2nd Viscount, succeeded to the estates and title in 1789, when he was aged 28. He also inherited his father's debts which amounted to £48,000. Attempting to pay these debts meant that the 2nd Viscount had to become economical in his ways. A number of years later, in 1802, he received part of a

---

Robert Butler's mansion. Over 500 Whiteboys attended on the night, some from Gowran and Callan, both Agar strongholds.
[37] Burtchaell & Dowling in *Kilkenny History & Society*
[38] Malcomson in *Archbishop Charles Agar*
[39]

windfall when he became the heir of his grand uncle, Welbore Ellis, Lord Mendip[40]. He also inherited the title. His fortunes took a decided turn for the better in 1815 when he inherited the Ringwood estates of his cousin George Agar who died without legitimate heirs.

Henry Welbore then took the additional name of Ellis. His full title was Henry Welbore Ellis Agar 2nd Viscount Clifden and 2nd Baron Mendip. According to himself he risked his life and spent a lot of his money in suppressing the rebellion of 1798. He was at the head of his yeomanry corps from mid April until mid October patrolling the countryside and in late June he wrote 'I have not been in bed for three nights and yesterday spent eighteen hours in the saddle'. He also stated in September that though he wished to return to England, he would remain another two or three weeks in the area. After the Union he seems to have spent most of his time in England.

He married Lady Caroline Spencer, the daughter of the Duke of Marlborough and had a son and a daughter who died young. His son, George, who was created Baron Dover in 1831, predeceased the 2nd Viscount and died in 1833 aged 36. George had married Lady Georgiana Howard, the daughter of the 6th Earl of Carlisle and they had four sons and three daughters. Two of the daughters married but only one, Lucia, who was married to Lord Bagot, had children. The third and fourth sons found careers in the Army and in the diplomatic service but both died relatively young and unmarried. The first and second sons, Henry and Leopold became the 3rd and 5th Viscounts.

When Henry Welbore the 2nd Viscount died in 1836 he was succeeded by his grandson Henry, a young man of twenty, who became the 3rd Viscount. Henry was also the 2nd Baron Dover. It is probable that he spent most of his time in England as he married Eliza Seymour, a highly decorated lady who was one of the ladies of the bedchamber to Queen Victoria.

Henry the 3rd Viscount died at the age of 41 and was succeeded by his only son Henry George in 1866. Henry the 3rd Viscount had an only daughter, Lilah Georgiana who married Baron Annaly in 1884.

It is probable that Henry George now the 4th Viscount Clifden lived at least some of his time in Gowran. In 1884 when Bassett visited Kilkenny he gave a good account of Gowran House the residence of Lord Clifden. While he didn't say the Lord was in residence the implication was that at least he was taking care of his

---

[40] As part of the Act of Union settlement Henry was paid £15,000 by the Government for the disenfranchisement of the borough of Thomastown, which they had controlled despite not owning any land in the town. He also received a similar sum for Gowran – T.P. Power in *Kilkenny History & Society* ed. William Nolan

property. Writing of Gowran this is what Bassett had to say about the Clifden residence –

'Lord Clifden's residence gives to this village its chief attraction. It is a plain cut limestone mansion and stands in a demesne of six hundred acres, all in grass, and handsomely planted. Three artificial ponds are supplied by a little stream which rises in the Earl's bog, one mile distant and runs through the demesne, greatly enhancing the beauty of its scenery. The view from the front of the house also takes in a metal bridge, boat, boat-house and cascade.'

Henry George the 4thViscount Clifden died unmarried in 1895 and was succeeded by his uncle, Leopold, who was almost seventy at the time.

Leopold, the 5th Lord Clifden and 3rd Baron Dover, was a major in the Kilkenny Militia, a J.P. and an M.P. for Kilkenny for almost twenty years. A Trinity College Cambridge graduate he became a barrister. He was married to Lady Harriet Camoys and they had one son, who died young and three daughters[41].

When Leopold died in 1899 the title of Dover became extinct but that of Clifden passed to his cousin Thomas Charles the 2nd Baron Robartes and now 6th Lord Clifden. At this stage the family connection with Kilkenny seems to have almost ceased. The Land Acts of the late 1890s and the early years of the 20th century saw the break up of practically all the large estates in Ireland, including that of Gowran. Thomas Charles was an Oxford graduate and became a barrister. He was a J.P. and a Deputy Lieutenant in Cornwall and was an M.P. for Cornwall for a number of years, until he succeeded his father in 1882. He was married to Mary Dickinson from Somerset and they had five sons and four daughters, Mary, Julia, Edith and Constance.

The sons were Thomas, Francis, Arthur, Cecil and Alexander. Thomas pursued a career in the Army and Francis entered the Diplomatic Service

The Hon Rachel Mary the daughter of the 8th Viscount married Capt. Cromwell Felix Lloyd-Davies and has a daughter Ann, b. 1942, m. Colin Victor Williams from Surrey. They have two sons Andrew and Simon and one daughter Zara, all born after 1967.

Gowran Castle was left to Lady Annaly by her cousin the 6th Viscount Clifden. She was probably Lucy Emily, the daughter of Baron Annaly and Lilah Georgiana Agar, who had been married in 1884. She sold the Castle and eighty acres

---

[41] The three daughters were Caroline who married Lt. Col. Fawcett, Harriet, whose husband was Thomas Knox of London and Evelyn who married the Hon. Edward Vanden-Bempde-Johnstone the son of Lord Derwent. All three ladies had families.

to the late Mr. Jim Moran and his wife Mary in the mid 1950s. Mary is a very prominent member of numerous historical societies. She wrote a very fine article about the Agars of Gowran in the Duchas Tullaherin Publication of 1990 called *In the Shadow of the Steeple*.

Blunden of Castle Blunden

In its heyday in the last quarter of the 18th century Castle Blunden was above all the home of a generous and happy family. This is vividly remembered and described by Dorothea Herbert. She was ecstatic about her many memorable visits to Castle Blunden in the 1770s. She recalled boating on the exquisite lake 'while being serenaded by six fiddles' and the atmosphere of joy and merriment that prevailed. Dorothea's mother was Martha Cuffe. Her sister was married to Sir John 1st (Blunden). Dorothea's cousins were of course Sir John's children and both the Herberts and the Blundens had large families. These happy scenes were repeated at intervals during the 19th century and during the last quarter of the 20th also. It could be said without contradiction that the Blunden household down through the centuries was marked by a joyous happy serenity that was probably unusual in persisting for so long.

Sir John 1st and his wife Lady Susanna, the daughter of the 1st Lord Desart, had a large family including five daughters and in order to assist in finding suitable marriage partners for those ladies many lavish parties were held at Castle Blunden. Guests who had travelled far would stay the night and the young unmarrieds would share the barrack room, modesty being maintained by means of a curtain hanging across the room to segregate the sexes. Dorothea Herbert describes staying at Castle Blunden in 1780. Only the old nanny was there to protect the girls from the waggeries of the gentlemen. Routing them from spying on them en chemise the girls overturned the chamber pot whose whole contents meandered into the men's barrack – "immediately the house rang with their laughter and left us au desepoir."

Lake at Castle Blunden

According to Burke's Peerage Overington Blunden was given a grant of lands in Co. Kilkenny in 1667. He was granted Clanmore[42] or Glanmore "to be forever called Blunden's Castle". The lands originally belonged to the Shee family. He was also granted other lands in Co. Kilkenny together with lands in Co. Laois and in Co. Waterford. The Blunden name does not appear in the Fiants of the Tudor monarchs so it is safe to assume that the first member of the family to come to Ireland did so between 1603 and 1667 the year of the grant.[43] The first Blunden in Ireland may in fact have been Overington who is described as one of the

---

[42] Sir Philip Blunden believes that the proper name was 'Clonmoran'.
[43] Overington Blunden was listed as a Titulado (meaning he held title to lands) in the Census of 1659. He paid Hearth Money Tax in 1664, in Kilkenny.

Cromwellian 'adventurers' in an article in *Kilkenny History and Society*.[44] Overington was granted the lands in lieu of the money he had adventured. He was originally from Southwark in Surrey and was by profession a whitster or cloth bleacher[45]. He had some connection with the Blundens of Shropshire and the Irish Blundens share the same coat of arms with that family. The actual Kilkenny land in Blunden ownership was less than 500 Irish acres at that time. They appear to have had other estates in Co. Laois and Co. Waterford. When they took possession of the Kilkenny lands they lived in the tower house which was to the rear of the present house which was not built until almost one hundred years later.

Overington was married to a lady called Elizabeth and they had two sons and four daughters. Three of the daughters married. Mary's husband was John Lloyd, Dorothy married an Arthur Brereton and Sarah married a Thomas Richards of Goslingtown. Lydia died unmarried. After Overington's death in 1685 the eldest son, John, inherited the estates in counties Kilkenny and Waterford and the Co. Laois lands were willed to the second son Robert[46]. John appears as the purchaser of a house or houses in Kilkenny city in the first decade of the 18th century when the 2nd Duke of Ormonde was struggling to have his family debts reduced.[47] John died intestate and papers of administration were granted to his son John.

John, the grandson of Overington, was the man who raised the family to the highest rank. He seems to have been a very able person and was most fortunate in his choice of a wife. He married Martha Cuffe the sister of the 1st Lord Desart. He was active politically and was an M.P. for Kilkenny city from 1727 to 1751. His wife died in 1726 but they had one son and one daughter who married Samuel Waring of Springfield, Co. Kilkenny. His son John was created a baronet in 1766.

Sir John 1st probably attended Trinity College as he became a prominent barrister. He represented Kilkenny in parliament from 1761 to 1776. Like his father he married well and chose as his bride his first cousin, Lady Susanna, the daughter of his uncle the 1st Lord Desart. They were married in 1755 and they had three sons and five daughters.[48] While the provision of dowries for the five ladies may appear

---

[44] *Kilkenny History & Society* pg.176 Ed. Wm. Nolan
[45] From documents in the possession of Lady Pamela Blunden.
[46] Robert's numerous descendants are spread all over the world and are professional people specialising mainly in Medicine and the Law.
[47] Ibid pg. 124
[48] The daughters were Martha, Araminta, Sophia, Charoltte and Dorothea. They all married and their husbands were with one exception from other gentry families in Co. Kilkenny. The exception was Dorothea's husband William Bolton from the Island in Wexford. The other men were Wemyss of Danesfort, Waring of Springfield, White-Baker of Ballytobin and Matthews of Bonnettstown.

to have constituted a substantial drain on the family finances, this was clearly not the case as Sir John was able to loan £10,000 to James Wemyss of Danesfort, the husband of his eldest daughter Martha[49]. The loan was secured by way of a lien on the Wemyss property and was to be repaid in six months, which in fact it was. He also gave the loan of a sum of £800 to the Herberts, the parents of Dorothea Herbert[50].

Castle Blunden

Sir John appears to have become somewhat tetchy with the passage of time and in 1780 he openly quarrelled with the Volunteers who proceeded to burn his effigy in Kilkenny. Sir John heated himself at the fire to show his contempt.[51] He died in 1783. Dorothea Herbert and her mother paid a visit of condolence to 'Aunt

---

[49] Blunden family papers.
[50] *Retrospections* – Dorothea Herbert
[51] Unpublished thesis in Rothe House.

Blunden' and found that the Blunden girls had 'the whitest hands, noses and teeth in the world, were dressed beautifully and had just become mistresses of large fortunes'. She thought that the new Sir John (2nd) was very handsome but with 'an overlove of the fair sex and the bottle'.

It was Sir John 1st who undertook the task of building Castle Blunden. It is not know if he had an architect - the style is reminiscent of Francis Bindon, the Limerick architect who finished Russborough and redesigned Carnelly House in County Clare. Bindon, however, had died in 1765. It is more likely that the work was carried out by a jobbing mason, who had worked for Bindon.

Bence-Jones (1988, 62-63) describes Castle Blunden as "a highly romantic mid 18th century house with water on both sides of it so that it seems to float; the water being two lakes probably formed out of the moat of the earlier house or castle here". It was built either for John Blunden, MP, or for his son Sir John Blunden, 1st Bt. It consisted of three storeys over a vaulted basement with a six bay front. There is a central niche with a statue below a square armorial panel and above it has a single-storey pedimented Doric portico. The back of the house consists of two gables with a projection between them containing the principal and secondary staircases. The decoration of the interior is late 18th century and was probably carried out by the 2nd Baronet after his marriage to his bride who, according to Dorothea Herbert, brought him 'a clear £8,000 a year.'[52]

The gothic ice-house in the grounds of Castle Blunden was probably built some time later. According to Howley (1993) this ice-house is the finest surviving example in Ireland. "This quaint little building is a most successful garden ornament, but, as part of its structure is above ground, it was probably not quite so successful at preventing ice from melting." He goes on to describe the little building – "externally the structure is all in rendered rubble stone, with a covering of slate to the vault and the conical roof of the ice chamber. The interior of the passage is finished with a stone-flagged floor and neat brick vaulting; and the ice chamber, which extends to a depth of about twelve feet below the level of the passage, is a splendid circular structure with a brick dome. It abuts onto a quarry and stands on the edge of an open field above a small stream".

Sir John's third son, Overington, as expected, joined the Army and rose to the rank of General. He died in 1838, apparently unmarried.

William Pitt was the second son of Sir John and he would appear to have stayed at home at least until his marriage to Harriet Pope of Popesfield in Co. Laois. They had two sons and a daughter Harriet (she married Rev. Joseph Carson, a senior

---

[52] The house was further enlarged in the 1970s under the supervision of the well known Dublin architect Jeremy Williams.

fellow of Trinity College). William Pitt's two sons were John who became the 3rd baronet of Blunden Castle upon the demise of his uncle and William Pitt of Bonnettstown.[53]

The Ice House at Castle Blunden

Sir John's eldest son, John became the 2nd Baronet when his father died in 1783. Although married twice Sir John 2nd had no children but initially he substantially improved the family finances by marrying an heiress, Frances Robbins of Ballyduff, as his first wife. Frances died in 1808 and in 1812 Sir John married Hester Helsham of Leggetsrath, Co. Kilkenny. However as his life progressed he became a spendthrift or a gambler and he mortgaged the estate. When he died in 1818 he was succeeded in his title and estate by his nephew, Sir John, the 3rd baronet[54]. His financial affairs looked pretty grim but his uncle Overington, the General, came to his rescue and paid off the debts on Castle Blunden. Lady Pamela seems to think that the money may have been prize money given to the General because of his exploits in the Peninsular Wars.

---

[53] William of Bonnettstown was a J.P. and a High Sheriff and his wife was Frances Knox the sister of Elizabeth who was married to Sir John 3rd. They had two sons Overington and Frederick and a daughter Catherine.
[54] The son of William Pitt.

Like his grandfather, Sir John 3rd became a barrister and married Elizabeth Knox of Castlerea, Co. Mayo, in 1839. They had six sons and three daughters. Three of the daughters married, Kate to Nicholas Richardson, Harriette to James Egan and Nicola to Rev. Becher of Bagenalstown, Co. Carlow. The six sons were William, John Overington, Edward, Maurice Robert, Arthur and Abraham. Edward seems to have died in infancy and Arthur died unmarried. The second of Sir William's sons, John, became a barrister. He lived in Killiney in Dublin and his wife was Frances Hone of Dublin. Maurice the fourth son married Eleanor Armstrong of Lismoher Co. Clare but they had no family. Abraham, the sixth son, became a surgeon in the army and was domiciled in Edinburgh. He married Mary Magee the daughter of a surgeon major in the Kilkenny militia and they had one son, Abraham.

Lady Pamela Blunden told a remarkable tale about Harriette who had been almost completely obliterated from the Blunden family memory. A phone call to Castle Blunden in the early 1960s from an elderly American lady, Harriet Egan, who claimed a near relationship to the Blundens, resulted in a visit by her to the Castle where she was warmly welcomed by a curious Sir William and Lady Pamela. She stayed in the Castle for a few days and told her story. Her mother, Harriette, was a daughter of Sir John 3rd (d. 1890). Following her education at home Harriette was trained as a nurse in St. Thomas's Hospital in London. When she arrived home to Castle Blunden, following her training, she met and fell in love with a local man named James Egan who worked on the Blunden farm. Knowing that her parents would never consent to her marrying James the young couple decided to elope. Shortly afterwards they made their plans and left Kilkenny for America. It is not known what James worked at in America but it would seem that they managed to get on reasonably well as they had three children who were well educated. Not alone was Harriette disinherited by her father but her name was never subsequently mentioned by the family. However when he died in 1890 Sir John left Harriette some money with which she bought a home she called Shamrock Lodge in Palmyra. Harriette and James had a son who became a lawyer and two daughters who became schoolteachers. One of the daughters was Harriet. Her cousin Abraham Blunden left Harriet a house in Courtmacsherry in west Cork and on at least one occasion Harriete and James came back from America to holiday in Ireland. They travelled steerage class. While they were in Ireland Harriette decided to go to Kilkenny and went to St. Canice's Cathedral where she knew her family went every Sunday. On coming out of church she went up to her brother and said "don't you know me Willy, I'm your sister Harriette". "I have no sister Harriette," replied William looking straight through her, as he walked away.

William the eldest son of Sir John 3rd became Sir William when his father, Sir John 3rd baronet, died in 1890. Sir William was fifty years old at the time.

William was a graduate of Trinity College and became a doctor. After his graduation he went to New Zealand and met his future wife Florence Shuttleworth there. They married in 1879 and they had two sons John and Eric and a daughter Muriel. He practiced in Timaru (South Island) and the family lived there. William was enthralled by the Maoris and was reluctant to come home. However after the death of his mother in 1900 he decided to return as the house was now left empty – apart from two servants[55]. In 1904 he was High Sheriff for the county during the visit of King Edward VII and Queen Alexandra to Kilkenny. His son, John, called 'Jack' ran the estate with his mother[56] and Eric remained in school graduating as an engineer. Muriel married her cousin Jack Richardson but they had no family.

Sir William died in 1923 and his eldest son became Sir John the 5th Baronet. He married Phyllis the daughter of Philip Creaghe, R.M. of Golden, Co. Tipperary. Sir John's only brother was Eric Overington, a Trinity graduate who found employment as an engineer with the North Midland Ministry of Transport. Eric was an Honorary Lieutenant and served in World War I where he was mentioned in dispatches. Eric's wife was Bridget Curtis and they had one daughter, Josettia, who married Colonel George Kenyon CBE.[57]

Sir John 5th died also in 1923 just three days after his father. Sir John died from pneumonia and was unaware of his father's death. He was only 43 years old. The two deaths coming together were catastrophic for the family, not alone because of the deep personal loss but as two lots of death duties had to be paid. Sir John's eldest son, William, then became Sir William the 6th Baronet. He was born in 1919 and was only four years old when his father died. Despite the financial hardship Lady Phyllis Blunden managed to have her two sons William and Philip educated at Repton. Sir William joined the Royal Navy Volunteer Reserve at the beginning of the Second World War and during the war he met his future wife Pamela Purser, the daughter of John Purser a Professor of Civil Engineering in Trinity College Dublin. Pamela was in the WRNS at the time[58].

Sir William retired from the Navy in 1958. He and his wife Lady Pamela have six daughters. During the time the children were growing up Castle Blunden

---

[55] The census of 1901 shows just two servants as residents.
[56] Sir William was reputed to have spent much of his time sitting under a tree reading the Bible while his wife and son managed the farmwork (Lady Pamela Blunden).
[57] Josephine and Colonel George have two sons Robin and Crispin, both born in the 1950s and educated at Charterhouse. Robin married Marcia Ludeke of NZ and they have children. Crispin's wife is Carolyn Drinkwater of Sacombe, Ware, Herts and they have a family. Josephine and George also have a daughter, Rowena.
[58] Lady Pamela's great aunt Sarah Purser was a distinguished artist who painted a portrait of Sir John Blunden.

became once more the hospitable, fun loving home, full of family affection that had been depicted more than two hundred years earlier by Dorothea Herbert. Sir William and Lady Pamela took an active part in the Kilkenny social scene hunting with the Kilkenny Hunt, shooting on Mount Leinster and playing cricket with the Bagenalstown and Mount Juliet clubs. One of the incidents that must have given them most pleasure was in 1968 when their horse, Jenny, ridden by Juliet Jobling Purser, Lady Blunden's cousin, took part in the Olympics in Mexico in the Irish three day event team.

Their eldest daughter, Sarah, married John Perceval Maxwell of Moore Hill, Tallow Co. Waterford and they have two sons and two daughters. Jane and Caroline are twins. They are much travelled ladies and both have published books relating to travel. Jane's book is a Travel Guide to Mongolia and Caroline's book is a Cultural Atlas of China. Caroline owns a unique company called Blunden Oriental which specializes in assisting Oriental artists to exhibit in the west. Rowena has one son and three daughters. Elizabeth's husband is Nicholas Marshall and they live in Australia. They have two sons and twin daughters. Lady Pamela's youngest daughter, Fiona, is married to John McGovern and they live in Vermont. Sir William carried out improvements to the Castle 'without violence to its character' as was noted in his obituary in the Irish Times.

When Sir William died in 1985 he was succeeded by his brother Sir Philip the 7th and present baronet. Philip also joined the Royal Navy and fought in World War II. His wife was Jeanette Macdonald of the Isle of Skye.[59] Lady Jane as she was known passed away in 1999. They have two sons Hubert and John and a daughter Marguerite. Hubert married to Eilish O'Brien and they have a son Edmond and a daughter Amelia. Hubert is now a Captain in the Merchant Marine while his wife Eilish is a remedial teacher. John is a well respected Antique Restorer and Marguerite is nurse who has recently embarked on a new career as a film producer. Edmond, like his grandfather has artistic leanings and Amelia is a scientist working in the pharmaceutical industry.

Sir Philip is a distinguished artist and his works have been given excellent reviews in one of the national newspapers recently. Exhibitions of his paintings are planned for later in this year (2004) in Galway and Glasgow. In his youth Sir Philip was a keen sportsman and still has an active interest in horseracing, attending numerous race meetings throughout the year.

---

[59] Passed away in 2000.

Blunden of Castleblunden

Bryan of Jenkinstown

Jenkinstown estate was situated on the banks of the Nore at Ballyragget, Co. Kilkenny. The rolling countryside and the sweep of the Nore at Ballyragget combined to make the Jenkinstown estate one of the most beautiful in the county.

Thomas Moore, the celebrated 19th century poet and songwriter, was a frequent visitor at Jenkinstown. It was while staying there he was inspired to write "The Last Rose of Summer" one of his best known songs set to an adaptation of "The Groves of Blarney". Thomas was very friendly with George Bryan and his social connections in Kilkenny where he attended and took part in the Kilkenny Private Theatre Productions initiated by the Powers of Kilfane. With the passage of time the friendship between the Bryans and Thomas Moore (and his wife Bessy Dyke) became deep and enduring. The Moores visited Jenkinstown many times and while both families were in Paris in 1822 they socialized on a daily basis, exchanging presents and dining together.[60]

The Moores were not the only ones entertained at Jenkinstown. There is a portrait of George Bryan that was presented to him by Mrs. Plowden of Rome. On the back of the portrait there was a note stating that Mrs. Plowden, nee Elizabeth Bryan, was an illegitimate daughter of George Bryan and Madamoiselle Wallstein, 'a lovely Austrian actress who came to Jenkinstown with the Covent Garden Cast, including Thomas Moore and his future wife, also an actress. Mrs Plowden (whose husband was a banker) was adored by her father who left her £150,000 of 'unencumbered estate.'

George Bryan from a portrait

The fact that the Bryan family kept a brass of Sir William Bryan (1395) of Seal, near Seven Oaks, in Kent, is not in itself a proof of their ancestry. One school of thought on the subject holds that they were of Irish descent, Bryan being a corruption of Byrne or O'Byrne. If they were in fact descended from an Irish Byran, it is more than likely that the Bryan in question was a member of the Bryans or Breens of the Duffry near Enniscorthy in Co. Wexford. The remnants of this once powerful Gaelic clan still clung to their ancestral lands until as late as 1654.[61]

---

[60] *Old Kilkenny Review* – Tom Moore and George Bryan, Jenkinstown – by Rev. John Brennan

[61] The clan called the Sil Brain descended from Bran Dubh the King of Leinster in the 6th century. They were settled in the Hook Peninsula. They were disturbed by the Vikings in the 9th and 10th centuries and moved away en masse to the safety of the mountains settling

It is significant that in the family pedigree in Burke's Landed Gentry it is noted that they descended from one Lewis Bryan who was the father of a John Bryan and the grandfather of another John Bryan. This Lewis, it was stated, had a grant of lands from Thomas the 10th Earl of Ormonde.

In the 1552 Fiant of Queen Elizabeth[62] outlining a grant of lands to Sir Richard Butler (Lord Mountgarret), Lewis Bryan is mentioned as being a sergeant of the Earl of Ormonde. A pardon was granted to Lewis Bryan, gent., of Damaghe, in 1566. He was in company with numerous other people. It was not stated why they were pardoned.[63] Gerald Fitz Lewes Bryan received a pardon (with about 300 more people) in 1602. He is described as a gent., and it is stated that he was from Listerlyn.[64]

John Brennan, in the Old Kilkenny Review, tries to make the case that Lewis was at least known to Sir Francis Bryan, if indeed he was not related to him. Sir Francis was a courtier at the court of Henry VIII and later during the reign of King Edward VI he was appointed Lord Marshal of the garrison (in Ireland) and was made Justice of the Realm during the King's pleasure.[65] He also managed to marry the widow of James the 9th Earl of Ormonde, who outlived him and later married her first cousin, the Earl of Desmond. If this Sir Francis Bryan was indeed an ancestor of the Bryans of Jenkinstown it is most likely that it would have been noted in Burke's Landed Gentry.

To revert to Lewis it would appear that he was very friendly with 'Black Tom' and was given some lands by him, on a lease basis, we assume.[66] However, his association with Bawnmore and Whiteswall began when he married an heiress. She was Ellice White the only daughter of a Mr. White of Whiteswall.[67] In 1582 his son Brian Bryan of Whitwall was granted livery.[68] He was described as the son of Lewis Bryan of Whitwall. A few years later in 1587 Brian's brothers Gerald and Charles

---

in the Duffry or Dubh Tir west of Enniscorthy and bordering on Counties Carlow and Wicklow. In later times they were called by various names Bryans, Breens, Brains and Briens.

[62] Fiants of the Tudor Monarchs no. 1078
[63] Fiant Elizabeth no. 912
[64] Fiant no. 6706 (Listerlin is near Rosbercon, New Ross, Co. Kilkenny)
[65] Fiant Ed. VI no. 426
[66] At an inquisition in Kilkenny dated 1557-8 Lewis Brian is seised in his demesne as of fee tenure of the town of Whiteswall with its appurtenances by demise of James De-Butler late Earl of Ormond, and the manor of Damagh with its appurtenances by demise of Thomas De Butler, Earl of Ormond etc., (Cal. Ormonde Deeds).
[67] This was probably Nicholas White who was appointed a commissioner to execute martial law in Kilkenny in 1565. See Fiant Eliz. 724.
[68] Fiant Elizabeth no. 3957

Fitz Lewis Bryan of Whitwall were granted pardons.[69] Gerald received another pardon in 1594. The family was still in possession of Listerlin in 1601 as Gerald received a pardon in that year as of Listerlin.[70] In addition to his two brothers Charles and Brian, Gerald seems to have had at least two more brothers who received pardons at the same time, in 1601. They were Teig Fitz Lewis Bryan and Barnaby Fitz Lewis Bryan. All are described as gentlemen. According to Burke and Brennan (in Old Kilkenny Review) there was another son John known as John of Kilkenny who was the man from whom the Bryans of Jenkinstown descended.

John married Margaret Walshe. Records show he died in August 1607 and his wife in August 1610. It is John Fitz Lewis's grandson, also called John of Kilkenny, who is directly concerned with the Jenkinstown connection. He married a lady called Anne Staines who was the heir to Jenkinstown.[71] Her father, Henry Staines may well have been a descendant of Richard Staines, constable of Longford in the reign of Queen Elizabeth.

They were married about 1640 and tradition has it that it was a love match. John became an Alderman and Sovereign of Kilkenny. They lived in a house situated nearer to the river Dinin than that of later times which occupied the present site. They lived through troubled times. The Confederate war was followed by the Cromwellian conquest. During that time their house at Jenkinstown was made the repository for some precious articles for Catholic Divine Worship. The recorded list of these includes the David Rothe silver monstrance as well as five chalices and several sets of elegant vestments.[72]

John Bryan died in 1671 and was buried in St. Mary's Church in Kilkenny[73]. James Bryan, the eldest son and heir was for a time a student at Lincoln's Inns. He was a Captain in King James's army. He was appointed an Alderman of Kilkenny by the Charter of James II in 1687. He became an M.P. for

---

[69] Ibid no. 4993

[70] Ibid no. 6564

[71] According to the Down Survey the lands of Jenkinstown were owned by the Earl of Ormonde. The Shee family also owned lands in the area. A John Bryan, an Irish Papist, was noted as the owner of various parcels of land in the Urlingford area – Rathbane 251acres, Whitswall 510a., Rathreagh 267, Waterslands 38, Tankardstown 89, Part of Brickanagh 92, Bawnmore 1310 plus wood and bog 880 acres. John Bryan was also noted as having 'a faire stone house'.

[72] All these were kept in safe custody and after 200 years were presented to Most Rev. Dr. Walsh, Bishop of Ossory on the completion of the new St. Mary's Cathedral: It was consecrated on October 4th 1857. (Burke & Brennan in *Old Kilkenny Review*)

[73] Eleanor Bryan of Bawnmore, who married Sir Pierce Butler the 2nd Viscount Ikerrin, was probably a sister.

Kilkenny city in 1687 together with John Rothe who was also Alderman and Mayor. This was in the Parliament of James II which met in May 1689 but was dissolved on 28th July 1689.

Jenkinstown House

James Bryan was in considerable trouble when King William arrived in Ireland. He had been on Ormonde's side before William landed in England but Ormonde changed sides and went over to William in the English struggle. In the meantime back home in Kilkenny James Bryan had raised a troop of horse for Ormonde. Despite his attachment to James and the Jacobite cause, he was not disturbed from his estate or home at Jenkinstown, because of the Ormonde influence at court.

James married Rose, younger daughter of Edward Rothe and Catherine Archdeacon his wife.[74] Her father was one of the four Commissioners who finally negotiated the surrender of Kilkenny to Cromwell in 1650. Rose's brother was

---

[74] Rose brought with her a substantial dowry which included properties in Kilkenny city.

Lieutenant General Michael Rothe K.C.S.P., and Colonel of the Rothe Regiment in the Irish Brigade of the French service.

In 1702 James acquired 1,250 acres at Aughatubrid and Clogh in the Castlecomer area. By 1704 he had acquired the northern portion of Dunmore Manor. These acquisitions gave him a considerable estate.

James had three children, two boys Pierce and Henry and a daughter Catherine. Nothing much is known about the lives of the younger children Henry and Catherine[75] but Pierce went on to become a barrister, having studied in London.

Pierce married Jane Aylmer of Lyons Co. Kildare[76] and went to live in Jenkinstown after his father's death, possibly in the early decades of the 18th century. His estate increased significantly when he inherited from his kinsman James Bryan of Bawnmore, who died in 1740.[77] Pierce and Jane had four sons and three daughters. It would appear that only one of the daughters got married. This was Mary the youngest, who married her cousin, William Wall of Coolnamuck, as his second wife.

The most interesting of the four sons was Aylmer the 3rd son who joined Rothe's regiment in France as a cadet and later rose to the rank of Brigadier. He was made a Knight of St. Louis by the French monarch Louis XV, a very prestigious award made only to officers who served with distinction in the army or navy. At that period France was involved with the War of the Austrian Succession (against Austria) and, after a switch of alliances that realigned (1756) France with Austria, in the Seven Years War.

George the 2nd son of Pierce went to London where he received an education. He lived in London having married Catherine Xavaria Byrne only child of Henry Byrne of Oporto,[78] and his wife, a daughter of James Eustace,

---

[75] Catherine died in 1770, in Kilkenny, according to Brennan. It is very likely that Henry died young as succession by one son was forbidden to Catholics at this time.

[76] The Aylmers were a very significant Kildare family who also came into the possession of the Courtown estate there.

[77] The lands of Bawnmore and Galmoy were regranted to John Bryan in 1660, but he in fact was not allowed to take possession, while he was allowed to remain on his former property. His son James was given the ownership. John however had married twice and had another family when he died. In his will he begged his son not to 'molest or hinder his second wife (Ursula Walsh) in the enjoyment of the property during her life and not to trouble or prejudice her or her children in anything....and providing that he perform my will I forgive him for all things wherein he offended me...' Those lands passed to Pierce Bryan (a Protestant) in 1696 and then to Pierce's son James (High Sheriff of the county in 1732). James had no children and left his property to his kinsman.

[78] Henry Byrne's mother was Alice Fleming the daughter and co-heir of Randall the last Lord Slane. She married Gregory Byrne of Timiogue, Co. Laois, in 1690. She died in 1753.

Yeomanstown, Co. Kildare. They were married in the church of St. Clement Danes in Westminster. Their eldest son, also called George was born in his parent's London house in Devonshire Square in 1770. The young George was destined to inherit the estates of Jenkinstown as his uncle, James, was unmarried and died childless in 1805.

George the younger was sent to the Continent to receive an education. At first he went to Liege, but later his uncle Aylmer, Brigadier and Knight of St. Louis, brought him to Strasburg. There he was joined by his younger brother, Eustace who died at Metz in 1786 when George was 16 years of age. In 1787 George visited Munich and Vienna, but by the spring of 1792 he was in Paris and witnessed the massacre at the Tuileries. At that time he was 22 years of age and his fiancée was Countess Louise de Rutant, daughter of Count du Rutant of Nancy.

Louise was Lady-in waiting to Marie Antoinette and was imprisoned with her under the French Commune. George is said to have become a kind of Scarlet Pimpernel in his efforts to rescue both ladies. He failed, however, and came under the suspicion of the authorities and was imprisoned for sixteen months. Even the Count de Rutant was lucky to escape with his life in those dangerous days. On his release from prison George again turned to the de Rutant family. Louise, in the meantime, had been executed during the Reign of Terror, and accordingly he sought the hand of her sister, Countess Maria Louise Augustine. He was accepted and he married her secretly at Nancy in 1794.

They escaped to London where on the 8th August 1795 he married her publicly at Maria de la Bone (known now as Marylebone). George was very lucky in his choice of wife. A contemporary account says that she "from her highly polished education and kindness of heart diffuses happiness not only throughout her own immediate family but the respectable circle in which she moves and the whole neighbourhood in which she resides".

After his father's death in 1797 George bought a Commission in the British Dragoons. Later he was promoted to the rank of Captain, but when it was discovered he was a Catholic he was informed he could not hold such a Commission. He promptly resigned and moved from London to Ireland. He purchased a house at 12 Henrietta Street, Dublin and with his wife, son and daughter he came to live there in 1802.

In post Union Ireland the Catholic Committee was again active in its efforts to obtain relief from the penal restrictions still imposed on Catholics. The Catholic Emancipation Movement was beginning to gather momentum. George Bryan entered wholeheartedly into these activities, especially that of the Catholic Committee. He was a

---

George Byran later instigated a court case claiming the title of Lord of Slane in the right of his grandmother Alice Fleming but the case was lost.

friend of Daniel O'Connell and letters written by the great Liberator are still in the possession of a family member.

Besides his work in the affairs of national importance he was also very active in the affairs of his parish and local community. He took a leading part in the purchase of land for a new St. Michan's church in North Ann Street. He personally laboured hard to raise funds for this while subscribing generously himself. The Church was completed in 1817 and was at that time the second largest church in Dublin. The local community expressed its gratitude to George Bryan for his work and financial assistance by having the Bryan coat of arms emblazoned at the gallery stairs of the church where it stands to the present day.

As the heir presumptive George and his family stayed long and often in Jenkinstown and they were fully accepted into the social scene of the time including the amateur theatricals of Kilkenny which was popularised by the Power brothers from Kilfane.

When his uncle died in 1805 George moved to Jenkinstown with his family. Because of his inheritance he was rated one of the richest Commoners in Ireland. Besides owning Jenkinstown he inherited the Byrne fortune in Oporto. His mother had been an only child and the Byrne fortune was very considerable. To his already large land holding he added a further lands at Ballyrafton which were purchased at a cost of £3,042.

George Bryan became a Major in the Kilkenny Militia, a rank by which he was familiarly known. He was also known as "Punch" Bryan or simply "Major Punch". In 1830 he was appointed High Sheriff of County Kilkenny the first Roman Catholic to hold such an office since 1690. He was elected M.P. for Kilkenny County from 1837 to 1841 and again from 1841 to 1847.

It is probable that George Bryan built or greatly extended the Jenkinstown mansion. It is unlikely his eccentric Uncle James did any work of that nature. George built Gragara House as a residence for his son. A racecourse and Grand stand were also built.

George had a son and a daughter. The daughter, Mary Napoliana, married Colonel Sir Miley Doyle K.C.B. M.P. for Co. Carlow in 1817. The son and heir, George was born in London on 25th October 1796 after his parents arrived there safely in their escape from France.

Major George Bryan is buried in the family vault at Old St. Mary's Kilkenny. An altar tomb bears the inscription "George Bryan of Jenkinstown, Co. Kilkenny, died 8th October 1843 aged 73 years".

His successor is better known as Colonel George Bryan. He had lived with his parents and sister in London, Dublin and Jenkinstown until his marriage in 1820. He married Margaret Talbot, second daughter of William Talbot and Mary O'Toole of Castle Talbot, near Blackwater, Co. Wexford. Margaret Talbot, besides being no ordinary person herself was a member of no ordinary family[79]. She had eight maternal (O'Toole) uncles - all officers in the French service. Some of her brothers held important military posts on the Continent as well.

'Naughty' Margaret

Margaret was a famous beauty and wit.[80] She is said to have dined and danced with all the Crowned heads of Europe. She was a friend of Madame Bonaparte and of Pope Pius IX. The Pope is said to have donated the special 17th century glass panel depicting the Last Supper to Jenkinstown Oratory. A very fine portrait of Pope Pius IX is kept at Barmeath Castle. Margaret was also a friend of Leopold, King of the Belgians, who became godfather to her only surviving son, George Leopold Bryan.

Colonel George Bryan and Margaret Talbot had a family whose names are listed in the Bellew family Missal kept at Barmeath Castle, Co. Louth. There were three sons and six daughters. Of the sons - James and Eustace died in infancy while George Leopold was to survive to become the heir to the family estates.

---

[79] Her elder and only sister Maria Theresa married John Talbot of Warwick in 1814. He was to become the Earl of Shrewsbury of Alton Towers in 1827, inheriting property worth £400,000 and extended landed estates in Ireland. It is worth noting that the Wexford Talbots were distantly connected with the Shrewsbury Talbots. For more information on the Wexford Talbot family see *The Wexford Gentry Vol.1* by Art Kavanagh and Rory Murphy.

[80] She was known as 'Naughty Margaret' in family circles.

Of the six daughters only one survived into adulthood. She was Augusta Margaret Gwendoline who was born in 1830. She married Edward Joseph Bellew, 2nd Baron Bellew of Barmeath Castle, Co. Louth.

Possibly because of the delicate health visited upon their children, Colonel George and Margaret spent a lot of their time on the Continent. A number of their children are buried in Italy.

Colonel George did not inherit Jenkinstown until 1843. Gragara House had been built for them by Major George, but they never actually lived there. When they came back to Jenkinstown they decided to extend the mansion. It is said that Margaret wished to emulate the architecture that was used to build Alton Towers. Battlements were superimposed on the building but during the construction part of the wall fell killing some workmen.

The Bryans had come home from one nightmare (of their young children's deaths) to another – the Famine. Fortunately for the people of Kilkenny the famine did not affect their county with the ferocity experienced farther west. But the scarcity of food was felt and the workhouses were crowded leading to outbreaks of disease. Landlords like the Bryans did their utmost to offer support to their tenants by foregoing rents and working tirelessly on relief committees.[81]

The Colonel's efforts came to an abrupt end when he died, somewhat suddenly and prematurely in 1848 in his fifty second year. He was succeeded by his only surviving son George Leopold, who was born in 1828.

Within a short time George Leopold took over the responsibilities of running the estate and continued the improvements to the house and demesne, putting in new entrance gates and gate lodges and improving the drives. In 1878 George Leopold Bryan, of Jenkinstown House, Co. Kilkenny, owned 12,891 acres and other Bryan estates, mainly in Counties Wexford and Kilkenny, amounted to another 13,000 acres.

During the land agitation of the later decades of the 19th century George Leopold, known as Captain Bryan, was reputed to have been sympathetic to the plight of the tenants and reduced rents in many instances. He was active politically and was an M.P. for Kilkenny from 1865 to 1880. He was also a J.P. and a Deputy Lieutenant for the county. He was appointed High Sheriff for the county in 1852.

A year after his father's death he married Lady Elizabeth Conyngham.[82] They had one daughter Mary who died in her twentieth year. She was very popular

---

[81] A further example of the Colonel's philanthropy was the provision of a stained glass window for Kilkenny's St. Mary's Cathedral and the building of a school for the children of his employees. The school later became the gate lodge and is still in use as a residence.

[82] She was the granddaughter of another Lady Elizabeth Conyngham the mistress of King George IV. That Lady Elizabeth was a great beauty and socialite of her time. She was an

in her community. The accounts of her charity, kindness and concern for all and especially for young people live on even to this day. She was a frequent visitor to the school, probably that at Gragara, to help with the religious instruction of the children there.

Captain George Bryan was a well known figure in sporting circles. He was one of the stewards of the Kilkenny Four Day Annual Races. He is said to have owned a Derby Winner.[83] He was master of the Kilkenny Hounds in succession to Sir John Power.

Bryan hunting party

The Captain only outlived his daughter by eight years, dying in 1880. After the death of Captain George Bryan his widow later married the 11th Earl of Winchilsea.

George Leopold Bellew, a nephew of Captain George, inherited Jenkinstown and the estates. George L. Bellew was the third son of Edward Joseph Bellew and Augusta Margaret Gwendoline Bryan of Barmeath Castle - she being Captain Bryan's only surviving sister (as above).

---

accomplished harpist. As an heiress and only child of a very wealthy banker, named Denison, she was independently wealthy.

[83] He certainly did not own an English Derby winner but he may have owned the winner of an Irish Derby. The first Irish Derby was held in 1866 at the Curragh but I was unable to find the names of the owners of the winners from 1866 to 1880 – A.K.

George L. Bellew was 23 years of age and unmarried. On taking over ownership he was required to take the name Bryan as well. This he did by Royal license in 1881. Having undertaken a British Army career he spent very little time at Jenkinstown. Stewards and agents looked after his property and rents. Sometimes harsh treatment was meted out by these to the tenants.

In spite of his long and frequent periods of absence, George Bellew did much reconstruction work towards the end of the nineteenth century. The present cut stone castellated structure, still standing on the mansion site, was built by him. It was he, too, who built the single storey parish priest's house at Conahy, the parish in which Jenkinstown is situated.

During this time George's brother, Richard, had taken over and lived on the estate property at Mount Firoda, Castlecomer. At one stage he and his family came to live at Jenkinstown and many of his children were born there. Richard's first wife was Ada Gilbey a person noted for her great charity and friendliness. He had married her in 1887 and they had four children -Edward Henry, Bryan Bertram, Gwendoline and Ada Kate. She died, however, in 1893. He married, secondly, Josephine Gwendoline Herbert. They had two sons George Rothe and Patrick Herbert. Richard and his second wife left Jenkinstown and went to live in England.

In 1911 George Bellew succeeded his brother to become 4th Baron Bellew of Barmeath and was henceforth known as Lord Bryan Bellew. Once more the estate was cared for by agents and stewards in the continued absence of Lord George Bellew who was still touring in the Middle East. On a trip to Libya in 1927 he met and married Elaine Dodd, widow of Herbert Lloyd Dodd who had died in 1914. Elaine was daughter of John Leach, Queenstown, South Africa. It was then they returned to Jenkinstown to live there and restore what was for so long neglected. Lady Bellew proved herself an efficient if demanding manager and administrator.

Lord Bellew died on the 15th June 1935 without issue. Since 1911 he had owned not only the Jenkinstown property but that of Barmeath Castle as well, becoming 4th Baron Bellew. The properties passed to Edward who got Barmeath and Bryan Bertram who got Jenkinstown. By this time Edward Henry was 46 years of age, married and engaged in his life's work in London. He was not prepared to take up the Irish property and so he gave it to his younger brother Bryan Bertram Bellew. Edward retained the title 5th Baron Bellew until his death in 1976.

Bryan Bertram was at this time married and living at Troyswood, Kilkenny. He chose to live at Barmeath Castle, to retain the estate there, and to sell Jenkinstown. The Land Commission purchased it and subsequently divided it amongst farmers rerouting some internal roads and erecting boundary fences.

Due to this sale Elaine Lady Bellew was obliged to vacate Jenkinstown. She retired to live first at Kilcreene and later at Butler House, Kilkenny on an annuity of £500 per year. In her new situation she became active in the public affairs of the city and was elected as a Co. Councillor. She died on the 7th March, 1973 aged 88 years and is buried at St. Kieran's cemetery.

The Bryan arms were granted to James Bryan in 1684. The arms consist of a red shield with three lions and the crest is a sword erect with pommel and hilt in gold between two lions.

Butlers (Lords Carrick) of Mount Juliet

"To those who know this place, the very name evokes memories of green meadows sweeping down to the river Nore, groves of trees clothed in summer richness or stark against a winter sky, with groups of horses congregating under a row of pruned lime or spreading beech and all reminiscent of a scene by Herring or Stubbs. Happily, the great house of the earls of Carrick still dominates the demesne. This place, now well into its third century of existence, maintains that well bred air of aristocratic privilege which was so essential for its creation."

When the noted Kilkenny historian John Kirwan penned those words he may have been vaguely aware that today Mount Juliet would be synonymous with World Class Championship Golf Course. Not alone was the famed Golf Course developed in the last decade but the splendid and elegant Mount Juliet House has been carefully restored and is now a Hotel of enviable international repute. In addition the entire 1500 acre estate is fully utilized to make it a veritable heaven for guests. The long list of pursuits available to the visitor includes riding, fishing, hunting, shooting, archery and of course golf.

The story of the Butler family, who built Mount Juliet, began, not in Kilkenny but in Tipperary.

Edmund the 6th Butler (f. 1280 – 1320), from whom descended the Ormonde line, had at least two sons and his second son, John was the ancestor of the Viscounts Ikerrin, later Lords Carrick. He was settled in Tipperary in an area in and around Ballingarry, at Lismolin Castle. His neighbours were the fierce, determined O'Meaghers whose homeland was adjacent in Clonakenny in the barony of Ikerrin (an Anglicisation of the Gaelic *Ui Chairin*). The Butlers were able to survive in their castle at Lismolin because of their willingness to adapt and because of the power of their cousins who were the lords in Kilkenny Castle and Palatinate Lords of much of Tipperary. Another tenacious family of Norman descent, the Fannings ruled from their strong castle in Ballingarry, nearby.

Little is known of this branch of the Butlers until the year 1600 when Sir James Butler of Lismolin and his son Pierce Butler were pardoned by Queen Elizabeth, presumably for being in rebellion. In the notice of the pardon they were in the company of many other Butlers including Lord Dunboyne.[84] It will be remembered that the Nine Years War, as it known, between the Irish and the English was nearing its finale, culminating in the Battle of Kinsale in 1601. In another pardon of the same year Pierce was again pardoned and this time he was in the company of many members of very prominent Kilkenny families of Norman descent, such as the Shortalls, Shees, Rothes and Cantwells.

Lismolin Castle

Pierce, now Sir Pierce, was created Viscount Ikerrin in 1629. At this period he was in possession of over 20,000 acres of land in Tipperary. His marriage to Ellena, a daughter of Walter, the 11th Earl of Ormonde was significant, as it gave Sir Pierce and his descendants a close tie with the very powerful 1st Duke of Ormonde.[85]

---

[84] Fiant s of the Tudor Monarchs no. 6441
[85] He was the eldest son of Walter and therefore a brother to Ellena.

Their son, James, who may have been killed in the rebellion of 1641,[86] was married to a daughter of the 3rd Lord Dunboyne and it was their son, Pierce, who inherited the title and estates when Sir Pierce died in 1659.

Sir Pierce was caught up in what was known as 'the Great Rebellion' that was begun in the north of Ireland in 1641 and spread rapidly throughout the land. The Great Rebellion was a religious war and Sir Pierce being a leading Catholic in Co. Kilkenny had no option but to side with his kinsman, Lord Mountgarret. This move put him in direct conflict with his brother-in-law the 1st Duke of Ormonde who for the first eight years of this complex and confusing war was on the opposing side. Sir Pierce was made a Lieutenant General of the Leinster forces of the Catholic Confederacy and as such must have been present at the battles of Kilrush (Co.Kildare) and Ballinvegga (Co. Wexford) where the Confederate forces were heavily defeated by the armies commanded by the 1st Duke[87].

After the comprehensive defeat of the Irish/Confederate forces (now led by the 1st Duke of Ormonde) by the Cromwellians in 1649-50, Sir Pierce, with most of his Butler relations was subjected to forfeiture of his lands. He was allocated lands in Connaught, in counties Clare, Galway and Mayo in 1654 and given instructions to remove there with his wife and family and livestock. However prior to the removal of his entire household he was ordered to attend the government offices in Athlone to ascertain the exact location of his new lands and he was further ordered to build a stone house there prior to moving his wife and chattels. Whether by good fortune or by contrivance Sir Pierce fell sick and requested permission from the Cromwellian administrator to go to Bath, in England, to recover. This permission was granted and it is probable that he spent the winter of 1654-55 in Bath with his wife and family. They returned to Ireland in 1655 and, somehow, managed to avoid having to comply with the transportation order, perhaps feigning illness. The following year Sir Pierce wrote to Cromwell requesting an interview and this request was granted. He went to England and met Cromwell and petitioned him to return at least some of his lands as he was facing dire poverty. Cromwell instructed his deputy in Ireland to make some provision in Tipperary for Sir Pierce. During the entire upheaval of the period, Sir Pierce's grandson, also called Pierce, had been brought up as a Protestant in an English school.

When Sir Pierce died in 1659, he was succeeded by his grandson, now Sir Pierce the 2nd Viscount Ikerrin. This man lost no time in claiming back the lands lost by forfeiture. He claimed as an Innocent, being but two years old in 1641. His

---

[86] He was dead by 1642.

[87] For more information about this period see that chapters on the Butlers of Mountgarret and the Butlers of Ormonde.

claim was further advanced by his grand uncle the 1st Duke of Ormonde, who became the most powerful man in Ireland after the Restoration of Charles II in 1660. Most of the Ikerrin lands were restored but some areas in Co. Tipperary were left in the hands of Cromwellian grantees such as Langley[88] in Coalbrook and Jesse of Jessfield.

A strange story is still remembered in Tipperary about a priest called Father William Kelly and his persecution by the 2nd Viscount Ikerrin. Father William was the son of Ellen Butler and William Kelly. Ellen was the 2nd Viscount's aunt. According to the tradition the 2nd Viscount coveted the Kelly lands and to that end sought to have Father Kelly either killed or transported. A reward was offered for his capture. Fr. Kelly went on the run and hid in the houses of sympathisers. He moved from house to house and managed to stay ahead of the posse so to speak, for the rest of his life. The 2nd Viscount died either before or shortly after 1680 and the 3rd Viscount continued the vendetta. He died in 1688 and his successor, according to the story persisted unsuccessfully with the hunt. Fr. Kelly died c.1713 and on the night his coffin was being carried to the graveyard in Lismolin soldiers were spotted waiting in the graveyard, anxious to get the reward. The coffin bearers turned and brought the coffin back to the house where the priest had died and he was buried in the haggard of that farmstead. According to the Thurles historian, Michael Fitzgerald, the body was, at a later time, exhumed and buried in Lismolin.

Whatever the merits of the story, the 2nd Viscount recovered most of his ancestral lands, married a daughter of John Bryan[89] of Bawnmore, in Co. Kilkenny and had at least one son, his heir, James Butler.

Sir James, who succeeded as the 3rd Viscount Ikerrin, was reputed to have served in the Army of King James. He was fortunate in his marriage as his wife, Eleanor, was the daughter and co-heir of Colonel Redman, who had received 17,000 acres of land in Ballylinch in Co. Kilkenny[90]. Sir James died at a comparatively young age in 1688. His successor was his eldest son, Sir Pierce, who became the 4th Viscount.

Ballylinch, the property of the Butlers of Ikerrin, initially belonged to the Cistercians, based at Jerpoint Abbey. This foundation preceded the Norman conquistadors of the 12th and 13th centuries and was established by the

---

[88] See more about the Langleys in *The Tipperary Gentry Vol.1* by Art Kavanagh and Wm. Hayes
[89] See the chapter on the Bryan family in this book.
[90] Colonel Redman was a Parliamentarian officer who, at the instigation of his brother-in-law, John Otway, changed allegiance back to Charles II. Colonel Redman was married to Abigail Otway, John's sister. John Otway's cousin, another John, a Cromwellian officer was rewarded with a large estate in Templederry in Tipperary (See the *Tipperary Gentry Vol. 1*).

MacGiollaPadraig (FitzPatrick) ruler of the Osraighe on the eve of the Norman invasion. Their tenure of the properties was undisturbed, until the Protestant reformation of the 16th century despite having come under the jurisdiction of the Norman overlord William the Earl Marshal. In 1540 the Abbey and lands were granted by Henry VIII to James Butler the 9th Earl of Ormonde. Two decades later the lands were leased by Black Tom Butler, the 10th Earl, to one Oliver Grace, a descendant of one of the original Norman invaders. The property remained in the possession of that family for almost another hundred years until the Cromwellian Confiscations took place. The Grace incumbent of the time was caught up in the maelstrom of the Great Rebellion and lost his life at the Battle of Kilrush in Co. Kildare. His lands formed part of the parcel of properties granted to Colonel Redman. According to the Down Survey, his Kilkenny property consisted of the townlands of Ballylinch with "a very fair and large house, built English-wise, in good repair"[91]; Legan with "a castle"; Rathduff and Killarney, with "a castle in repair". The two former townlands were granted by Cromwell to Colonel Daniel Redman, the latter two, to Robert Myhill.

It was Somerset Butler, the 8th Viscount, a grandson of James Butler and Eleanor Redman who moved the family seat from Lismolin to Ballylinch. The townland named Mount Juliet involved the renaming of the townland of Waton's Grove[92] across the river (Nore) from Ballylinch. Somerset had inherited the title and lands in 1721when he was just three years old[93]. His father, the 6th Viscount Ikerrin, had died in 1719 at a comparatively young age. Since the 6th Viscount was a chaplain general in the army of the Duke of Ormonde in Flanders this meant that the young Somerset probably lived on the continent for some of his childhood. His mother was

---

[91] "Ballylinch castle was probably one of those ubiquitous tower houses which the gentry and aristocracy built in large numbers from the middle of the fifteenth century, until they became redundant in more settled and prosperous times, when they were considered uncomfortable and old-fashioned. It was probably built by the monks of Jerpoint or by a lay tenant of the abbey. The Graces may have added 'a very large castellated mansion' to this tower" – John Kirwan in an article entitled Mount Juliet in *Old Kilkenny Review 1998*

[92] This Waton family had been in Kilkenny since at least 1364 and occupied the lands continuously until the Cromwellian era. After that time the lands were confiscated and in 1660 were granted to the brother of Charles II. He sold the lands to a Stephen Sweet who in turn sold them on to Charles Kendall. Upon this man's death in the 1730s the lands were left to Thomas Bushe, a clergyman. He sold the lands to Hannah, the widow of Thomas Davis of Enniscorthy (founder of Davis's Mills) in 1753 and shortly after this the lands were acquired by Somerset Butler.

[93] Somerset's elder brother, James, inherited before him in 1719, but he died at the age of 8 in 1721. According to Lord Dunboyne he died of smallpox.

Margaret Hamilton from Co. Down. Somerset's wife was Juliana Boyle, the daughter of the Earl of Shannon[94]. In what must have been a most romantic gesture he named the townland of Mount Juliet after her.

Mount Juliet (courtesy College Books)

Somerset (b. 1715) had two sons, Henry and Pierce and two daughters, Henrietta and Margaret.[95] Pierce was an M.P. and although married he had no family. One of the greatest events of the life of the Butlers of Mount Juliet must have been the elevation of Somerset to the Earldom of Carrick in 1748, three years after his marriage to Juliana. His crowning achievement was the establishment of Mount Juliet demesne and the building of the fine mansion[96] which is still a jewel of 18th century architectural accomplishment. The Earl was considered to be a most

---

[94] He was Henry Boyle the 2nd son of the Hon .Henry Boyle who was killed in Flanders in 1693. The Hon. Henry's father was the Earl of Orrery.
[95] Henrietta married the 11th Viscount Mountgarret and Margaret married Armar Lowry-Corry, Earl Belmore. The Earl Belmore was from Co. Tyrone, where the Scottish Lowry family had settled during the plantation of Ulster. John Lowry the heir of James, the original planter, was present at the siege of Derry.
[96] John Kirwan thinks the house was built c.1769-71 (O.K.R. 1998)

influential figure in his time and was in receipt of a pension worth £1000 p.a. from the Irish exchequer during the viceroyalty of Lord Townshend. He was also instrumental in the destruction of the Freney gang by persuading Freney to rat on his comrades in return for a king's pardon[97]. Like many of his contemporaries he was very active in suppressing any kind of disorder. In 1770 three hundred Whiteboys had kidnapped a man called Patrick Shee, intending to bury him alive[98] at Dungarvan. However in the melee he fell off his horse and was badly injured. He died later from his injuries. Swoops were made in the area and eleven men were lodged in jail by Lord Carrick.[99]

Somerset died in 1774 and was succeeded by his eldest son, Henry, who became the 9th Viscount Ikerrin and the 2nd Earl of Carrick. He married an heiress, Sarah Taylor of Askeaton and they had four sons and four daughters. Henry must have been pleased with the matches made for his daughters Anne, Juliana, Harriet and Sarah. Their respective husbands were Rev. Henry Maxwell the 6th Lord Farnham, the 2nd Earl Belmore, [100]Frances Savage (and secondly Col. Matthew Forde) and finally the Hon. Charles Butler Wandesforde who was the brother of the 1st Marquess of Ormonde. Of course such prestigious marriages meant considerable dowries that must have put a strain on the family finances. His eldest son, Somerset Richard was groomed for the Earldom but the second son Henry Edward chose a career in the army. The two younger brothers both took Holy Orders and became parsons.

Henry Edward and three of his four sons were distinguished Army Officers, while his other son, Pierce, was in Holy Orders. Henry Edward, himself became a General and was Colonel of the 94th foot. His three remarkable Army Officer sons all died in 1854 two of them fighting in the Crimean War. The eldest son, Henry Thomas, who had served in the campaign in China, fell at the Battle of Inkerman in

---

[97] This notorious gang robbed the houses of the wealthy in Kilkenny and surrounding counties. On Freney's evidence seven men were tried and executed. Freney himself was pardoned in 1749 and his autobiography was published in 1754. Through the good offices of some person of influence, possibly Lord Carrick, he was given a small government post in New Ross in 1776 where he remained until his death. The autobiography was printed seven times and was used as a text in hedgeschools all over Ireland. (*Kilkenny History & Society* – ed. Wm Nolan, pg. 264)

[98] This did not mean they intended to kill him. Burying alive meant being buried up to the neck and left overnight or longer. It was meant to terrify but not kill.

[99] Burtchaell & Dowling in *Kilkenny History & Society*

[100] Juliana married this man, her first cousin.

1854, where the combined French and British armies defeated the Russians[101]. His fourth son, James Armar, was in Silistria, in 1854, when it was besieged by the Russians. The town was defended by the Turks who were commanded by Major Nasmyth and Captain James Butler. It was a desperate defence and lasted for a month. In the last action of the siege Captain Butler was severely wounded. Eventually the Russians moved away. Nasmyth and Butler became heroes. Captain James Butler later died of his wounds[102]. Charles George was a Captain in the 86th foot and he died of fever in Bombay.

Although married Henry Thomas had no family but Captain Charles George whose wife was Jane Prosser, had a son Charles Henry Somerset who later became the 6th Earl. Pierce, the 3rd son of General Henry Edward was an army chaplain for a time and was later the rector of Ulcombe in Kent. He had a son, Pierce Armar, also a rector, who married and had four sons and two daughters.

Henry Edward the 9th Viscount and 2nd Earl died in 1813 and was succeeded by his eldest son Somerset Richard.

Somerset Richard became the 10th Viscount and the 3rd Earl. His first wife, whom he married in 1811, was Anne Wynne of Haslebrook, Co. Sligo and they had two daughters. Anne died in 1829 and four years later Somerset Richard married Lucy French of French Park. He was actively involved in attempting to promote industry in Kilkenny. In 1817 he was on a committee with the Hon. Thomas Butler that set up a school to train linen workers. Unfortunately that project eventually ended in failure. He died in 1838 leaving his widow[103], two young sons and a daughter.

It is unclear as to how the family finances took such a serious downturn but within weeks of his death a Sheriff's Sale was held at Mount Juliet. The main creditors were Rev. Edmond Cronyn, Benjamin Alcock, Henry Gore, Stephen

---

[101] This famous victory was achieved despite the British and French being vastly inferior in numbers. The Russians had over forty thousand men in the battle while the allies had less than ten. The Russian dead and injured and those taken prisoner numbered over 12,000 while the allies lost less than 1,000 killed and about 4,000 injured.

[102] Field Marshal Lord Raglan had this to say about Captain Butler – 'by his prudence, courage, skill, stability and intrepid daring, this young volunteer assisted by his gallant friend and brother officer, infused into the garrison that spirit of heroic resistance which led to its triumphant defence.'

[103] Four years later, in 1842, Lucy married again. Her 2nd husband was the Hon. Charles Butler Wandesforde the brother of the 1st Marquess of Ormonde. It was his second marriage also. He died in 1860 and Lucy died in 1884.

Wright and Robert Madigan[104]. The notice of the sale was published in the Kilkenny Journal of the 24th February 1838 as follows –

> To be Sold by Auction, at Mount Juliet on Thursday, the 1st day of March next, at the hour of 12 o'clock at noon, and following days, the entire household furniture, plate, and plated ware, valuable paintings, books, piano forte, china, glass, &c. Also the entire stock, horses, carriages and farming implements, comprising 225 sheep, 242 ewes in lamb, 208 hoggets, 11 rams, 28 fat cows, 7 fat bullocks, 9 cows, 8 heifers in calf, 2 new milch cows, 6 dry cows, 10 two, three and four year old heifers, 11 three and four year old bullocks, 6 store Kerrys, 5 bulls, 10 calves, 17 other cows, 21 carriage, saddle, and draft horses, 4 brood mares, 13 one, two and three year old colts, 2 foals, 1 pony, 30 pigs, and about 100 deer, about 170 tons of straw, 200 barrels of wheat, 170 barrels of oats, 300 barrels of potatoes, 25 acres of growing wheat. 2 carriages, 2 jaunting cars, 1 pony car, 1 cab, with harness complete to each, saddles, bridles, horse clothing, &c. *The Farming Implements* comprise threshing and winnowing machines, ploughs, harrows, scufflers, drill and cleaning machines, cars, carts, drays, rollers, plough and car tackling; a quantity of timber, with numerous other articles.

It is probable that the sale raised sufficient funds to help the widow maintain a reasonable life style. She did manage to marry off one of her two step daughters[105], and her own daughter. Her step daughter, Anne Margaret was in her forties when she married George Lloyd of Strancally Castle, Co. Waterford. The dowager's own daughter, Lucy Maria, married Lord Massy[106] in 1863.

A further sale of property occurred in 1852 when much of the family property, excluding the 1500 acre Mount Juliet estate, was sold by the Encumbered Estates court. The sale realised over £40,000.

The 4th Earl of Carrick died when he was still a teenager and the title and estate passed to his younger brother, Somerset Arthur, who became the 5th Earl. This man pursued a career in the Army and joined the Grenadier Guards as an ensign in 1856. He took part in the siege of Sebastopol during the Crimean War and was suitably decorated. He retired from the Army as a Captain in 1862 and took up

---

[104] John Kirwan in O.K.R. 1998

[105] Somerset Richard's daughters by his first marriage were Sarah Juliana and Anne Margaret. Sarah Juliana was married in 1832 to the 3rd Earl of Clancarty and her descendants continued the line of Clancarty to modern times. The 8th Earl of Clancarty, a world famous ufologist died in 1995.

[106] This very prestigious family owned properties in many places including Limerick and Dublin.

residence in Mount Juliet. There he entered into the social life of the gentry of his time, hunting, shooting and fishing. He was said to have been a very charming, dashing young man but he never married. In later life he became almost a recluse. He died in 1901 and whatever personal fortune he possessed was given to the Plymouth Brethren[107] of which he was a member.

His successor in 1901 was his elderly cousin, Major Charles Henry Butler, mentioned above, who became the 6th Earl. He never lived at Mount Juliet and he gave legal possession of the estate to his son and heir, Charles Ernest Butler[108], who in 1909, on the death of his father, became the 7th Earl of Carrick.

The 7th Earl found that after paying the death duties he was unable to maintain the estate. He decided to lease the property and he found a ready purchaser in General Sir Hugh McCalmont whose family had been very successful London bankers. The 7th Earl moved to London and was there created an Earl in England which gave him the entitlement to sit in the House of Lords and presumably an annual emolument. Prior to that he had been a Colonel in the army and had served in the First World War. He was given an OBE in 1918 in recognition of his military prowess. He had married two years before the turn of the century and his wife was a daughter of Colonel Henry Lindsay of Glasnevin[109]. They had five sons and two daughters.

The two daughters both married. Lady Rosamund was married twice. Her first husband was Lionel Robertson and they had one son, Patrick Somerset who later took his step- father's name Gibbs. Lady Rosamund was a well known person in her community in Hertshire where she was a J.P., a founder of the Care of Children group attached to Ware Park Hospital and President of the Church Councils for Hertshire. Patrick Somerset, her son, was a Lt. Col. in the army and served in that capacity during the Second World War. He married and had a

---

[107] This was a splinter group of the Church of Ireland. Its members yearned for a more disciplined and simple type of religion. They believed in the power of austerity and prayer. It was begun in Dublin in the early 1800s.

[108] Charles Ernest had one sister, Kathleen who married Col. Walter Lindsay of Glasnevin in 1897. He was a descendant of the 6th Earl of Balcarres.

[109] Colonel Henry Lindsay of Glasnevin was a brother of Col. Walter (above) who had married Kathleen Butler, the 7th Earl's aunt.

family[110]. Her second husband was Major Bryan Gibbs and they had a son[111] and a daughter[112].

Lady Rosamund's sister was Lady Irene and like her sister she was married twice. Her first husband was John Charlton of Tunbridge Wells and her second husband was Colonel Anthony Hobson from Sussex. They had one son Michael, a captain in the army. He married Marie Feuilherade in 1953 and they have a son John and a daughter Marie.

All five sons of the 7th Earl pursued careers in the armed forces. His eldest son and heir, Theobald was in the Navy and the other four in different regiments of the army and airforce.

The second son, Horace Somerset earned himself an Indian Frontier medal and was an Honorary Magistrate in Rangoon. He was also a member of the House of Representatives in Burma in the years prior to the Second World War. He was married to Barbara Hood from Befordshire and they one daughter, Georgina, who became a celebrity in the fashion world as Gina Fratini the famous fashion designer[113]. Her second husband was Renato Fratini from Rome. She later married James Short, an actor from Glasgow, whose stage name was Jimmy Logan, and her final marriage was to Anthony Newly who died in 1999 in Florida.

Guy Somerset the 3rd son was a major in the Royal Canadian Dragoons and he was married twice. His first wife was Mrs. Patricia Tennant and they had two sons, Rupert and Dermot. Rupert became an RAF officer. Rupert's wife is Jennifer Rush from Surrey and they have four children all born in the 1970s[114]. Dermot who was educated in England was married twice and has one daughter, Tara, by his first wife Lorna Menzies.

The 4th son Godfrey does not appear to have married but the 5th son, Pierce, a Major, was married twice. He had a son, David, and a daughter, Helen, with his first wife, Leri Llewelyn-Jones from Anglesey. David is a farmer and company director and he and his wife Anne Haigh have a son Michael and a daughter Hilary.

After the death of the 7th Earl in 1931 Theobald became the 8th Earl of Carrick. He was Commander in the Navy and was a life Vice President and later Deputy Governor General of the Roy Stuart Society. He was married twice. He and

---

[110] His wife was Mairi Zoe Evans and they have five children all born in the 1950s – Andrew, David, Alexander, Teresa and Georgiana.

[111] Somerset Bryan Gibbs married Elspeth Russi and they have four children all born in he 1950s –Brian, Anthony, Matthew and Kathleen.

[112] Brigid married Lancelot Hannen and they have a son Peter and a daughter Caroline.

[113] She designed clothes for Princess Diana and many other famous people.

[114] Piers Somerset, Eli Somerset, Matthew Somerset and Sebastian Somerset.

his first wife, Marion Donoghue of Philadelphia had one son Brian Stuart Butler who on the death of his father, in 1957 became the 9th Earl of Carrick.

The 9th Earl was born in 1931 and received his education at Downside. He was associated with the cotton industry and a member of a large number of boards of directors of such companies as the Liverpool Cotton Association, the Khartoum Cotton Association and Cotac, Le Havre. He was married twice and he and his first wife, Mary Turville-Constable-Maxwell had one son, David James and a daughter Lady Juliana.

The 9th Earl died in 1992 and was succeeded by his son, David who became the 10th Earl. David was educated at Downside. He is married to Phillipa Craxton of Hantshire and they have two sons Thomas Piers (Lord Ikerrin) and Piers Edmund and one daughter Lady Lindsay, a twin to her brother Piers.

Butlers of Maidenhall

As Hubert Butler, that exceptional man of great insight and international fame said modestly, 'the Butlers of Maidenhall were minor gentry'. Maidenhall is near Bennetsbridge in Co. Kilkenny. The family took up residence there in the mid 1800s. Before that it was built and occupied by a Henry and Frances Griffith in the mid eighteenth century.[115] Henry was an intellectual and an entrepreneur[116] and his wife was a writer[117]. Hubert Butler found them a most extraordinary couple and in his book *Escape from the Anthill* he devoted the first chapter to them under the title *Henry and Frances*.

---

[115] On a Taylor and Skinner Map of the 18th century it was noted as being in the ownership of the Flood family.

[116] Henry got a grant from parliament for starting linen manufacturing on the Nore. He built a factory and his house – Maidenhall c. 1745. An expected second grant did not materialize and as Henry was heavily mortgaged his business was ruined. He and Frances turned their hands to novel writing and Frances, in particular, was quite successful. Henry was also able to make a living from his writings.

[117] She was the first English translator of Voltaire.

Hubert in concluding the chapter went on to say 'Last year the Nore flooded, as it often does, and flattened out the remaining wall of Griffith's flaxmill, which has been used for some generations as a boundary fence. The mill-stream has long been choked up and it was only quite lately that poking about on the banks of the river I found traces of its stone built sides. The cottages that housed the mill-hands as well as the sixty one harvesters[118] have gone without trace, but the elm trees which Henry planted are still standing. As for Maidenhall, it has not changed very much; its successive owners have always been poor and never had any money to make many of those lavish improvements which were admired in Victorian times.'

Maidenhall – an overview

One of Hubert's most fascinating essays in the same book was that entitled 'The Artukovitch file' which outlined Hubert's crusade to find out how Croatian Artukovich, a mass murderer of many thousands of Serbs during the Second World War, had managed to find asylum in Ireland for a year (1947-48) and was then

---

[118] This is a reference to Henry who used to sit among the stooks in a barley field, writing to Frances and reading Pliny's Letters. Watching the binders and stackers he counted forty seven women and fourteen men.

provided with a visa to enable him to go to America. Hubert's detective work leaves Sherlock Holmes in the ha'penny place. In the concluding section of the article Hubert tells how attempts were being made to have Artukovich extradited to Yugoslavia in 1985.

It must have been gratifying for Hubert to have lived to see that in 1986 Artukovitch was in fact extradited, tried in a court in Yugoslavia for war crimes and sentenced to death by firing squad. He escaped the firing squad but died in prison there in 1988.

Hubert's other published works include *Ten Thousand Saints: A Study in Irish and European Origins (1972); Wolfe Tone and the Common Name of Irishmen; Children of Drancy ; Grandmother and Wolfe Tone; The Sub-Prefect Should Have Held His Tongue* and *In the Land of Nod* which was published posthumously.

Perhaps his greatest achievements were not in his books and ideas but in his actions. He worked in Vienna for the liberation of the Austrian Jews after the Anschluss – the annexation of Austria by Germany in 1938; his investigation of the deportation of four thousand children in Vichy, France; and his efforts to expose the Vatican's complicity in a campaign to forcibly convert Orthodox Serbs in Catholic Croatia.

Neal Ascherson, the distinguished Scottish writer wrote a foreword to *In the Land of Nod* and in that essay he wrote that the material in the book 'will confirm Hubert Butler's international reputation, already brilliant but still spreading....by the time of his death in 1991 readers throughout Europe and America were asking in amazement why he had not been part of their common culture before. Among his early admirers was the most beloved of Russia's exiled poets, the late Joseph Brodsky.'

Roy Foster in his essay 'Butler and his Century' in *Unfinished Ireland (Essays on Hubert Butler)* had this to say: *By the end of Hubert's century, he was recognized - in the USA and Britain as well as in Ireland - as one of its key commentators, who had at once kept pace with history and kept faith with his "ethical imagination", transmuting his observations of the great world-historical cavalcade, or the inexorable juggernaut, into beautifully worked and mercilessly clear-sighted essays which bear reading and re-reading.*

Hubert Butler loved Kilkenny and he loved Maidenhall. This strong attachment comes through in his writings. In his essay Beside the Nore (*Escape from the Anthill*) he wrote – 'I have lived most of my life on the Nore and own three fields upon its banks, some miles before it turns to the south-east and forces its way under Brandon Hill to join the Barrow above New Ross. In sixty years it has changed remarkably little. From a top window, looking across the river towards the

Blackstairs and Mount Leinster, I can still see the same stretch of cornfields, nut groves and mountain slopes. Beside the woods of Summerhill and Kilfane I can spot the round tower of Tullaherin and Kilbline, the sixteenth century castle of the Shortalls.'

Hubert Butler

In another essay, in true Hubert Butler style, he gives us a glimpse of his in depth knowledge of the place of his birth. 'One of our favourite places was Annamult Woollen Factory, a very stylish and spacious ruin on the King's river just before it joins the Nore. Before the king-cups and the bullocks took over, it was in 1814 one of the most progressive factories in the British Isles. Its owners, Messrs Shaw and Nowlan, rivalled Robert Owen, the Utopian industrialist, in their concern for their 400 work people. The children all had free schooling and lesson books, their fathers and mothers had health insurance cards, and every Sunday they danced to the fiddle in the large courtyard. George Shaw and Timothy Nowlan were stern but just, and rather quizzical. (Shaw was, I believe, a great great uncle to George Bernard.) Employees who misbehaved were punished but not sacked. Sometimes the offender, dressed in a yellow jacket, was obliged to roll a stone round the courtyard in full view of the Sunday merrymakers. The factory, while it lasted, was hugely successful. The Prince Regent and all the employees of the Royal Dublin Society dressed themselves in its woollens and the fields around Annamult were white with a flock of 600

Merino sheep, vast bundles of wool with tiny faces, which the Prims, a famous Kilkenny family with Spanish relations, had imported from Spain.'

Hubert's ideas and his uncompromising stance in relation to matters such as the forcible 'conversion' of the Serbs and the Fethard Boycott in Co. Wexford led to clashes with the Irish establishment and the Catholic Church. As a result Hubert became a *persona non grata* in many quarters. However he was totally vindicated when the Mayor of Kilkenny, Paul Cuddihy, publicly apologized on the occasion of The Hubert Butler Centenary Celebration, eight years after Hubert's death. In his opening remarks the Mayor said *"This evening I wish to apologise publicly for the treatment the late Hubert Butler received in Kilkenny in 1952. I wish to apologise because it is important to do so when you are in the wrong and we were in the wrong. I am not here to pardon him as he did nothing wrong."* He went on to explain how the situation had come about and the background of ignorance and insularity that had led to Hubert and his family being ostracized.

The Butlers of Maidenhall descended from the Butlers of Dunboyne, who resided at Kiltynan Castle[119] in Co. Tipperary until the time of Cromwell, when the castle was battered by cannon and was later granted with part of the Dunboyne estate to Edward Cooke, an adventurer.

The first Baron of Dunboyne was Edmund Butler, who was the son of James Butler and Joan the daughter of Piers Roe, the 8th Earl of Ormonde. James, himself was the 9th Lord Dunboyne[120] as distinct from his son who was the 1st Baron. The Barony of Dunboyne was conferred on Edmund by Henry VIII in 1541. The title was conferred as a 'grant to Edmund Butler, esquire, and the heirs male of his body;

---

[119] Kiltynan had come to the Butlers when the Lord of Dunboyne (who was killed in a duel in 1420) married a de Bermingham heiress. The duel was extraordinary in that Lord Dunboyne was killed by his kinsman the son of the Prior of Kilmainham, an illegitimate son of the 4th Earl of Ormonde. The Prior had been granted Kiltynan by his father, the Earl, so in order to settle the matter the Earl, who was conveniently also Lord Lieutenant, decided the matter should be settled by mortal combat. The Lord of Dunboyne lost his life and the Prior's son was grievously wounded, but Dunboyne's descendants continued on living in Kiltynan – from a lecture given by Lord Dunboyne and reproduced in the *Old Kilkenny Review* of 1966.

[120] He descended from Sir Thomas Butler, a first cousin of James the 1st Earl of Ormonde. Sir Thomas was married to Synolda le Petit whose father was Lord of Dunboyne and Molyngar (Mullingar). During the reign of Richard the 1st Hugh de Lacy was replaced by William le Petit who was granted huge territories in Westmeath and Meath and was given the title Lord of Dunboyne and Westmeath. As Synolda was the sole heir of William his successor, the titles were acquired by Sir Thomas Butler. He was slain in 1329 and his son became the 2nd Lord Dunboyne of the manor of Grenagh in county Kilkenny.

of the dignity of baron of Dunboyne.'[121] Edmund was given a further grant of lands in Tipperary in 1543 – 'grant to Edmund Butler, knight, baron of Donboyne (sic), in consideration of the sum of £110 of silver; of the site of the monastery of Augustin friars of Fyddert, Co. Tipperary; land etc., in Fyddert, Ballyclowan and Crosarde. To hold for ever, by the service of a twentieth part of a knight's fee, and a rent of 5s. 4d.'[122]

Sir Edmund died in prison[123] in 1567 and was succeeded by his son James the 2nd Baron of Dunboyne (d. 1624). James was married twice. His first wife was a daughter of Fitzpatrick the Lord of Upper Ossory and his second wife was a daughter of the O'Brien Earl of Thomond. He had families by both his wives and the 7th son of the second marriage was the ancestor of the Butlers of Maidenhall.

He was Theo Butler who was settled at Priestown in Co. Meath. This man had a son, Pierce, a Doctor of Divinity and rector of Glenbeigh, who in turn was the father of Theobald who was born c.1690. Theobald's wife was the daughter of Sir Nathaniel Whitwell, Lord Mayor of Dublin in 1727. He had a number of sons of whom James Butler of Priestown, Co. Meath was the eldest.[124]

It is not clear when the main branch of the Butlers became Protestant (in name at any rate) but towards the close of the 17th century the Catholic Bishop of Cork, the Right Rev. and Hon. John Butler succeeded to the Dunboyne title and estates at the age of 67. He promptly turned Protestant, in order that no obstacle could be put in the way of his succession and took his cousin as a wife, hoping to produce a successor, but in this he failed. After his death the title went to his cousin James Butler who became the 13th Baron. The Bishop left a valuable endowment to Maynooth College still know today as Dunboyne House.

James Butler of Priestown who was born in the middle of the 18th century was married to a daughter of Sir Richard Steele. They had one son, Richard, a Doctor of Divinity and Vicar of Burnchurch Co. Kilkenny. He was married to Martha Rothwell, of Rockfield, Co. Meath and they had at least six sons and a daughter[125]. Briefly these were James of Priestown, Very Rev. Richard, Dean of Clonmacnoise and Vicar of Trim, Thomas a Captain in the Army, Whitwell of Staffordstown the man who carried the colours at Waterloo (and survived to tell the

---

[121] *Fiants of Henry VIII* no. 194.
[122] *Fiant of Henry VIII* no. 397
[123] He had taken part in a rebellion at that time which was led by the sons of the Earl of Ormonde. The Earl's sons escaped the scaffold because of the Earl's influence.
[124] The other very interesting son was the second son Whitwell who became the ancestor of the Butlers of Waterville, Cobh and Anner House, Fethard, Co. Tipperary.
[125] She is not mentioned in Burke's pedigree but Rev. Richard, the Dean of Clonmacnoise, mentions her in correspondence – *Memoir of the Very Rev. Richard Butler* NLI

tale dying in 1877), Rev. Edward of Llangoed Castle, Brecon (who was married four times and had children by all his wives) and John of Maidenhall. John of Maidenhall was the father of George who despite having five uncles had less than seven cousins. It was no wonder that Hubert Butler, George's son complained of a scarcity of cousins on his father's side!

The Bishop of Ossory was a very good friend of Rev. Richard senior, who had settled at Burnchurch and when the Bishop was removed from Ossory to Meath he presented the parish of Trim to the Rev. Richard. However Richard had built a house for his family at Burnchurch and was reluctant to move. He wrote to his son in Oxford, Richard junior, asking him to take up the duties of the parish of Trim. Richard junior agreed to do this. He was ordained in 1819 and took up his post the same year. There he became quite friendly with many of the gentry families including the Edgeworths and within a short time he was married to Harriet Edgeworth. His uncle John Rothwell died about the same time and left him a small estate.

In 1831 when the anti Tithe movement found expression in what was known as the 'Hurler' gatherings[126], the quiet of Burnchurch was seriously disturbed. A huge crowd gathered in front of Rev. Richard's house demanding the reduction of the tithes. When Doctor Butler went outside and addressed them, 'neither fearfully nor angrily, the mob seemed awed by his dignified presence and left the place without having broken a shrub or trampled on a flower'.[127] But as the protests continued unabated, with the gentry of the county standing aloof, the Vicar and his family were forced to leave their home and go to England. They did not return until 1834 and from that time onwards they lived there peacefully.[128]

Meanwhile, Richard in Trim was facing his own battles. There the demand for tithe reduction was negligible but an outbreak of cholera in 1832 compelled the young pastor to expose himself as he made the very many sick calls to the dying. In addition large numbers of Protestants were emigrating to Canada. The anti tithe movement did find its way to Meath, but fortunately for the Rev. Richard it exhibited itself in a very mild form only and he was not embroiled in any controversy.

In Trim, the famine, as in Co. Kilkenny, while it did visit many hardships on the poor was not so severe as in other areas and nobody died of hunger. A relief committee was formed and carried out much charitable work. Rev. Richard of Trim

---

[126] In order to give the impression that the gatherings were legal, the anti Tithe organisers pretended that the crowds assembling were in fact going to attend a hurling match.
[127] Dr. Richard died in Burnchurch in 1841. *Memoir of the Rev. Richard Butler, Dean of Clonmacnoise* – N.L.I.
[128] Ibid.

was appointed Dean of Clonmacnoise in 1847. It was a title only and had no remuneration or duty attached. Maria Edgeworth died in 1849 to the great grief of the Dean to whom she was the author of much kindness[129]. Richard of Trim was a noted antiquarian and contributed to the Irish Archaeological Journal which was founded during the middle of the century.[130]

George Butler of Maidenhall was the son John of Maidenhall and grandson of Dr. Richard of Burnchurch. George had two sisters, Harriet and Florence who, when they had passed unmarried into middle age settled at Lavistown[131], a small country house a few miles from Maidenhall. Hubert wrote lovingly and very wittily about his maiden aunts. Harriet had deserted the Protestant religion and turned to Christian Science. 'Aunt Harriet became a Christian Scientist because a certain Dr. Davis had failed to meet her under the clock on the platform at Kingsbridge station in Dublin.' She also became a Gaelic Leaguer because of the passionate involvement of Otway Cuffe and his sister-in-law, the Countess of Desart, in the same movement.[132] Florence, on the other hand, was a Martha to her sister's Mary. She looked after the worldly necessities such as managing the gardener and making sure they got fed properly.

In a rare insight into how families gradually lose their wealth and prestige Hubert revealed that 'we had forebears called Kingston who owned a shipyard in Cork and when it closed retained the ground rents of the buildings that went up on the quays beside the Lee. The ground rents passed on to their descendants, getting less and less with each generation, together with some good miniatures of themselves in a blue velvet frame, by Frederick Buck of Cork. We got the miniatures and my aunts got the ground rents.'

George, according to Hubert, was a farmer. He was also a J.P. and High Sheriff of Kilkenny in 1901. The Butlers had over 600 acres of land and were in fact gentlemen farmers. The whole was comprised of two separate lots of about 300 acres each. One farm was at Burnchurch, near Bennetsbridge and the other was six miles north east of Kilkenny city at Drumherin. The lands were looked after by the Phelan brothers. George took a keen interest in all the farming activities and managed the operation, deciding on crops, stocking levels and going to fairs. George

---

[129] Maria was a half sister of the Dean's wife Harriet. She was the author of several novels including *Castle Rackrent, The Absentee* and *Ormond*.
[130] He also compiled a history of Trim which was republished in 1978 by the Trim Archaeological Society.
[131] Lavistown was built by William Colles, the founder of the Kilkenny Marble Works as a residence for his manager, but was bougth for the Butler ladies after the marriage of their brother.
[132] *Independent Spirit* by Hubert Butler

was married to Harriet Neville Clarke from Co. Tipperary and they had four children, Cicely, Hubert, George Gilbert and Joanna Vernon.

Sir Tyrone Guthrie

Hubert inherited Maidenhall after his father's death in 1941. His wife was Susan Guthrie from Annaghmakerrig, Co. Monaghan, a sister of the renowned director, playwright and actor Sir Tyrone Guthrie[133]. They had one daughter, Julia whose husband is Richard Crampton. Julia and Richard have four children, Thomas, Cordelia, Suzanna and Katherine.

The Tyrone Guthrie Centre at Annaghmakerrig

---

[133] This very distinguished man was the grandson of Tyrone Power the famous 19th century actor and he was a great grandson of the famous philanthropist and preacher of the same name (Guthrie), whose statue now stands in Prince's Street in Edinburgh. The Tyrone Guthrie Centre in Annaghmakerrig in Co. Monaghan was the home of the Guthrie family.

Butlers of Maidenhall

Cicely Marion was married to Herbert Doudney of Ceylon but they had no family. Joanna Vernon's husband was Gerald Lenox – Conyngham, originally from Co. Louth was a tea planter in Ceylon (now Sri Lanka). Joanna and Gerald had three children, Melosina (Melo), Vere and Eleanor. Vere and Eleanor are both married. Eleanor's husband is Professor Nicholas Grene. Melo, a much travelled lady, lives in Co. Kilkenny and is the administrator of the now very famous Butler Society.

George Gilbert's wife was Noreen Pomeroy from Corkagh, Co. Dublin and they had one son James and one daughter Jessica. James is married to Gillian Becher and Jessica's husband is Benjamin McClintock Bunbury the 5th Baron Rathdonnell.

Butlers Viscounts of Mountgarret

The 17th Viscount Mountgarret who passed away in 2004 was a most colourful character. He sat in the House of Lords and he certainly did not endear himself to those whose political persuasion inclined to the left. He rejoiced in not being dependent on the whim of electors. "I do not have to curry favour with constituents" he stated tritely in the House much to the chagrin of the *New Worker* which reported his comment and went on to say "Just a few weeks ago an industrial tribunal ordered him (Viscount Mountgarret) to pay £20,000 compensation to a gamekeeper who had suffered eight years of his (Mountgarret's) *unpredictable, irrational and intolerable rages*".

Another remarkable incident was noted in a brief comment about the Viscount in an article on the Internet. *"The 17th Viscount Mountgarret, who has died of a heart attack aged 67, claimed descent from King Henry VII and regularly behaved as though living in the 16th century. His most famous exploit was to take a shotgun to a hot-air balloon manned by tourists, which floated too low for his liking over his Yorkshire grouse moor in 1982. He was fined £1,800 by Skipton magistrates, amid much testy harrumphing."*

While the Viscount may have claimed descent from Henry VII it would appear from all the relevant documentation available that this claim was incorrect.[134] He was in fact descended from Edward Longshanks insomuch as a granddaughter of that monarch was married to the 1st Duke of Ormonde, in the early 14th century and bore his children.

The first Viscount Mountgarret was Richard, the second son of Piers Roe Butler the 8th Earl of Ormonde. Piers Roe himself was the son of Sir Richard Butler of Polestown and Sadbh Kavanagh the sister of Art Bui Kavanagh the McMurrough and King of Leinster. Piers Roe was given a Gaelic upbringing by his Kavanagh mother but his Fitzgerald wife, the famous Lady Margaret soon brought him back to 'civility'. She was the daughter of the Great Earl of Kildare but when she married Piers Roe she soon became a dedicated Butler and used her not inconsiderable talents and influences to further the interests of that family. Her eldest son was James who became the 9th Earl of Ormonde and Richard was her second son.[135] She strove with all her maternal instincts to ensure that Richard became a very powerful lord also.

The 16th century in Ireland was a very exciting time for the entrepreneurial English and Anglo Irish such as the Butlers. Huge swathes of church lands were taken by Henry VIII and leased or sold to members of the powerful ruling families. In 1541 Richard Butler was given leases of lands in Wexford and Kilkenny, notably in Inistioge, Thomastown and Shankill.[136] Two years later, in 1543 he got a grant of all the Augustinian lands in and near New Ross.[137] He was created Viscount Mountgarret and Baron of Kells in 1550 in direct response to his plea to be given a title that would outshine that of the McMurrough. "For the next two centuries those Viscounts had a noble record of supporting losing causes with considerable gallantry, culminating in 1793 with the death of the 11th Viscount from a surfeit of strawberries and cider!"[138]

---

[134] It might be possible that Henry VII had an affair with Margaret Fitzgerald the wife of Piers Roe, the 8th Earl but if this is the case it is certainly not information that is in the public domain, while it may have been part of the family lore. It is well known that Margaret made every effort to advance her son Richard, but from what we know of her character this was to be expected.

[135] Her third son, Thomas, was killed in a battle with his Geraldine cousins, at Jerpoint Abbey in Co. Kilkenny in 1532. Lady Margaret's niece, Lady Alice Fitzgerald, was married to Cahir McArt Kavanagh of Borris, Co. Carlow, ancestor of the present day Kavanaghs of Borris.

[136] Fiants of Henry VIII no. 239

[137] Fiant no. 396

[138] Lord Dunboyne's talk at Kilkenny Castle (*Old Kilkenny Review*)

Richard the 1st Viscount was not among that unhappy band. The forays of his father Piers into the territories of the Fitzpatricks of Upper Ossory, trained him in the exercise and knowledge of those military operations, which he afterwards turned to good account in defending the King's lands against the "Irish enemy," especially in Wexford, against the Kavanaghs. It was in recompense for such services to his Sovereign that King Edward VI gave directions to have him created a Viscount. He had already been installed in Mountgarret Manor and castle, on the outskirts of New Ross, and it was from this that the name Mountgarret derived. The Manor was formerly Church lands and the Castle was the home of the famous Bishop Barrett in the late 14th and early 15th centuries, after he had removed from Ferns, the traditional residence.

Mountgarret Castle

In addition to the Augustinian lands of New Ross that he had acquired earlier, Mountgarret bought the lands of Kayer (Davidstown to Glynn) from Foulks

Denn in 1556. The Kayer lands were later demised to Piers Butler his son. The Butler family of Kayer was subsequently dispossessed by the Cromwellians.

During the reigns of Edward and Queen Mary, prior to being created Viscount Mountgarret, Richard was made keeper of the Castle of Ferns. He was also in two commissions for the preservation of the peace, in the Counties of Tipperary, Kilkenny and Wexford. He was present in the Parliament of 1560 which met in Dublin and which ended in passing the Statute of Uniformity, which made Queen Elizabeth head of the Church, in Ireland, and re-established the reformed worship, as it had existed under Edward VI. Richard was buried in St. Canice's Cathedral, Kilkenny, in 1571.[139]

By his first wife, Eleanor, daughter of Theobald Butler of Neigham, he had a daughter Margaret[140] and a son, Edmund, who became the 2nd Viscount. He followed in his father's footsteps of persecuting and hunting down the 'mere Irishry'. He was ever ready to spill blood, in quarrels and in defence. He renewed the old animosities with the Fitzpatricks, the Princes of Upper Ossory. Edmund later married Grainne, the daughter of Lord Ossory (Sir Barnaby Fitzpatrick). Marriage alliances in those days were often used in an attempt to patch up old enmities.

The 2nd Viscount was a significant political player in his time, siding with the Earl of Ormond and Lord Justice Pelham against the Earl of Desmond. He played a prominent role in the 'plantation of Munster. He accompanied the Lord Deputy in his Munster Expedition in 1579 against the Spaniards and James Fitzmaurice, who was leader of the Desmond insurgents. He sat in Perrott's Parliament in Dublin (1585-6) which attainted the late Earl of Desmond. One hundred and forty of his followers confiscated 600,000 acres of land, to be distributed among English undertakers, who peopled it with English families.

Strange as it may seem the Ormondes and the Mountgarrets were closely related to the Desmonds of Munster as Edmund's uncle, James, the

---

[139] The Viscount was not without his enemies and one such may have been Colclough of Tintern in Wexford who complained to the Lord Deputy that Sir Richard refused to attend a hearing to answer for complaints against his men. The complaints were that they were responsible for ' taking of preyes, Bordragges, wounding of men by night and taking Gentilwomen prisoners' (Hore – *History of the town & county of Wexford* Vol. 6 pg. 35)

[140] Married to Sir Nicholas Devereux of Ballymagir in Co. Wexford. This made her the mother-in-law of Catherine, the daughter of Brian McCahir Kavanagh of Polmonty, the ancestor of the Kavanaghs of Borris in Co. Carlow. Catherine was married to Walter Devereux the son of Sir Nicholas.

9th Earl of Ormonde, was married to Lady Joan Fitzgerald the daughter and heir of the 11th Earl of Desmond. It was even stranger to note that some of the sons of the 9th Earl were involved in what was known as the Desmond Rebellion, which found expression in a battle fought for Kilkenny city. And yet stranger was the fact that Piers and James, two brothers of Edmund the future Viscount Mountgarret also sided with the Desmond faction, then led by James FitzMaurice the son of Sir Morish Fitzgibbon, the White Knight.[141]

The rebel Butlers all took an active part in the battle of Kilkenny in 1568. The Butler participation in the rebellions of the period stemmed from two grievances – the loss of land suffered by the Butlers of Cloghgrennan, Co. Carlow[142] and the pressure being put on them to renounce Catholicism.

The battle of Kilkenny was a serious affair involving the Butlers allied to the Gaelic clans of the region, the Kavanaghs, O'Byrnes and O'Nolans. The rebel Butlers with their Gaelic allies took over the city and defended it against the Crown forces led by Sir Peter Carew and probably the Mountgarret forces. The defenders numbered two thousand. Carew defeated them with great slaughter, killing over four hundred.

Following this defeat the Butlers were arrested but were released on the orders of Black Tom the 10th Earl who enjoyed almost unlimited influence at court.[143] They were in rebellion again the next year (1569) and together with their old allies sacked the town of Enniscorthy. After this the rebellion seems to have fizzled out and the Butlers were again arrested but once more because of the influence of their brother (who claimed they were mad) they were released.

---

[141] Edmund Fitzgibbon, the last White Knight, was granted possession of Kilbehenny Castle after the defeat of the Geraldine Rebellion in 1583. The White Knight already owned a large territory, known as the White Knight's Country, in south-east Limerick and in the Mitchelstown area. He died in Kilbehenny Castle on April 23 1608. His son and heir, Maurice Fitzgibbon, had died the previous day. Father and son were interred in the old Dominican priory in Kilmallock, which had been founded and endowed by their ancestors.

[142] The Cloghgrennan Butlers were Sir Edmund (a son of James the 9th Earl of Ormonde) and his sons. They were Piers of Ballysax and James. Both Piers and James were executed for their part in the Nine Years War.

[143] See the chapter about the Butlers of Ormond.

Edmund the 2nd Viscount Mountgarret lived through the Nine Years War[144] but died in 1602.[145] He was succeeded in his estates and titles by his eldest son Sir Richard Butler the 3rd Viscount.[146]

At only twenty four years of age, the young Richard was already inured to the hardships of war. He and his father had sided with the O'Neills of Tyrone in the Nine Years War and Richard was married to Margaret the daughter of Hugh O'Neill the Earl of Tyrone.[147] In a bewildering change of allegiance the Butlers, father and son, sided with the Earl of Essex who arrived in 1599 to put down the rebellion. This was probably done because of the urgings of the Earl of Ormonde. When the Nine Years War was finally brought to a conclusion by the defeat at Kinsale the Mountgarret Butlers had their lands intact.

Richard continued as a loyal subject under King James I and sat in the Parliament of 1615 in his capacity of Viscount. He continued as a solid citizen and loyal to the crown and was again in Parliament in 1634 when Wentworth was Lord Deputy.[148] However in 1641-2 he resurrected his ancient armour, mounted his old war steed, and joined the Confederacy in support of the Catholic cause. At this time he was the owner of a huge amount of land in Kilkenny, Wexford and Carlow, said to have been in excess of twenty thousand acres.[149]

This move by Mountgarret was a staggering blow to the government side and his second cousin James the 12th Earl of Ormonde. The old warrior now in his

---

[144] The Earl of Ormonde in writing to the Privy Council, in 1598, stated that Viscount Mountgarret was in rebellion. (Hore – *Chronicles of Ross* – page 284)

[145] Edmund had at least three brothers : Piers ancestor of the Butlers of Kayer, Moneyhore and Munfin (Wexford) and Tullow (Co. Carlow), John: ancestor of the Butlers of New Ross and Wells (Co. Carlow), Thomas: ancestor of the Butlers of Castlecomer & Coolnaheen (Co. Kilkenny)

[146] Richard had at least one brother, James who was ancestor of the Bealaborrow (Wexford) and Tinnehinch (Carlow) Butlers. He also had a sister, Eleanor, (one of three) who was married to Morgan Kavanagh of Polmonty, a nephew of Fiach McHugh O'Byrne.

[147] Sir Richard was married three times. His second wife was a daughter of Sir William Andrews of Buckinghamshire who died in 1625 and his third wife was the widow of Sir Thomas Spencer. She survived Sir Richard and died in 1656.

[148] Joan Butler a daughter of Lord Mountgarret was murdered in 1639 by her husband John Butler. She had a daughter by a previous marriage Mary Poulett and there was much effort by her grandfather to make sure her property was not stolen. In 1642 he also requested the Confederacy to enforce payments to Mary by her tenants. (NLI Ms. 3172-85)

[149] Sir Richard Butler, Lord Mountgarret paid £800 for lands in Co. Wexford in 1640. He bought the lands from Nic Bussher. At this time he owned over 20,000 acres of land in Kilkenny and over 3,000 acres in Co. Wexford. Mountgarret Manor, just outside New Ross, comprised a castle and 380 acres in demesne.

early sixties commanded such huge respect that all the Catholic gentlemen of the county with their cohorts flocked to his standard. He swept into Kilkenny city and seized it for the Confederacy. One of his first acts was to extend his protection to all the Protestant citizens and their property. Of course the wife of the 12th Earl was also a Protestant and she made every effort to help her co-religionists by giving them sanctuary in the Castle. These moves did help to quell the tide of religious hatred that was a hallmark of that particular period.[150] However in the aftermath of the Cromwellian invasion Sir Richard was accused of attacking Protestants as the following deposition shows

'Deposition of Simon Sellers of the city of Dublin, gent, sworn, etc., sayth *that* about the 1st December 1641, he, being at Eniscorfy in the Co. of Wexford, was then and there, with his wife and children, forceably deprived and expelled from their house dwelling and farmes there, and of two mills, and was then and there also forcibly robbed and dispoyled of Cowes, horses, mares, young cattle, household goods, hay, a tanyard with a great quantity of leather in it, bark, and other goods and meanes to the value of £800 at the least. In debts also this Deponent is perswaded he hath lost also £540 at least. He sayth that the Rebels in the County that rose up in armes and deprived and despoyled him of his houses, etc., were Pierce Butler late of Clonekerry,[151] Esqr, Joseph Farrell of Eniscorfy aforesaid, merchant, the Lord Mountgarret and the friars of Wexford.'[152]

Viscount Mountgarret was very much involved militarily during the period and in 1642 he seems to have had joint leadership of the southern Confederate Army with General Preston. This army suffered serious defeats at the hands of the Marquess of Ormonde, his second cousin, in that year at Kilrush, Co. Kildare and at Ballinvegga near New Ross.[153]

---

[150] In another instance he prevented 'the Irish' from hanging a Richard Fitzhenry from near New Ross, who was accused by them of hanging 'three or four' Kavanaghs, who according to him had murdered and robbed 16 English men and women and sucking children. Fitzhenry at the time had a Commission from Lord Ormonde to execute martial law in the county. (Hore's *History of the town & county of Wexford* Vol.6 pg. 483)
[151] Cloghnakeeragh now called Wilton near Enniscorthy.
[152] Hore's History of Wexford and county Vol. 6 pg. 480
[153] Over 700 of the Irish force were killed on the day, including Sir Morgan Kavanagh of Clonmullen, Co. Carlow – a distant cousin of the Marquess. A Lt. Col. Butler was captured and this may in fact have been Richard Butler of Kilcash the brother of the Marquess. The prisoners were brought to Dublin but the gentlemen were very well looked after by the Marquess and on his orders were not sent as prisoners to England. One writer complained that they were treated as if they had been the victors!

Sir Richard, who was elected President of the Council of the Confederates, headquartered at Kilkenny, was sidelined by the Machiavellian Rinuccini, the Pope's envoy to the Confederates, possibly because he was a near relation of the Duke of Ormonde – a committed Protestant. However he still commanded loyalty and respect from his old comrades. Because of the interference of Rinuccini the Confederacy was deeply divided about its policies and aims and any attempts by the more moderate Confederates to find a solution to the impasse were thwarted by that worthy. An example of his overbearing and meddlesome behaviour was his opposition to the terms of peace negotiated between Ormonde and the Confederates in 1646. The majority of the Confederates opted to agree to the conditions which promised to guarantee them some freedom in the area of religious worship, relief from the oath of supremacy and concessions in the areas of land ownership and education rights. The brave bishop used his mighty mitre and threatened to interdict every town and parish that allowed the terms of the peace to be made public.[154] Furthermore he forbade church services to be held and silenced any clergy who opposed him.[155] To his credit Viscount Mountgarret was not overly impressed and he sent his son, Edmund, with a party of horsemen to ensure that the terms of the peace would be promulgated in the city of Kilkenny and in the surrounding towns.

It is not clear what subsequent role Lord Mountgarret played in the Confederacy or in the campaign against Cromwell, but he died a natural death in 1652.[156] Edward one of Mountgarret's younger sons who had been living in Urlingford Castle was arrested in 1652 and taken to Dublin. He was tried for the murder of people in the Freshford area ten years earlier. He was believed to be innocent but on the testimony of Major Warren he was found guilty and executed.[157]

---

[154] In May of 1648 when a peace deal was finally agreed between the Confederacy and the King's representatives (but not by Owen Roe O'Neill) the nuncio excommunicated all those who were party to the arrangements.

[155] Such was the superstitious nature of the people at that time many really believed they would have to endure hell's fires if they opposed the wishes of the Church Hierarchy.

[156] After the Cromwellian campaign he fled to Galway where he took refuge and died there. His castle at Ballyragget was taken over by Major Abel Warren. Warren's father, Rev. Edward Warren, the rector of the parish was ousted from his living by Mountgarret's soldiers in 1641. Rev. Edward had three sons, two of whom were officers in Cromwell's army.

[157] Abel Warren had a brother Edward who was a Colonel. After the Restoration they were involved in a plot to take the Lord Lieutenant as a hostage and compel him to change the law relating to the restitution of lands. The plot was discovered and the Colonel was hanged for his part. Abel escaped but died two years later. The notorious Captain Blood was also involved in this escapade.

Lord Mountgarret's successor was his eldest son, Edmund, who became the 4th Viscount Mountgarret. Edmund, like his father, was a key player in the Confederate Army and saw action at Kilrush and Ballinvegga and in Co. Wexford, where he was for a time Governor of Enniscorthy and then of the entire county of Wexford.[158] He was also Governor of Kilkenny in 1646. Sir Edmund was taken prisoner when Wexford was captured by the Cromwellian Army.[159] It is unclear how he came to be in France with Charles II where he was a Captain in that monarch's army. In the subsequent land grabbing fever the lands of the Mountgarrets were declared forfeit and were earmarked for distribution to the land hungry Cromwellian soldiers and adventurers.

However this arrangement was declared null and void in 1660 when Charles II was restored to the throne of England. The Duke of Ormonde was his most trusted advisor and probably the most powerful man in Ireland. One of his first acts was to restore their lands, almost in total to his relatives. In this way Edmund Butler the 4th Viscount Mountgarret was reinstated in most of his Kilkenny lands. In addition he received further lands in 1667 in an Act of Settlement grant. Those lands were in the barony of Knocktopher.

Sir Edmund was married twice and by his first wife, Lady Dorothy Touchet, he had two sons and two daughters. His second wife was a widow, Elizabeth Conyers, who was the daughter of an heiress Lady Simeon, whose mother was the heiress of Baron Vaux of Harrowden. Sir Edmund and Elizabeth had a son, Edward. Edward was the grandfather of James Butler the Archbishop of Cashel.[160]

After Sir Edmund's death in 1679 he was succeeded by his eldest son, Sir Richard the 5th Viscount Mountgarret. Richard, who served as a Captain in the French army was imprisoned in Liverpool in 1658 and also in Dublin Castle in the

---

[158] Hore Vol. 6 pg. 488

[159] Hore Vol. 5 pg.280

[160] Edward was willed the lands of Ballyragget, with other properties, by his father Sir Edmund. At some period, possibly in the late 1670s, Edward was found guilty of the manslaughter of a man servant in Dublin (Cal S.P. 1669-70). Edward's mother was the daughter of Edward the 4th Lord Vaux of Harrowden. Lord Vaux died in 1662 and the estate went into abeyance. It was restored almost two hundred years later, in 1832, by Royal assent, to George Charles Mostyn a descendant of Edward Butler. Edward's wife was a daughter of George Mathew of Thomastown, Co. Tipperary (for notice of that family see *The Tipperary Gentry* by Art Kavanagh & Wm. Hayes). Through various marriage alliances the Butlers of Ballyragget were connected to the Kingstons, the Talbots of Malahide and the Bellews (all aristocratic families). Edward's great grandson, George Butler, had no male heirs and he transferred most of his property to his brother-in-law, Walter Kavanagh of Borris, Co. Carlow in 1813. George had one daughter Maria Lucinda and it was her son, George Charles Mostyn who became the 6th Lord Vaux of Harrowden as mentioned above.

same year, because of his religion.[161] He claimed his seat in Parliament in 1692 and took the oath of allegiance but refused to take the oath of supremacy.

Ballyragget Castle

The 5th Viscount was married twice. His first wife was an English lady Emilia Blundell and his second wife was the widow of Gilbert Butler and daughter of Richard Shee of Shee's Court. The Viscount was lucky in that his relation, the 2nd Duke of Ormonde, was a committed Williamite, who entertained that monarch in his castle of Kilkenny after the defeat of King James at the Battle of the Boyne. In the Jacobite confiscations that followed the Mountgarret Butlers emerged unscathed. They still remained Catholic and produced children too numerous to mention in this short article[162]. The 5th Viscount died in 1706. His son and heir was

---

[161] The Duke of Ormonde wrote of him as 'the weakest young man both in body and mind that I know, living without a guardian, if he may be said to be so, who has a good discreet woman to his wife' – Ormonde Mss vol. IV pg. 234

[162] Edmund and Richard Butler sons of the 5th Lord Mountgarret were reared in England and tutored by their grandfather Blundell – a royalist and a Catholic. Both the 6th Viscount and his father sought refuge from persecution in Ormskirk near Crosby. (*Cavalier's Notebook* – Wm. Blundell)

educated at the Jesuit Colleges of Flamstead, St. Omer and La Fleche. He was a Lt. Colonel of Horse in the Army of King James II at the siege of Derry but was captured and outlawed. The outlawry was reversed in 1721 but while he took the oath of alliegience he would not take the oath of supremacy and withdrew from the House of Parliament.

A succession of Mountgarret Viscounts followed[163] and the next man of note was Edmund the 11th Viscount who finally succumbed to the pressures of the Penal Laws and took the expedient step of becoming a Protestant. He was born in 1745 and was an M.P. for the County of Kilkenny from 1776 to 1779. His father had died in 1779 and the 11th Viscount took his seat in the House of Lords. His wife was Henrietta, the daughter of Somerset Hamilton Butler the 1st Lord Carrick. They had four sons and one daughter who married a Colonel John Smith. The sons were Edmund, Somerset Richard, Henry and Pierce. The 11th Viscount must have been a man of impetuous temper as in 1790 he fought a duel with a Counsellor Bushe with the result that Bushe was seriously, though not mortally wounded, in the stomach.[164]

After the death of the 11th Viscount in 1793 the following strange entry appears in the private diary of Lord Clonmell, an enemy of his: 'died Lord Mountgarret, as wicked a malignant selfish monster as I ever knew, a victim to his brutal appetites and thirst for blood; a lesson to vice and a caution to be civil to all, obliging to many, to serve few and offend none, as the safest, wisest, pleasantest mode of going through life'. The Gentleman's Magazine was more complimentary and stated that he 'was an excellent scholar, a man of strong intellect, of a violent disposition...an excellent parliamentary speaker who had been for several years a staunch and dauntless patriot.'

The 12th Viscount had a memorable year in 1793. He was married in June, to Mildred Fowler the daughter of the Archbishop of Dublin, his father died in July[165] and in December he was created Earl of Kilkenny. Edmund had no children and he was in turn succeeded by his nephew, Henry Edmund as the 13th Viscount. The Earldom became extinct on the death of the 12th Viscount (in 1846) who according to Lord Dunboyne was insane for most of his adult life. Of the widow of

---

[163] These included four Viscounts who were brothers. The 6th Viscount was outlawed in 1716 after his cousin the Duke of Ormonde was attainted. However he seems to have been able to escape having his lands declared forfeit.

[164] This must have been Gervase Parker Bushe of Kilfane, an eminent lawyer and politician who died in the early 1790s. He was married to a sister of Henry Grattan. It would appear that the Bushe family left Kilfane at around this time and settled at Glencairne in Co. Waterford.

[165] 'From a surfeit of strawberries and cider' according to Lord Dunboyne in his talk in Kilkenny Castle.

the Earl it was said 'Her manners would be fascinating were it not too evident that she labours to be so. She had great remains of beauty; but she is a deep character, insincere and consequently always to be feared'. Referring to her husband it was said 'the old man in a brown scratch-wig is a queer, specious old Irishman'[166] However 'the specious old Irishman' had his moments as recounted by Barrington.

Lord Mountgarret, the Earl of Kilkenny, had a great number of lawsuits with his insolvent tenants and having lost a number of cases he decided on a course of action which involved challenging the attorney and all the counsel on the opposing side. The first duel was with a Mr. Ball an attorney and in this Lord Mountgarret was wounded. He was hit in the arm and in the side but neither wound was dangerous. The Hon. Somerset Butler the brother of Lord Mountgarret now proceeded to challenge the first of the counsel, a Mr. Peter Burrowes. The duel took place one cold frosty morning near Kilkenny. On his way to the duelling ground Peter bought some spiced gingerbread nuts from a peddler and put the nuts and the change in his waistcoat pocket. They met and the ten paces were measured. Somerset fired first and hit Peter in the body. Peter dropped to the ground and Somerset fled. However the shot had by an extraordinary coincidence hit the coins in his pocket. That saved his life.

When his Lordship was sufficiently recovered he challenged the next counsel, John Byrne. On this occasion the nobleman was the victor and John Byrne was struck in the body but not mortally.

Next to take on the counsels was Captain Pierce Butler, Somerset's brother. His intended protagonist was Dick Guinness but following various procrastinations this duel never took place. Captain Pierce was known as a most courageous man and a fine marksman. Pierce actually attacked Dick in an open court and pandemonium broke out. Pierce narrowly escaped being jailed for his assault. After this the Earl was persuaded to finish his crusade of duels and he decided to let the law take its course in the future.

Lord Dunboyne went on to say that Henry, a younger brother of the Earl, 'as a dashing, dissipated young man of fashion who having sown his wild oats in Ireland, drifted to England, a hunted debtor and in Regency Brighton formed an attachment with an affluent and attractive widow.' They eventually ended up in Edinburgh where they parted. Henry decided to head for calmer climes 'but in the Yorkshire snow his horse fell near Harrowgate, where as luck would have it, he was found by the daughter and heiress of the local land owner John Harrison. She promptly married him and their son, the 13th Viscount (Henry Edmund), in turn,

---

[166] *Private Correspondence of a Woman of Fashion* vol.1 pg 49

married a Yorkshire heiress, the only child of Thomas Rawson of Nidd Hall, near Ripley.'

Pierce, the Earl's youngest brother was a more serious type and as well as becoming a Colonel in the Kilkenny militia became an M.P. from 1832 onwards. Pierce who married Anne March of Lisburn had seven sons and three daughters (all three died unmarried).

His eldest son was involved in a bitter dispute with his cousin Henry the only son of his uncle Henry. The strange case of Pierce Somerset claiming that he was entitled to sit in the House of Lords in the place of his cousin Henry Edmund the 13th Viscount was first entered for hearing by the Committee of Privileges in 1847, the year after the death of the 12th Viscount. In addition Pierce Somerset had sought an ejectment order against Henry Edmund from the Castle of Ballyconra and from the hereditary lands. The case did not come up for hearing until 1854 and many witnesses were called who proved that Henry's father was in fact older than Pierce the father of Pierce Somerset. Birth certificates and death certificates were produced. The case was postponed in 1854 because the ejectment case was then being heard in Co. Kilkenny. Pierce Somerset won the ejectment case but it was appealed and overturned. When the case before the Committee for Privileges was resumed no witnesses for Pierce Somerset were produced on the grounds that two of them had died and another was incapacitated and the case was dropped. Henry was then declared the legitimate 13th Viscount.[167]

Most of Pierce's sons and grandsons were in the Army or Navy and that family is represented today mainly by the descendants of Walter the 7th son. Walter's eldest son by his wife Maria Farrell was Theobald who was born in 1853. Theobald was married twice. Most of the descendants of Theobald and his first wife have died out, but his only daughter who married Capt. John Percy Groves had a family some members of which may still be alive. By his second marriage to Elizabeth Frazscher of Sweden he had a son Pierce and a daughter Dorothy who married Edward de Fine Sucht and had a family.

Pierce the son of Elizabeth Frazscher became a medical doctor and was a pioneer in geriatric research. He married Kerstein Samuelson of Sweden in 1923. They had three sons and one daughter, Kerstin who was born in 1923. Their sons are Pierce Torsten, Carl Somerset and Lars Theobald.

Both Pierce Tolsten and Lars Theobald married. Pierce married Dagmar Hakansson and Lars married Ulla Bergh. Pierce has one son Pierce and two daughters Jenny and Anne all born in the 1960s.

---

[167] Ms in the National Library

Lars and Ulla have one son Pierce Anders and one daughter Anna Christina both born in the 60s also.

While 13 may be an unlucky number it proved to be a very lucky one for Henry Edmund the 13th Viscount who had married Frances Rawson of Nidd Hall. Not alone did he win his legal battles but his wife's aunt left him over half a million pounds. This was a huge sum of money, equivalent in today's terms to about fifty million sterling. In addition his son, the 14th Viscount, was left considerable properties in Yorkshire.

Nidd Hall

In 1883 the Mountgarret estates were as follows. In Kilkenny they owned over 14,000 acres, in Wexford over 500 acres and in Yorkshire 120 acres. The estates in Ireland were valued at almost £10,000 per annum. The Rawson estate which came to the family in 1891 consisted of almost 8000 acres in Yorkshire, 1300 in Herefordshire and 160 in Lancashire. That estate was valued at over £12,000 per annum.

Henry Edmund, who succeeded as the 14th Viscount, in 1900, was educated at Eton and Oxford was High Sheriff of Yorkshire in 1895. He was a Lt. in the Life Guards and later in 1911 was created Baron Mountgarret of Nidd. He married Mary Charlton (of Apley castle). They had one son and three daughters, two of whom married. Elinor married Andrew Lawson of Aldborough Manor and had daughters, co-heirs, one of whom married Sir Thomas Selby Tancred who later assumed the name Lawson Tancred. Ethel married Henry Wilson of Bromhead Hall, Yorkshire and they had a family. The transfer of the Irish properties to the tenants, begun in the lifetime of his predecessor the 13th Earl was completed during the tenure of the 14th Earl who died in 1912.

His only son by his first wife was Edmund Somerset Butler the 15th Viscount. Edmund, although married had no children and when he died in 1918 his titles and estates passed to his half brother Piers Henry who became the 16th Viscount. Piers Henry was the son of Henry Edmund the 14th Viscount and his second wife Robina Hanning-Lee of Bighton Manor, Hants.

The 16th Viscount who inherited in 1918 was educated in the Royal Navy College and in Cambridge. He was a J.P. and was twice married. His first wife was Elizabeth Christie of Jervaulx Abbey, Yorks. and they had one son and one daughter. The daughter is The Hon. Mrs. Sarah Raynar who has two sons Rupert and James.

The 16th Viscount's son, Richard Henry Piers Butler the 17th Viscount, is the man we wrote about at the start of this chapter. He served in the Army and the Navy. He was married three times. He had two sons and one daughter by his first wife, Gillian Buckley of Chelsea[168].

Their sons are Piers James Richard (now the 18th Viscount), born in 1961 and educated at Eton, and Edmund Henry b. 1962. Piers the 18th Viscount married Laura William of Illinois in 1995 while Edmund Henry married Adelle Lloyd of New York.

Henrietta the only daughter married Robert Cluer of South Africa in 1991.

---

[168] She later married Baron Howard de Walden

Butlers of Ormonde

One of the Rolling Stones, with three bedraggled friends, was present at the handing over of Kilkenny Castle to the State on August 12th 1967. The Butlers were well represented, dressed immaculately in contrast to the 'rockers'. The eighty year old Lord Ormonde himself was there with his Lady. Mr. Charles Butler, his heir, from America was there. So too were Lord Carrick, Lord and Lady Mountgarret and Lord and Lady Dunboyne. Slightly lesser Butlers were represented by Sir Thomas of Ballintemple, Co. Carlow, Hubert the historian and a brace of Vicomtes from France. German and Austrian Butlers were represented by the Barons von Buttlar-Elderberg. The government party of officials was headed by the colourful Minister for Finance, Charles Haughey. Members of the public and a large contingent of Butlers attending the Butler Rally were present.

This was one of the most momentous occasions in Irish History. It marked the end of a feudal system that had lasted from the 13th century right down to the 20th. The Butlers present knew it. The government party knew it. The Rolling Stone didn't give a damn. He was there to have his photograph taken in front of the Castle.[169] When the press photographers got wind of the word that a Stone was present they lost interest in the Lords and Ladies and the 600 years of history and

---

[169] Bence Jones in *Twilight of the Ascendancy*

switched their focus to the new aristocracy of rock. Followed by the Irish version of the 'paparazzi' the Stone legged it out the gate and away, causing a ripple of raised eyebrows among the glum set who were standing as at a burial, which in fact they were.

The magnificent Kilkenny Castle was the main residence of the Butlers of Ormonde from the time of its purchase in 1391 by the 3rd Earl right up to the middle of the 20th century. The stone castle was originally built by William the Earl Marshall in 1260 on the site of the older wooden structure erected there by Strongbow. Over the centuries the castle was extended and improved until by the end of the 18th century the edifice that stands today was in place. In addition the graceful and ancient town of Kilkenny grew under the patronage and stability offered by the Butler family in every century.

Kilkenny Castle

It was the first Duke who changed the character of the castle in the later 1600s. He fashioned the old castle into a chateau in the French taste which was prevalent after the Restoration. At this period the large windows, high-pitched roofs and tall chimneys were added and inserted into and placed upon the old work. The ducal crowns upon the towers were added also. The present castellated style of the castle was imposed upon the site in the 1800s between 1825 and 1860. It would seem that this style was made fashionable by its adoption at Windsor.[170]

Dunmore Park (adjacent to the Dunmore Caves) became the residence of Lady Ormonde when her husband the 1st Duke was out of favour after the Cromwellian debacle. She spent huge sums of money on Dunmore House. She thought she would outlive the Duke and as she felt strongly about the head of the household (the Duke's heir) occupying Kilkenny she determined to have a sumptuous property for herself. A man called Dillon was with the Duke on the roof of Kilkenny Castle viewing the countryside when Dillon remarked with a pun, 'Your Grace has done much here but yonder you have Done more.' 'Alas,' replied the Duke, 'it is incredible what that house has cost; but by wife has done so much to that house, that she had almost undone me!'[171]

John Dunton writing about Dunmore in 1698 described it as 'the finest house in Ireland. On some of the floors I reckoned twenty four rooms; the staircase that leads to them is hung with curious landscapes and is so large that twenty men might walk abreast. It may boast of more rooms than are to found in some whole towns'. Dunmore Cottage now occupies the site of the former mansion.

No money was spared on Kilkenny Castle either when the first Duke was reinstated. When he returned to Ireland from France in 1661 he was the greatest man in Ireland. He was a Duke of England and Ireland, steward of the royal household, chancellor of Dublin and a confidential adviser to the young king Charles. All his estates were restored and he was given grants of further confiscated lands in addition to a grant of £30,000 from the Dublin Parliament. Despite all this apparent wealth the Duke was deeply in debt. This situation was not helped by the extravagance of his wife, already alluded to.

It could be said without contradiction that the house of Ormonde was the most powerful family in Ireland from the time of Theobald fitzWalter who was made chief Butler of Ireland by Henry II in 1177, down to the 18th and possibly the 19th century. Granted there was the occasional hiatus when their power was at a low ebb such as the periods after 1654 and 1715 when the Earls were attainted. The fact that the family managed to survive these assaults on their power and property is a tribute to their tenacity and determination and to a fortuitous succession of male heirs.

Theobald's numerous grants of lands included Upper and Lower Ormond in Tipperary. He established his principal seat in Nenagh castle. From there he organised his baronial lands into seven seigniorial units at Nenagh, Dunkerrin,

---

[170] Kilkenny Castle by Rev. T.J. Clohosey in Old Kilkenny Review no. 17
[171] Ibid

Thurles, Caherconlish, Gowran, Tullow and Arklow. He died c. 1206 and was succeeded by his son Theobald who assumed the surname Butler in the second decade of that century. His fortuitous marriage to a de Marisco heir ensured that his descendants enjoyed further huge estates both in Ireland and in England. Theobald's son also married well and his de Burgo wife brought him considerable landed property.[172]

A succession of Theobalds followed until Edmond a brother of Theobald the 5th butler succeeded. This able man was at various times Chief Justice of Ireland and Lord Deputy and was created Lord Carrick in 1315. He served under Edward Longshanks in the war against the Scots and he was centre stage in the war against the Bruces in Ireland. He was married to a daughter of the 1st Earl of Kildare. Edmond died having come home from a pilgrimage to Spain to the shrine of St. James of Compostella, in 1321. His son James was only a boy when his father died.

James succeeded to the title and estates when he came of age and by another most fortuitous marriage launched the family into the mainstream of aristocratic society in England. His wife was the granddaughter of Edward Longshanks. As a result of this strategic alliance James was created 1st Earl of Ormonde in 1328. He was given many honours and it was during his period as Earl that the Ormonde properties in Tipperary were constituted a Palatinate. He had only one son and one daughter Petronilla. She married the 3rd Lord Talbot and was therefore the ancestor of the Earls of Shrewsbury. The son, James became the 2nd Earl of Ormonde when his father died in 1337 at a comparatively young age. James the 2nd Earl was known as the Noble Earl because Edward Longshanks was his great grandfather. Like his predecessors the 2nd Earl held high offices in the administration in Ireland.

The 2nd Earl died in 1382 and was succeeded by his son, James the 3rd Earl. This was the man who built Gowran Castle and lived there for a time until he purchased the Castle of Kilkenny from the heirs of the Earl of Gloucester in 1391. Kilkenny Castle has been the main seat of the Butlers of Ormonde from that time right up to the middle of the 20th century. He had three sons James the 4th Earl, Richard of Polestown,[173] and James Gallda, an illegitimate son, who was the ancestor of the Butlers of Cahir.[174]

---

[172] Burkes Peerage.
[173] The great grand father of Piers Roe the 8th Earl.
[174] James Gallda Butler, the illegitimate son of the 3rd Earl of Ormonde was born around the year 1400. His mother was Catherine, the daughter of the Earl of Desmond. James Gallda, of Cahir, was appointed by his brother, the 4th Earl of Ormonde, to be the keeper of the county with the right to maintenance of the necessary troops. This appointment was disastrous as James Gallda had his own agenda and was closely involved with the Desmonds

The 4th Earl, know as the White Earl, a scholarly man, held all the high offices in Ireland for long periods, during the first half of the 15th century, as Justiciar, Lord Deputy and Lord Lieutenant. It was he who prevailed upon the King (Henry V) to establish a King-of-Arms for Ireland.[175] Being scholarly did not prevent him from being militarily inclined and, apart from having served in the wars in France, his stewardship of the Earldom of Ormonde was tempestuous. He feuded with the Talbots (his kinsmen) and with many English officials who tried to blacken his name at court with charges of corruption and fraud. He was twice married and his second wife, a widow, was the daughter and heir of Gerald the 5th Earl of Kildare.[176] As a result of this marriage he acquired a large portion of the Kildare properties. The 4th Earl (the White Earl) was succeeded by his son, James the 5th Earl, whose mother was Elizabeth Beauchamp.

The 5th Earl succeeded his father in 1452 and was immediately appointed as Lord Deputy of Ireland for ten years. In the Wars of the Roses in England the Earl supported the Lancastrians. He was captured after the battle of Towton and beheaded by the Yorkist supporters.[177] His lands and title were declared forfeit but were restored to his brother, John, the 6th Earl by King Edward IV. John had been present at Towton also. He survived until 1478 dying in the Holy Land where he had gone on pilgrimage. John was reputed to have been one of the most accomplished gentlemen of his time. Edward IV said of him that 'if good breeding and liberal qualities were lost in the world they might all be found in the Earl of Ormonde'.[178]

John was succeeded by his brother Thomas the 7th Earl. Thomas had been also attainted with his brothers but was restored by Henry VII in 1485. He was the father of two daughters one of whom Margaret married Sir William Boleyn. Sir William had one son, Sir Thomas, who was the father of Ann Boleyn. Thomas the 7th Earl died in 1515 and the peerage passed to Piers Roe Butler, the son of Sir Richard Butler of Polestown, mentioned above.[179] However in 1527 Henry VIII

---

who were rivals of the Ormondes in Munster. See *The Tipperary Gentry Vol.1* by Wm. Hayes & Art Kavanagh

[175] This title was later changed to Ulster King-of-Arms, an office set up to record and register the Heraldic Arms of the various noble and gentry families.

[176] The 5th Earl of Kildare was succeeded by his brother, John, who became the 6th Earl of Kildare.

[177] James the 5th Earl of Ormonde was not married but he had an illegitimate son, James Dubh, who was slain by Piers Roe, later the 8th Earl.

[178] Burkes Peerage.

[179] All the English properties passed to the Boleyns and the St. Ledgers, husbands of the 7th Earl's daughters.

deprived Piers Roe of his title and granted it to Sir Thomas Boleyn, his prospective father-in-law. Piers Roe was then given the title of Earl of Ossory. He was also made Lord Deputy. The short marriage of Henry VIII and Ann Boleyn ended when she was beheaded in 1536 and the following year her father died. As he had no male heirs his title was granted to Piers Roe who then became the 8th Earl of Ormonde.[180]

Ormonde Effigy in St. Canice's Cathedral

One of the turning points of the fortunes of the Butlers of Ormonde was the marriage of Sir James Butler of Polestown[181] to Sadbh Kavanagh. Sadbh was the daughter of Donal Reagh Kavanagh and sister of Art Bui the McMurrough and King of Leinster. She was also the widow of the chief of the O'Nolans of Forth in Carlow. As a result of this marriage Sadbh's son Piers Rua Butler (later the 8th Earl) managed to persuade the Kavanaghs to hand over huge swathes of land to him and his heirs.

---

[180] Queen Elizabeth I was therefore a third cousin once removed of Piers Roe and she would have been quite informed of the relationship.
[181] James Butler was a grandson of James the 3rd Earl. His mother was an O'Reilly of Cavan, the daughter of Gildas O'Reilly, Lord of Breffni.

Butlers of Ormonde

The lands included the town of Arklow and its hinterland, the Rower in Kilkenny, the lands of Duiske Abbey and the lands of Forth O'Nolan in Carlow.[182] This move by Piers Roe may well have been an attempt to counteract the very real alliance that existed between the Kavanaghs and the Fitzgeralds of Kildare. The Fitzgeralds were destroyed in the 1530s following the rebellion of Silken Thomas and from this time onwards most of the Kavanagh clan members gave their allegiance to the Ormondes.[183]

Piers Roe must have had mixed feelings about the fall of the House of Kildare, as his wife was Lady Margaret, the 2nd daughter of Gerald the 8th Earl of Kildare.[184] They had three sons and six daughters. All six daughters were married to Irish lords and this network of relations helped to keep the peace in the Ormonde territories. Joan and Elinor were married to Lords Dunboyne and Cahir respectively, both Butlers. This cemented the agreement, known as the Composition of Clonmel, drawn up by Piers Roe to prevent the bitter inter familial wars of earlier decades.[185] Another daughter, Margaret, was married to the son of the Earl of Desmond and after his death to the Fitzpatrick Lord Upper Ossory. Katherine and Ellen were married to Lord Power of Donoughmore and to the Earl of Thomond. These powerful alliances further enhanced the prestige and effectiveness of the House of Ormonde. The sons of Piers Roe were, James who succeeded as the 9th Earl, Richard Butler created Lord Mountgarret[186] and Thomas who was killed in 1532 in a fight at Jerpoint in Co. Kilkenny.[187] Piers Roe died in 1539 and his title and estates passed to his eldest son James.

James the 9th Earl was sensationally poisoned at Ely House, Holborn, in 1546. Not alone was the Earl poisoned but his steward and sixteen servants died at the same time. They did not die immediately but within a period of two weeks they were all dead. It is not known who was responsible or why. This was a time of

---

[182] *The Kavanaghs Kings of Leinster* by Art Kavanagh

[183] For more details about the Butler/Kavanagh connection see *The Kavanaghs Kings of Leinster*

[184] Margaret was said to have been a very formidable woman who had many of her enemies hanged from her castles. On the credit side she founded the first grammar school in Kilkenny, later known as Kilkenny College.

[185] The peace in Munster was short lived however as Thomas, the 10th Earl, grandson of Piers Roe was involved in a protracted and bitter war with the Earls of Desmond later in the 16th century.

[186] Richard was the ancestor of the Butlers, Lords Mountgarret, a noble and notable family that continued down to modern times.

[187] This was in fact a skirmish between the Fitzgeralds led by Silken Thomas and the Ormondes led by Thomas Butler his cousin. It is not known what caused the confrontation.

intrigue and change. Henry VIII, who was to die the following year, had introduced the new religion which was covertly opposed by families such as the Butlers. Thomas, the eldest son of the Earl was at school in the court.[188] He was being educated as a Protestant. From Henry's point of view, possibly, the death of the Earl of Ormonde would have been timely. With young Thomas being nurtured and formed within his court the House of Ormonde would be most amenable to the King's bidding. This experience confirmed Thomas in his loyalty to the Crown and indeed impressed him so deeply that, when he returned to Ireland as tenth Earl of Ormond, he built a beautiful manor house at Carrick-on-Suir in County Tipperary and decorated the walls with stucco representations of himself and Queen Elizabeth (who called him ambiguously her 'Black Husband'). He resumed the longstanding feud with Earls of Desmond over boundaries in the Clonmel area of Tipperary. As we have seen this Ormond-Geraldine quarrel was a century old. Finally it came to an armed confrontation in 1565 at Affane on the River Suir. Desmond was defeated in what was the last private pitched battle in Ireland and England. Because of his close friendship with Queen Elizabeth Thomas was made Treasurer of Ireland in 1559. It was also because of this friendship that his brothers escaped being executed following their rebellion in 1568.[189]

Black Tom was married twice and while his second wife, the daughter of Lord Sheffield, had three children, only the daughter, Elizabeth, survived her father.[190] She inherited all his lands, while his titles passed to a nephew, Walter Butler of Kilcash, (the 11th Earl) a grandson of James the 9th Earl.[191] After years of

---

[188] He was known as Black Tom because of the darkness of his complexion. He had six brothers - Edmund of Roscrea and Cloghgrennan, John of Kilcash, Walter of Nodstown, James of Duiske, Edward of Cloughinche and Piers of Grantstown.

[189] Edmond of Roscrea and Cloghgrennan, Co. Carlow, went into rebellion after the Kavanagh lands which had been given to his ancestor Piers Roe were claimed by and granted to Sir Peter Carew. He was aided by his brothers, the Kavanaghs and a son of the Earl of Desmond. He had three sons, one of whom Theobald later became Viscount Butler of Tullowphelim (in Carlow), and Piers of Ballysax and Sir James who were both beheaded for taking part in the Desmond rebellion of the late 16th century.

[190] Black Tom had 12 illegitimate children (Lord Dunboyne in Old Kilkenny Review no.18). Piers Butler of Duiske was said to have been an illegitimate son of Queen Elizabeth by Black Tom. His will very much favoured Piers and Lord Dunboyne in his lecture, drew his conclusions from this.

[191] Kilcash, in Tipperary, was at its zenith at this time and is best remembered in the old Gaelic poem of that name, which tells of its glory and the munificence of the Earl and his wife. Walter, who died in 1633, was imprisoned from 1617 to 1625 for refusing to surrender the Ormonde estates to his cousin Elizabeth, the wife of Sir Richard Preston (Baron Dingwall) and the only daughter of the 10th earl. He was deprived of the palatine rights in

disputes and claims, this was resolved in 1629 when Walter's grandson, James Butler the 12th Earl of Ormonde married his cousin, Elizabeth Preston.[192] This meant that the Butler titles, wealth and lands were reunited and in Butler ownership once again.

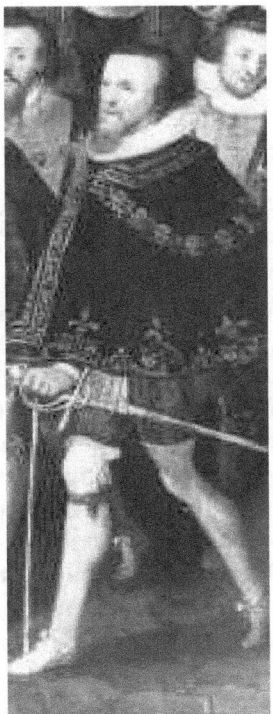

Black Tom

Walter, the 11th Earl, known as Walter of the Beads and the Rosary,[193] was married to his cousin Helen Butler and he had two sons and eight daughters. All eight daughters married various noblemen and gentry including Joan who was twice married (to George Bagenal of Dunleckny and Sir Thomas Esmonde of Gorey). His

---

the county of Tipperary, but he recovered most of the family estates after his release from prison in 1625. Preston was Elizabeth's second husband – her first husband was Theobald of Tullowphelim.
[192] She was his second cousin once removed.
[193] Lord Dunboyne in a lecture to the Kilkenny Archaeological Society (Old Kilkenny Review no. 18)

eldest son, Thomas, Viscount Thurles, who had married Elizabeth Poyntz, was drowned crossing over to England. According to Lord Dunboyne he may have been murdered because of his religion and on the orders of the authorities. It was Thomas's son James who became the 12th Earl.[194]

James was created the Marquess of Ormonde in 1642 and then granted the title of Duke of Ormonde in 1661. During the aftermath of the Cromwellian period he was attainted for a time as he gave his allegiance to the monarchy but was fully restored to his estates and titles after the Restoration. James was a colossus in his time and his influence on the affairs of Ireland for the forty years from 1642 to 1682 bordered on the unbelievable.[195] As a man he was brave, energetic, intelligent, shrewd and fair minded. In the course of his career he made many enemies who were envious of his abilities, his power and his influence[196]. Not all historians have admired the 1st Duke. This is what Gerard Doyle had to say about him. 'The first Duke of Ormonde in his youth passed through that indoctrination centre known as the Court of Wards where he was brain washed into political and theological conformity and became "a member of Christ and his Commonwealth".[197] He emerged on the Irish stage as a man who was subtle and sinister and a master of real-politik. He had slight knowledge of Irish but never became a speaker of the language. He contributed powerfully to the establishment of the English language as the language of public life in Ireland during his two terms as Lord Lieutenant. O'Brudair when he said "woe for him that lacks lisping English, since the Earl's coming into Ireland" must have had Ormonde in mind'.

The appointment of Ormonde firstly as Lieutenant General of the Army in 1640 and as Lord Deputy in 1643 was something of a poisoned chalice.[198] He was a Protestant and a loyalist. He was a Butler and was related to many of the leading

---

[194] Elizabeth then married George Mathew and so began the very famous family of Mathew of Tipperary. See *The Tipperary Gentry Vol.1*

[195] Among the many accomplishments of the Duke on his home sod he was responsible for building Kilmainham Hospital in Dublin.

[196] The Earl was appointed Chancellor of Dublin University in 1645 and held that post until 1653 and after the Restoration he again occupied that post from 1660 until 1688.

[197] The first Duke of Ormonde writing about his family said that his parents 'lived and died Papists, and bred all their children so, and only I, by God's merciful providence was educated in the true Protestant religion' (Ormonde Mss Vol.2 pg. 280)

[198] He was forced into immediate confrontation with his cousin Lord Mountgarret in 1642 when the latter joined the Confederacy and was appointed Commander-in-Chief of their forces. He defeated Mountgarret in two important engagements at Kilrush, Co. Kildare and at Ballinvegga near New Ross in 1642-43.

Confederates.[199] His wealth lay in his Kilkenny and Tipperary properties. He represented Charles I in Ireland. His was an impossible situation. It must be remembered that at this time the Parliamentarians were baying for Charles's blood. The Civil War in England was imminent but Ormonde did manage to arrange a peace with the Confederates through the good offices of his cousin Mountgarret, the President of the Council. Matters dragged on for the next five years with very little being achieved by any side so complex were the politics of the time.[200] Eventually in 1648 Ormonde himself was acknowledged as the Lord Lieutenant, appointed by Charles II (in exile). His position was accepted by the Confederates who by now were hopelessly split following the machinations of Rinuccini, who might best be described as a sinister, ignorant, meddling manipulator from Rome. Ormonde managed to conclude a peace deal with the Confederates. The terms of the peace agreement were much the same as those offered in 1646 - some freedom in the area of religious worship, relief from the oath of supremacy and concessions in the areas of land ownership and education rights.

An arrangement was agreed between Ormonde and Owen Roe O'Neill the commander of the Northern Irish forces and after O'Neill's mysterious death in 1649 Ormonde, now the sole leader of the Confederate/Royalist forces had the unenviable task of facing Cromwell's army on the soil of Ireland. He divided his army and gave command of one section to Lord Inchiquin. He himself was defeated at Rathmines in Dublin in the autumn of 1649. Following this defeat he went into exile in France where he became the chief advisor of Charles II.

As already mentioned earlier he was responsible for the development and restoration of Kilkenny Castle and Dunmore[201], through the efforts of his wife Elizabeth, who ignored the massive debts accruing.[202] Despite these huge liabilities he lived like a lord, after his return and it was not uncommon that over two hundred gentlemen sat down to dinner in the Castle on any given day. The lavish décor of

---

[199] His brother Richard of Kilcash was appointed Governor of Wexford during the period of the war and was appointed a lieutenant general in the Confederate army. Richard also fought at Rathmines as a Colonel in his brother's army. Richard was the ancestor of the Kilcash dynasty and his great grandson John became the 15th Earl in 1758. The Ormonde Lords thereafter descended from John the 15th Earl.

[200] Of course the city thrived during this period and the Catholic clergy in particular strove to renovate and improve their churches. Even St. Canice's Cathedral, which had been deserted by the Protestant bishop, was taken over and given a facelift.

[201] All this work took place after the Restoration of Charles II to the throne of England.

[202] He also maintained Carrick on Suir Castle, where he occasionally stayed. His hobbies included hunting, fishing, falconry and reading so it is probable that Carrick was maintained to a very high standard also.

both the Castle and Dunmore further increased his debts but brought an economic boom to the city and its inhabitants. No money was spared in fitting out the two establishments where the household items were bought from the finest craftsmen of Europe and the Far East. These included Chinese and Japanese porcelains, Italian furniture and English plate. His library in Kilkenny was said to be the finest in Ireland. He restored and reinstated the grammar school, now known as Kilkenny College, which had been established by Piers Roe, the 8th Earl. The Duke also attempted to establish industries in the city and in the towns of Kilkenny by bringing in foreign craftsmen.[203] In addition to his beloved Kilkenny houses he also owned houses in Richmond and St. James Park in London, where he stayed on his visits to the English capital.

James the 1st Duke survived an assassination attempt by a scoundrel called Blood.[204] He died in 1688 and was buried in Westminster Abbey.

His grandson, James, became the 2nd Duke of Ormonde and was arguably the most controversial man in the family.[205] The 2nd Duke, like his grandfather, was a statesman and a soldier. Unlike his grandfather he spent very little time in Kilkenny.[206] When he succeeded to the Earldom in 1688 he threw in his lot with William of Orange and commanded a force of cavalry at the Battle of the Boyne. His exploits in the war against France and Spain are legendary and he was amply decorated by Queen Anne.[207] He was viceroy in Ireland for four years (1703-07).

His financial affairs, which were mishandled by his agent, went from bad to worse and finally in the first decade of the 18th century the Duke was compelled

---

[203] *Kilkenny History & Society* – ed by Wm. Nolan pg. 121

[204] It was rumoured that the Duke of Buckingham was behind the assassination attempt and that the King gave him his covert support. Colonel Blood, a Clareman, may well have been a secret agent of some kind and his attempt to steal the Crown Jewels may well have been a smoke screen. In the event he was captured and imprisoned for that crime but was released on the orders of the King who went to see him in prison. In addition to giving Blood his freedom the King restored him to his estates in Ireland and gave him an annual pension of £500.

[205] The eldest son of the 1st Duke died in infancy. This is how Lord Dunboyne described his demise – 'he came to an untimely end at the age of six months when his Nanny, out for a drive near Dublin, tossed him out of the carriage window, in the agitation of the moment when the horses bolted near Phoenix Hill.'

[206] He spent time there during the Williamite Wars and entertained King William in the castle. He also lived there during the times he was Lord Lieutenant.

[207] He was wounded at the Battle of Landen and taken prisoner. A French guard spared his life when he saw the diamond ring on his finger. He was afterwards exchanged for the Duke of Berwick. He later commanded the navy which sunk the French fleet and destroyed the Spanish navy and captured the very important fort of Redondella. – Ormonde Mss Vol.2

to sell off considerable amounts of his properties in fee farm. Most of his lands, prior to this had been leased to the tenants who now seized the opportunity to become *de facto* freeholders. He sold off lands in Kilkenny and Tipperary and raised over £20,000 on the Kilkenny properties alone.[208]

After 1707 he was made a captain general and served mainly on the continent becoming embroiled in the Netherlands War. During this period he seems to have become involved in the Jacobite attempts to have the 'old pretender' James, the son of King James II, restored to the throne. He was removed from office in 1715 and impeached by King George I and fled to France. His estates were confiscated but later resold to his brother, Charles, the Earl of Arran. The 2nd Duke continued to reside on the continent until his death in 1745. He was buried in Westminster Abbey in the family vault.[209] Although married twice his wives and two daughters pre deceased him.[210]

Charles, the Earl of Arran was now the 14th Earl of Ormonde but the other titles which had been stripped from his brother were not restored. According to Burke's Peerage Charles was the *de jure* 3rd Duke. Charles, too, like his brother, was an army officer and served with distinction in the various campaigns of the period. He was made Master of the Ordnance for a period in the second decade of the 18th century. He was also a lord of the bedchamber to William III.[211] He died in 1758 and though married he had no family so the claim to the title of Earl of Ormonde and the estates passed to his first cousin once removed, John Butler of Kilcash, a great grandson of James 1st Duke.

Although the title was not recognised by the administration it passed on to John's first cousin, Walter of Garryricken and then to Walter's son John who became and was acknowledged to be the 17th Earl of Ormonde.

When Walter received the honours in 1766 he promptly moved himself and his household into the Castle and assumed a leading role in Kilkenny society.[212] He set about restoring the castle and its contents, most of which had been left intact and

---

[208] *Kilkenny History & Society* – ed by Wm. Nolan pg. 123
[209] His bones were interred in Westminster about seven years after his death.
[210] Between the time of his attainder in 1715 and their deaths they were treated generously by the government. Huge sums of money and lands were allocated to them during the period.
[211] Burke's Peerage
[212] Walter's famous daughter was Eleanor, who with her friend Sarah Ponsonby fled to Wales to escape family persecution. Sarah was being pestered by her godmother's husband, Sir William Fownes and Eleanor was the object of the wrath of her Catholic step-mother (Eleanor was a Protestant). They became famous as 'The Ladies of Llangollen'. (see *The Tipperary Gentry Vol.1* for more information of the two ladies).

spent huge sums entertaining. When he died in 1783 he was succeeded by his son John.

John of Garryricken was an M.P. for Gowran 1776-79 and was elected for Kilkenny in 1790-91. He was formally recognised as the 17th Earl in 1791 and moved into the House of Lords. The fact that his wife was Lady Frances Wandesforde the sole heir of the Earl of Wandesforde probably helped his cause. John was very much admired by his fellow citizens in Kilkenny where he was an enthusiastic alderman. When his titles were restored in 1791 the whole city was given over to festivities for a week. Concerning Lady Ormonde Barrington said that, 'as lady of the castle she was careful to keep up at least her due importance. It is not impossible for women or men either, to mistake pomposity for dignity. True pride is accompanied by an amiable condescension; cool unbending ceremony is the result of false pride and not of dignity. I thought perhaps erroneously that her ladyship made this mistake.' The Earl, in his opinion was the opposite extreme. 'He was well read and friendly and an incessant talker.'[213]

But despite the posturing of the Lady the power of the Ormondes was quite diminished. They would never again occupy the same dominant positions as they enjoyed during the reigns of the two Dukes and before. Jonah Barrington recalled a case where he had to defend the Earl at the Kilkenny assizes.[214] The Earl and his retinue, which included his sons, had occasion to retire to Mrs. Madden's public house, where the Earl was wont to frequent. There he had the usual hangers on. As they became somewhat inebriated one of the party mentioned the apothecary Mr. Duffy, who had offended the Ormondes some time previously. The conversation centred on the hurt and the perceived injustice became palpable. Some of the more hot-headed of the group suggested that Mr. Duffy should be left in no doubt about where the loyalty of the citizens of Kilkenny lay. A group moved into the street and proceeded to the shop where Mr. Duffy carried on his business. They tore up stones from the road and not a window was left intact. The next morning the Earl, having had time to reflect on the occurrence sent workmen to repair the harm, but Mr. Duffy refused to allow them to do so. He decided to take the Earl and his companions of the night's drinking to court. The Earl employed Barrington to defend himself and his sons and friends. The upshot of the case was that the jury acquitted the Earl but found the other defendants guilty and fines were imposed. In recognition of his gratitude to Barrington the Earl invited him to a banquet in the Castle, attended by all the local gentry and there presented him with a gold snuff box, suitably inscribed.

---

[213] Barrington *Personal Sketches Vol.2*
[214] Ibid.

Butlers of Ormonde

Walter, John's eldest son succeeded to the title and estates, as the 18th Earl when his father died in 1795. He had three brothers, John, James and Charles and two sisters, Elizabeth and Eleanor[215]. John died when he was in his twenties and James succeeded Walter as the 19th Earl. Charles of Castlecomer and Kirklington, York, had three sons[216] and a daughter Sarah. She married Rev. John Prior of Mount Dillon, Co. Dublin, the son of the vice- provost of Trinity College, Dublin, in 1836 and they had a family. She and her children were subsequently granted permission to use the name and arms of Wandesforde in addition to Prior – a quo the Prior Wandesforde family[217]. This occurred in 1882 after she had succeeded to the estates of Castlecomer and Kirklington on the death of her nephew, Charles.

Walter the 18th Earl was only 25 when he inherited. Lord Dunboyne stated 'he was an engaging young man of high promise; but he became a companion of the Prince Regent and his talents were wasted in the fashionable society he frequented.' It was the young Earl (created a Marquess in 1815) who sold the prisage of wines to the Government for a sum in excess of £200,000. That valuable asset had been in the family from the time of the first Butlers in Ireland. Although married he had no family and he died at the comparatively young age of 40 at Ulcombe in Kent, in 1820, where he was buried. His title and estates passed to his brother James who was then 45 years old.

James the 19th Earl of Ormonde, an Eton old boy, was an M.P. for Kilkenny both county and city for almost thirty years. Like his brother he was created a Marquess, in 1825. It is not known how he voted when the Act of Union was passed nor whether he supported either Catholic Emancipation or the Repeal movement. It is unlikely that a man, who had fifteen children by his wife Lady Grace Staples the granddaughter of Lord Molesworth, had very much time for anything other than looking after his very considerable brood[218]. He died in 1838 in a Dublin hotel and was buried St. Mary's Church. At the time of his death he was lord lieutenant of Co. Kilkenny and a Colonel in the Kilkenny Militia.

---

[215] Elizabeth married Thomas Kavanagh of Borris, Co. Carlow and Eleanor married Cornelius O'Callaghan, Lord Lismore. Eleanor was involved in a bitter divorce case (for details see *The Tipperary Gentry Vol.1* by Art Kavanagh and William Hayes).
[216] John, Henry and Walter. John's wife was a McClintock of the Rathdonnell family (for details of the Rathdonnells see *The Carlow Gentry* by Jimmy O'Toole), but they had no children. Henry never married and Walter had one son, Charles, mentioned above, who succeeded to the Castlecomer and Kirklington estates after the death of his grandfather.
[217] See the chapter about the Wandesfordes in this book.
[218] Many of these children died in infancy or died as very young adults. Only one other son, James, an Army Officer, had a family and his children died without issue.

John, his eldest son, succeeded him as the 20th Earl and 2nd Marquess. He was 29 at the time of his inheritance. John was educated at Harrow and was a serious scholarly type of person. He was responsible for classifying and arranging the huge manuscript collection of the Ormondes in Kilkenny Castle. He wrote widely and his book *Autumn in Sicily* was quite popular at the time.

During the terrible period of the famine, he reduced the rents payable by his Irish tenants and in many cases agreed to forego them entirely[219]. He was Patron of the Kilkenny Archaeological Society and vice President of the Royal Dublin Society.

John married Lady Frances Paget in 1843 and they had four sons and two daughters[220]. Quite remarkably all four sons were named James – James Edward, James Hubert, James Arthur and James Theobald. Due to whatever weakness was inherent in the family John too, died young. He was bathing is the sea, with his children, at the coast, near Loftus Hall, in Co. Wexford, when he took ill and died suddenly.[221] He was buried in St. Canice's Cathedral where there is an altar tomb in him memory. He was 46 years of age. His eldest son James Edward was only ten years old at the time.

James Edward, now the 21st Earl, was educated at Harrow and took a commission in the Life Guards where he remained for a number of years. Like his father and grandfather before him he was a Knight of St. Patrick. He was also a Privy Councillor for Ireland, but he took no further part in public life. A portly jovial man he was well liked by his tenants in both Kilkenny and Tipperary despite the upheavals of the time due to the land agitation. He was a noted yachtsman and spent a week annually at Cowes where he was Commodore of "The Squadron" – a post formerly held by Edward VII prior to his coronation.[222] King Edward and Queen Alexandra paid a visit to Kilkenny Castle as recounted in the Langrishe chapter in this book.

It fell to the lot of the 21st Earl to oversee the dismantling of the huge land banks in Tipperary and Kilkenny that had brought in an income in excess of £20,000 per annum since 1790. Following the Land Acts of the late 19th and early 20th centuries the tenants were assisted by the state in purchasing their tenancies. While the landlords were compensated this movement of assets heralded the end of a way of life that had been the cornerstone of an autocratic system since the time of the Norman invasion.

---

[219] Woodham Smith – *The Great Hunger* pg. 117
[220] Mary was a lady in waiting to the Duchess of Saxe Coburg and she married William Fitzwilliam. Her sister Blanche married a son of Lord Kensington. Both ladies had families.
[221] He died from apoplexy according to *The Complete Peerage*.
[222] Lord Dunboyne in *Old Kilkenny Review*

The 21st Earl and 3rd Marquess was married and had two daughters Beatrice and Constance.[223] Lady Beatrice married Lt. General Sir Richard Pole-Carew and they had a family. After the death of George O'Callaghan, Lord Lismore, in 1898, both ladies came into the possession of Shanbally Demesne in Tipperary. Shanbally was formerly the home of the O'Callaghans, Lords Lismore. George's mother was Eleanor Butler, the great great grandaunt of Beatrice and Constance. The Earl died in 1919 and was succeeded by his brother, James Arthur, then a septuagenarian who lived another twenty four years dying in 1943.

James Arthur the 22nd Earl and 4th Marquess was a former Army Officer, having served in the Life Guards. His wife was Ellen Anson Stager the daughter of a General in the U.S. army and they had two sons and two daughters. The eldest daughter, Evelyn, married Edmund Drummond a brother of the Earl of Perth. Both sons pursued Army careers and when James Arthur died in 1943 he was succeeded by his eldest son James George Anson as the 23rd Earl and 5th Marquess.

James George had served in World War 1, and having been wounded was invalided home. He resigned from the Army in 1920. James George was in Kilkenny Castle in 1922, with his wife (Sybil the daughter of Lord Ramsay), when it was occupied by the Republican forces during the Civil War. The castle was immediately besieged by Free State troops and after two days the Republicans surrendered. According to Lord Dunboyne 'it all ended with both sides being proud of having defended and rescued Lord and Lady Ossory'.

The 23rd Earl and Sybil had a son, James, who followed in the family footsteps and became an Army officer. He served in World War II and was killed in action. When the 23rd Earl died in 1949 he was succeeded by his brother James Arthur as the 24th Earl and 6th Marquess. James Arthur, like his brother, fought in World War 1 and in 1918 he was awarded the Military Cross. He also served in some capacity in World War II.

---

[223] His wife was Lady Elizabeth Grosvenor the eldest daughter of the Duke of Westminster.

The Marquess in the foreground visiting Rothe House
Others in the picture include Mrs. Bligh, J. Delaney, T. Hoyne, Miss Birthistle, P. Farrelly, Miss Hegarty, Mrs. Kenealy, Mrs. Stopford, Lady Martha Ponsonby, P. Walsh, Mrs. Grattan Bellew, Mrs Murphy, R. Deloughry, R. Haughton, Mrs. Phelan, F.W. Cole, Mrs. Lanigan

    The 24th Earl of Ormonde sold the dilapidated castle to a Castle Restoration Committee for £50 in 1967 and auctioned its contents in 1967 and it is now being restored by the Office of Public Works. Most of the extensive collection of portraits and many of the hangings were donated back to the castle. The two most interesting rooms are the Long Gallery, where a huge Carrera marble double breasted fireplace is carved with the history of the Butler family, and the elaborately furnished Victoria drawing room.[224]
    James Arthur was married to Jessie Clarke and they had two daughters.

---

[224] *The Irish News*

Cuffes of Desart

In 1921 the treaty between Britain and Ireland led to the establishment of the Irish Free State, which gave Ireland the right to govern itself as a Dominion within the British Empire. Within a few months, Ireland again erupted in conflict, this time a bitter civil war between the Provisional Government of the Irish Free State and those who felt that the Anglo-Irish Treaty fell far short of Republican ambitions.

On the night of February 1922, the 5th Earl of Desart was in London when a small group of Republicans walked up the avenue to Desart Court armed with fire-torches. Why it was felt necessary to destroy the building is unclear. The Desarts had not done anything obvious to bring this destruction upon them[225]. The 5th Earl had been amongst the earliest Irish landlords to agree to the sale of his estate in the wake of the 1903 Land Act. Lady Sybil Lubbock maintained the burning was "for no personal ill-will towards them [the Desarts] but in reprisal for some measure of severity on behalf of the new government". That same night, the Ponsonby's house

---

[225] Hubert Butler in his *Escape from the Anthill* seemed to think the attack was carried out to punish Senator Lady Desart for her political leanings. The houses of 37 Senators were burnt and in the following year 139 country houses were destroyed with their fine libraries, priceless antiques and marvellous potential.

at Bessborough was also burned. However, there does seem to have been an element of malicious intent in the burning, for, when a truck escaped from Desart carrying various pieces of furniture and art, it was apprehended at Athy and its contents destroyed. One can only guess at the treasures lost - the furniture, the portraits, the diaries, letters and correspondence. Ham Cuffe was distraught at the news. That so few of his tenants had lifted a finger to stop the destruction hurt him deeply. Ten years later, he wrote to his granddaughter, Iris Origo: "I can't bear to think of Desart -it is sadness itself. All gone, all scattered - and we were so happy there". He never again returned to Ireland

In 1641, Hugh Cuffe's grandson, the Ennis-born Joseph Cuffe, joined a cavalry regiment raised to defend the interests of the new planters during what would become one of the most brutal wars in Irish history. During Oliver Cromwell's Protectorate, Sir Charles Coote, a first cousin of Joseph, became one of the most powerful men in Ireland. Another close family friend was Sir William Petty, the man entrusted with the redistribution of lands confiscated from Catholic Irish families to English officers. In 1654, Joseph Cuffe was awarded a substantial 5000 acre estate in the barony of Shillelogher, County Kilkenny. In due course his descendents would come to call the estate "Desart".[226] When a serious challenge to the Cromwellian land settlement was initiated by the administration of the Catholic James II, Agmondesham Cuffe, Joseph's son and heir, was amongst the first men to take up his sword for the Dutch Prince William of Orange.[227]

---

[226] In the twelfth century, Earl William Marshal granted the parish of Castleinch to the Anglo-Norman De Valle (or Wall) family. By the 17th century, Shillelogher was one of the wealthiest baronies in the country, held in the patrimony of the Earl of Ormond. In the 1640s the resident landholder, Gerald Comerford of Castleinch hosted Archbishop Rinuccini, the Papal Nuncio, before he entered Kilkenny City to meet with the Irish confederates there. In 1650 Kilkenny surrendered to Cromwell's forces, and in 1654 Gerald Comerford was attainted for treason. His castle and lands at Castleinch were forfeited to Joseph Cuffe, Esq. Following the restoration of Charles II, and the death of Sir Charles Coote in 1661, the Comerfords, perhaps encouraged by their friendship with the Duke of Ormonde, successfully appealed the forfeiture of their estates. Under the Act of Settlement & Explanation, Joseph Cuffe was granted 200 plantation acres including 1200 acres at "Tullaghane, to be called and known for ever by the name of Cuffe's Desart. In total his estate in Kilkenny came to 5425 acres, including 324 acres at Cuffe's Grange and 420 acres in Killaloe. See Ronald P. Larkin, *The Road to Knockeenbaun,* Kilmanagh. (2002), p. 46.

[227] Among the family portraits that perished during the burning of Desart Court in 1922 was an oil in good condition, of a man believed to have been Agmondesham Cuffe. The artist was reputed to have been the Dutch artist, Sir Godfrey Kneller.

Cuffe of Desart

The victory of the Williamite forces over the Irish Catholics was in many ways absolute. It set in motion an age where the new Protestant elite was able to settle down and develop the hitherto unruly island into a proper English colony.

Perhaps the greatest symbols of the age of the Protestant Ascendancy were the enormous mansions erected by individual landowners across the country. Desart Court was amongst the earliest such constructions. It was built on the Cuffe family estate in Kilkenny in 1733 for John Cuffe, later 1st Lord Desart, eldest son of Agmondesham Cuffe, the Williamite soldier.

Desart Court

A graduate of Trinity College Dublin, John Cuffe stood as MP for Thomastown, County Kilkenny, from 1715 to 1727. Desart Court has been described as one of Ireland's most outstanding architectural triumphs. Its original architect is increasingly believed to have been Sir Edward Lovett Pearce, the man who designed Parliament House in Dublin. The construction costs appear to have been partially met through the sale of a large quantity of silver plate seized during a raid on the French fortress of Quebec by the father-in-law of the 1st Lord Desart.[228]

Agmondesham's son, John, was educated at Kilkenny College where Jonathan Swift had studied a decade earlier.[229] Like Swift and his father before him, John Cuffe went on to study at Trinity College Dublin, founded just over a century earlier by Queen Elizabeth. He entered Trinity aged 14 on 7th August 1697, became a Fellow Commoner and graduated with a Bachelor of Arts in 1701. It was during this period that the Rubrics, the oldest surviving building in the college today, was built.

His brother, Maurice, was called to the Irish Bar in 1712, became a King's Counselor for four years and represented the City of Kilkenny in King George I's Irish Parliament from 1715 to 1726. In 1732 he built a house at Killaghy (or St. Alban's) near the Ballyspellin Spa in County Kilkenny. He married Martha Fitzgerald, daughter of John Fitzgerald of Ballymaloe, Co. Cork.[230] A third brother was Denny Cuffe, MP, who married Grace Wright of Dublin and was ancestor of the Wheeler-Cuffe family. There was also a daughter, Martha, who married John Blunden, MP, father of Sir John Blunden, 1st Bart.[231]

---

[228] In her recollections, Dorothea Herbert, grand-daughter of John Cuffe, wrote that the marriage settlement between her grandparents had included "ten thousand pounds worth of plate, taken by her father [i.e.: General Gorges] at the Siege of Quebec". However, as the Siege did not take place until 1759, this may be a mistake. Perhaps Gorges acquired the fortune during the English raids on the French fortress of Quebec in the 1690s.

[229] Alumni Dublinenses, Burtchell & Sadlier, Royal Irish Academy, 2001 reprint, Vol. 1, p.200.

[230] Maurice and Martha's daughter Anne (Nancy) Cuffe was, for a short time, the wife of Edmond Fitzgerald, 20th Knight of Glin, (1705 - 1773), a member of the notorious Hell Fire Club. Born in February 1721, she was the second of seven daughters. A contemporary described her as 'a popular Protestant beauty from Kilkenny'. It is thus a surprise that her husband, whom she married in March 1740, was the still Catholic Knight of Glin. For reasons unknown - perhaps the Knight's mounting gambling debts - the marriage was a failure. She subsequently married her second cousin, as his second wife, Denny Baker Cuffe of Cuffesborough, King's County (modern Offaly) but died soon after on 24th October 1776.

[231] Sir John seems to have been a difficult man. His niece, Dorothea Herbert, recalled how he let none of his sons go to a public school and "kept his beautiful daughters shut up in a nursery making lace under an old Governess and their Mammy nurse until they were 15 or 16". When he died in January 1783, Sir John's will expressed the memorable wish "that he may not be buried till his head begins to be putrefied or his head severed from his body, and laid without ceremony in the round part of the wood where the laurel is planted and the ditch of water surrounds it". The Castleblunden estate contained "a highly romantic mid 18th

Cuffe of Desart

John Cuffe's political career commenced in 1708, when, at the age of 25, he was appointed Sheriff of Kilkenny. Seven years later he began to make his mark in the Irish House of Commons when he became MP for Thomastown, a position he retained for 12 years from the accession of King George I in 1715 to the accession of King George II in 1727.[232] As to his character, we have a description by his granddaughter Dorothea Herbert who recalled him as "a remarkably handsome and good man".

His first wife, Margaret Hamilton, from County Down died childless and young and in 1726, John Cuffe married again. His second wife - the future 1st Lady Desart - was Dorothea Gorges.[233]

Within a year of John and Dorothea's marriage both their fathers and King George I were dead. So too was John's sister, Martha Blunden. As heir to Agmondesham Cuffe, John and his wife then moved to the family estate at Castleinch in County Kilkenny. Over the next twelve years, Dorothea bore her husband nine children, of whom seven survived childhood. In between all this, she spent her time weaving a tapestry representing the Rising Sun which her granddaughter, Dorothea Herbert, recalled seeing on a visit to Desart in 1773.

Perhaps it was the noise of so many children in his home or more likely it was the growing pretensions of the landed gentry that, in 1733, inspired John Cuffe to abandon the old tower house of Castleinch and commission the construction of a new country manor which he would call Desart Court.[234]

At any rate, Desart Court was built and was a classic example of early Georgian construction. It was built with blue limestone and comprised a central block with pavilions projecting on either side. Over the ensuing decades, the interior

---

century house with water on both sides of it so that it seems to float", built just outside Kilkenny City by Sir John. (Bence-Jones, 1988, p. 63).

[232] One of his contemporaries at Kilkenny College and sometime neighbour was the philosopher, Bishop George Berkeley, who was born at Dysart (not to be confused with Desart) Castle outside Thomastown in 1685. Berkeley achieved much fame when he visited the American colonies with the novel idea of establishing schools for "the instruction of the youth of America". His memory is enshrined in the name of Berkeley College, California.

[233] Through her mother Dorothea was connected with the Beresfords and the Powers of Curraghmore (the Earls of Tyrone after 1690). Marcus Beresford, Dorothea's half brother, who inherited Curraghmore, was created Earl of Tyrone in 1746. Her father, an Army officer from Co. Meath, went on to become a General. Her younger sister was married to William St. Lawrence, Lord Howth. Relationships between the families of Gorges and St. Lawrence must have come asunder in 1736 when Hamilton Gorges, brother to both Lady Desart and Lady Howth, killed Lord Howth's brother in a duel.

[234] Said to have been designed by Sir Edward Lovett Pearce (1699 - 1733) who was the architect for the stunning new Parliament House.

was fitted with sumptuous tapestries, oil paintings by Italian Masters, Chippendale chairs, dado wood paneling, rococo ceilings, Dutch walnut cabinets, bookcases "enriched with fluted pilasters", beautifully carved Oakwood balustrades and mantelpieces from Sienna. The Cuffe family fortunes were substantially reduced in the process.

Desart Court – rear

John Cuffe may have been fretting about the unpaid bills involved in the construction of his new stately home but he must also have derived considerable pleasure when, on 10th November 1733, he was elevated to the peerage as Baron Desart of Desart in the Irish Peerage. The preamble to the patent applauded his father and grandfather; particularly the latter's efforts to ensure the "Protestant succession".[235] He took his seat in the Irish House of Lords two days later, no doubt casting a nod at his brother-in-law, Lord Howth, seated opposite.

Lord Desart further indebted himself in 1735 with the purchase of the Ormond Estate at Callan from Charles Butler, Earl of Arran, for £11,120. Thirty

---

[235] Quoted in The Complete Peerage, GEC, but also in Lodge, Vol. VI.

years later his son was compelled to sell some 2000 acres of the Callan lands to pay off the family debts[236].

John Cuffe, 1st Lord Desart, died on 26th June 1749 and was buried alongside his father and grandfather at the Church of Inchiholaghan in Castleinch. He was succeeded by his eldest son, 19 year old John Cuffe, 2nd Baron Desart, then a student at Trinity College, Dublin.

His wife, the Dowager Lady Dorothea Desart, survived him for nearly eighteen years, finally succumbing "at her house in Henry Street" in 1777. Her daughter Susanna was married off to her first cousin, Sir John Blunden, son of the 1st Lord Desart's sister Martha. It was Sir John who built the original house at Castleblunden, perhaps seeking to emulate his father-in-law's creation at Desart Court. The second daughter Sophia was given to a Killarney-born lawyer named John Herbert and the third, Martha, to his brother, the Reverend Nicholas Herbert.[237]

With regard to Lady Dorothea Desart's sons, the eldest, John, 2nd Lord Desart, went to Trinity College Dublin and married a Cork heiress but predeceased her by 10 years. The second son, Otway, 3rd Lord Desart, later 1st Earl of Desart, was dispatched across the sea to Christ Church College, Oxford, and became a lawyer. As befitting the age, the third son, Hamilton, joined the church whilst the fourth, William, secured a commission in the army with the 17th Dragoons.

Known to his Irish contemporaries as "Sean an Chaipin", John Cuffe, 2nd Baron Desart was born on 16th November 1730, the eldest surviving son of John and Dorothea Cuffe. Like his father, John was educated at Trinity College Dublin. He had not long entered the college when his father died on 26th June 1749. Thus, at the age of 19, John succeeded as 2nd Lord Desart, an inheritance that brought with it one of the grandest country houses in Ireland. Showing every bit as much political pluck as his forbears, the 2nd Baron took his seat in the House of Lords on 25th November 1751, 9 days after his 21st birthday.

On September 2nd 1752 this most eligible of bachelors took as his bride a young widow from County Cork, Sophia Thornhill.[238]

---

[236] The purchaser was James Agar of Ringwood (see chapter 1 for details of that family)
[237] Dorothea Herbert's father
[238] Her husband was Richard Thornhill of St. Stephen's Green. Dublin. Her father was a wealthy landowner named Bettridge Badham of Rockfield, County Cork. Her mother was Sophia King, daughter of John King, 3rd Baron Kingston (1664 - 1728) and his wife "a pretty and persistent Irish scullery maid". It was while living at the King family's new house of Rockingham near Boyle in County Roscommon that the future 3rd Baron Kingston first developed "a more than ordinary and suspicious familiarity" with Margaret (Peggy) O'Cahan. By the time his elder brother, Robert, 2nd Baron Kingston, heard of the romance the "amour was well advanced" and the couple had married. The 3rd Baron's uncle captured

The 2nd Lord Desart and his wife, Lady Sophia, had three daughters. Sophia married Richard Cooke in June 1772; Catherine married Sir Charles Burton, of Pollerton, County Carlow, in August 1778 and Lucy married William Weldon in May 1792. These were first cousins of Dorothea Herbert and she has left us with this insight into the lives of the three sisters: "Mrs. Cooke was as good a Creature as possible but had a couple of Mischief making Servants who constantly tattled and put her out of Temper. She was a fine figure of a woman, large and handsome, though not so beautiful as her sister, Lady Burton, whom she greatly resembled. These two and Mrs. Weldon were co-heiresses to the late Lord Desart's alienable property." [239] Sophia was the Mrs. Cooke, mentioned by her relative Dorothea Herbert, who, when her husband died, painted all the flowerpots black, reupholstered the furniture in sable and tarred the stables turning an elderly visitor's horses piebald 'for which he whipped the stableboy.'

The 2nd Lord Desart was not a particularly wealthy man. His father had spent a considerable portion of the family fortunes on the construction of Desart and the purchase of the Callan estates from the Earl of Arran. In 1765 he sold 2,108 acres of this estate, including the town of Callan, to James Agar, sometime MP of Kilkenny.[240]

John Cuffe, 2nd Lord Desart died at Desart at the relatively young age of 37 on 25th November 1767, sixteen years to the day after he first took his seat in the House of Lords.[241]

Otway Cuffe was the second surviving son of John and Dorothea Cuffe. Four weeks after his brother's demise, he took his seat in the Irish House of Lords. He was educated at Christ Church College, Oxford. He was the first of his family to have studied at that University since Henry Cuffe, the Elizabethan gentleman

---

the essence of the King family reaction to the marriage in this manner: "Few of the nobility of English extraction have ever contracted marriages with Irish papists but none (up to this case) have married one who was at once an ordinary Servant Maid and an Irish Papist who had neither Charms of Beauty nor genteel behaviour nor agreeableness of conversation".

[239] In addition to these three girls, the 2nd Lord Desart recognised an illegitimate son, Joseph Cuffe who was packed off to live with the Herberts though the family "respected and loved him as much as if he had been Legitimated into it".

[240] See Chapter 1.

[241] James Hoban, the celebrated architect of the White House in the U.S.A. was born on the Desart estate during the lifetime of the 2nd Lord. Hoban had been born in 1762, in one of the tenant cottages at Desart, and educated in the estate school established by the 2nd Lord Desart. Showing much prowess at drawing, young Hoban then moved from Kilkenny to school in Dublin where he was awarded the prestigious Duke of Leinster's medal by the Dublin Society. He subsequently served as an apprentice to the Cork-born architect Thomas Ivory who, later worked on redesigning Westport House for the 3rd Lady Desart's father.

executed with the Earl of Essex 150 years earlier. Over the next 150 years, Christ Church was to be the destination for a number of his sons, grandsons and great-grandsons.

Stairway – Desart Court

Otway appears to have been an enlightened individual who did much to enhance the state of County Kilkenny during his time at Desart. In this regard he must have been much aided by a new high road, commenced in 1750, which linked Kilkenny and Callan. This formed the principal entrance into the city of Kilkenny from the numerous mansions of the Anglo-Irish families in the south and southwestern parts of the county. The 3rd Lord Desart stood as Mayor of Kilkenny from 1771 to 1772 and again from 1779 and 1780. During this time he introduced street-lighting and "scavenging" (i.e.: rubbish collecting) programmes to the city and, in 1773, oversaw the restructuring of the Linen Market there. His interest in horse racing was such that, in 1767, he was appointed Steward of the Kilkenny Races.

On 6th January 1781, Otway Cuffe was "advanced to the dignity" of Viscount Desart, probably in recognition of his political influence as patron of half the borough of Kilkenny. Four years later, he married 30-year-old Lady Anne Browne. Lady Anne was a wealthy lady 25 years his junior. The Brownes, Earls of Altamont, descended from the great Pirate Queen, Grace O'Malley.[242] Lady Anne Browne's parents were, Peter Brown, 2nd Earl of Altamont, who in 1752 married Elizabeth Kelly, heiress to one of the largest Jamaican sugar plantations.

In 1785 the marriage of Otway Cuffe to Lady Anne Browne must have brought a considerable fortune to the House of Desart. It also afforded them an intimate association with one of the great families in Ireland.[243] On 20th February 1788 Lady Desart bore her elderly husband a son and heir, Otway Cuffe the younger, later 2nd Earl of Desart. Lady Desart also produced two daughters - Lady Dorothea and Lady Elizabeth.

In the 18th Century the rise of the Protestant Ascendancy, and the growth of landlord's economic and political power, inevitably affected relations between landlords and tenants. Many tenants responded aggressively to specific issues including the enclosure of common land and payment of tithes on crops, and by the second half of the 18th Century agrarian violence had become a feature of life in the Irish countryside. By 1761 a movement known as the Whiteboys (they wore white shirts over their everyday clothes), began to mobilise by night in counties Tipperary and Kilkenny. Their methods of protest included the houghing of animals, destroying fences erected around the large estates, and intimidation of the despised tithe collectors. Although in succeeding decades, several Acts were passed through

---

[242] John Browne, 1st Earl of Altamont, also commissioned the eminent German architect Richard Cassells (or Castle) to build a new house for his family at Westport on Clew Bay.

[243] Anne's brother, John Browne, 3rd Earl of Altamont, succeeded to the title on the death of their father in 1780. Only 24 years old at the time, he was already regarded as one of the wealthiest men in the land. One of his father's last acts before his death had been to employ the architect Thomas Ivory to substantially enlarge the original Westport House (1776 – 1778). In 1781, the 3rd Earl continued the family trend by commissioning James Wyatt to design a town around the Atlantic port in order to encourage the development of the local linen industry. Two years later, in May 1787, the Earl of Altamont married Louisa Howe, youngest daughter of the celebrated Admiral Howe, later created 1st Earl of Howe, as a result of his famous victory over the French revolutionary fleet on 1 June 1794.

Parliament to control such outrages, there was a fresh outbreak or violence in 1791. Viscount Desart appears also to have been affected by this crisis, as in that year, he and his cousin George Beresford, Marquess of Waterford, mustered a force of Protestant militia and spent several months stamping out this form of protest in the area.[244]

On 4th December 1793 Otway Cuffe was elevated in the Irish Peerage as Earl of Desart. In addition he was made Viscount Castle-cuff, a junior title subsequently borne by his first-born son and heir. Otway Cuffe took his seat as Earl of Desart in the Irish House of Lords the following January.

The revolt of the United Irishmen - better known as the 1798 Rebellion - which was ultimately a disaster and a tragedy, had little impact in Kilkenny and even less on the Desart estate.

What it did in fact achieve was the arousal of much fear in the hearts of the Ascendancy. It also encouraged the British Parliament in London to view Ireland less as a self-sufficient province and more as a potential base from which Napoleon Bonaparte could launch an attack on England's western flank.

In 1800 the Irish Parliament voted itself out of existence and ceased to exist, an event formalised by the 1801 Act of Union. Ireland's five million strong population now found themselves in a situation where all major decisions on Irish affairs were henceforth to be concluded at Westminster, a situation that remained until independence was granted to the Irish Free State in 1921. There had initially been strong opposition to the Act from the Anglo-Irish elite but many found themselves re-evaluating their position when London offered substantial "compensation" to those of a wavering disposition.[245]

Discontent amongst the aristocracy was further quelled by the reassurance that their order - the peerage - would continue to exert an influence in London through the 28 "Representative Peers of Ireland" in the British House of Lords, of whom the 1st Earl of Desart was one. The 3rd, 4th and 5th Earls would also subsequently hold this honour. The 3rd Earl of Desart was possibly the first of his family to spend long periods of time in London, in order to occupy his seat in the House of Lords, and participate in the festivities of the Season. Most "Backwoods

---

[244] Otway's youngest brother, William Cuffe, a Major in the British Army, died of a fever while serving with the garrison at Athlone in 1790. Dorothea Herbert recalled him as a "headstrong and hot" man who caused much trouble in his youth with his argumentative nature. A portrait of him by Johan Zoffany was among those destroyed in the 1922 fire at Desart Court.

[245] Among the beneficiaries was the 1st Earl of Desart's brother-in-law, the Earl of Altamont, who was created Marquis of Sligo on 29th December 1800.

Peers" hired apartments or purchased houses for such periods, although when the 67-year-old 1st Earl died on 9th August 1804, his death took place at his house in Kildare Street, Dublin. He was succeeded by his 16-year-old son, Otway, Viscount Castle-Cuffe, then a school boy at Eton.

The 1st Earl's wife, Anne, Countess of Desart, survived her husband by ten years, before she succumbed to a "nervous fever" in 1814.

Otway Cuffe, 2nd Earl of Desart, had a short but eventful life. He was born in Dublin on 20th February 1788, the only son and heir of the then Lord and Lady Desart. Like his father before him, he studied at Christ Church, Oxford, matriculating on 29th April 1805. Another man who matriculated from Oxford that year became his good friend: (Sir) Robert Peel, a former Harrovian who would later become Prime Minister of Great Britain.

The 2nd Earl had two sisters - Elizabeth and Dorothea. The first married Henry Wemyss of Danesfort, County Kilkenny, and had a son, Otway Wemyss, who served with the Buffs (The Royal East Kent Regiment). Her great-nephew, Hamilton Cuffe, 5th Earl of Desart, recalled her as "a sort of cross between a housekeeper and a Grand Duchess [who] might have come straight out of the pictures in a Dickens's book." He described the second sister, his great-aunt Lady Dorothea, as "a very different type ... rather like an eagle, and very formidable and determined".[246]

Unlike his father, the 2nd Earl was not one of the Representative Peers sent to represent Ireland in Westminster. However, this did not preclude him from politics and, from 1808 to 1817, he stood as Tory MP for Bossiney in Cornwall, once the seat of Sir Francis Drake, and apparently the place in which King Arthur's Hall of Chivalry supposedly lay. In 1809 he accepted a post as Lord of the Treasury under Lord Portland's Tory government, which he retained until 1810. During that year he also stood as Mayor of Kilkenny, a city on the rise following its Georgian re-construction, which included the Club House Hotel built three years earlier.

On 7th October 1817 the 2nd Earl of Desart married 18-year-old Catherine O'Connor. She was perhaps a curious choice for the Earl of Desart for she hailed from one of the most ancient Celtic bloodlines in Ireland. In time this would ferment itself in the mind of her youngest grandson, Otway Cuffe, one of the leading proponents of the Gaelic Revival in Ireland. Born shortly after the conclusion of the 1798 Rebellion, Catherine was the eldest daughter and co heiress of Maurice and

---

[246] Her husband, Major General Sir James Campbell, KCB, had served in the Peninsular War under the Duke of Wellington, and later as Governor of Ceylon. Their marriage was an unhappy affair, made considerably worse when - in the face of a Chancery court order awarding custody of their four pretty daughters to their father Sir James - Lady Dorothea fled to France and kept the unfortunate girls there, for the next 15 years.

Maria Nugent O'Connor of Gortnamona (or Mount Pleasant) in the "King's County" (i.e.: County Offaly). Her great-grandfather, Maurice O'Connor, "heir to the principality of Ofelia", had been amongst the first of the Irish Catholics to conform to Protestantism in the wake of Cromwell's invasion and having earned himself a fortune at the bar in England, married a daughter of the Earl of Fingall.

Her father had been a prominent advocate of Roman Catholic Emancipation and on a lesser level was a celebrated breeder of red setters, establishing a kennel at Gortnamona in 1779. The setters from this kennel were considered amongst the highest quality gun-dogs in the British Isles.[247] However, the 2nd Earl cannot have had much time to discuss the hazards of emancipation or indeed of shooting dogs for within a year of his marriage to Catherine, his new father-in-law lay dead.[248]

Catherine's mother was Maria Burke, the eldest daughter of Sir Thomas Burke of Marble Hill, County Galway.[249] These then were the aunts and uncles of Catherine, Countess of Desart. The influence they may have had over her is unknown but it is surely relevant, for instance, that her "Uncle Percy" taught George IV how to sail and that, in 1852, his son, the 7th Viscount Strangford, a member of

---

[247] The bloodline was later transferred to the La Touche family of Harristown, Co. Kildare, after the marriage to one of the O'Connor daughters. It stayed at Harristown until the 1860s when sold at auction to Sir A. Chichester of Devonshire. The Cuffes were linked to dog breeding on several other occasions. The 3rd Earl of Desart's kinsman, the Duke of Buccleuch, pioneered the importation of Labradors in the 1830s. Lady Kathleen Pilkington, only daughter of the 4th Earl of Desart, is likewise credited with the boom in French bulldogs across London during the reign of Edward VII.

[248] Unusually, Gortnamona then devolved upon Maurice Nugent O'Connor's youngest daughter, Elizabeth, who married the Reverend Benjamin Morris. Their son, William O'Connor Morris (1824 - 1904) was one of the great Judges of the Irish Supreme Court in Queen Victoria's reign. Like Desart, the house was burned down by the IRA in 1922

[249] Among the family portraits destroyed in the 1922 burning of Desart Court were oil paintings of the 2nd Earl of Desart and his wife by the Irish portrait artist Thomas Clement Thompson, and of both Maurice and Maria Nugent O'Connor. Thompson's two pictures were exhibited at the Royal Academy in 1819. Sir Thomas must have been a man of much ambition for Maria was one of four daughters that married into the upper realms of the British aristocracy. In 1799, Maria's sister Elizabeth married John de Burgh, Earl of Clanricarde (1744 - 1808). Their daughter Hester would go on to marry the enigmatic Marquess of Sligo while a great-granddaughter, Margaret, would take up residence at Desart Court as the Countess of Desart. In April 1806, Maria's youngest sister, Anne, married Sir Henry Tichborne (1779 - 1845), a direct descendent of the man who first proclaimed the accession of James I to the crown of England on the death of Queen Elizabeth. The third sister married Percy Clinton Smythe, 6th Viscount Strangford and 1st Baron Penshurst (1780 - 1855).

Benjamin Disraeli's "Young England" group, fought the last duel in England against Colonel Frederick Romilly.

Drawing Room at Desart Court

In the autumn of 1818, Catherine bore a son and heir, John Otway O'Connor Cuffe, Viscount Castle-Cuffe, delivered at Desart. Happiness should have followed but, alas, on 23rd November 1820 the 2nd Earl died at Desart. He was 33 years old. Had he lived on, he would almost certainly have become a well known figure in Parliament. Aside from his intimate friendship with Peel, he was also a close colleague of Spencer Perceval, the British Prime Minister assassinated in 1812 by John Bellingham - a failed businessman from Liverpool, who blamed the Tory politician for his financial difficulties.[250]

---

[250] 55 A portrait of Spencer Perceval painted from a mask taken after his death was amongst those destroyed in the 1922 fire at Desart Court. It was painted by G.F. Joseph, ARA, and presented to the 2nd Earl in 1813.

Cuffe of Desart

The Countess married again in 1826 and again misfortune befell her. Her second husband died after less than two years. Catherine, herself, lived until 1874. She died in Dublin in the family home on Pembroke Road.

John Otway O'Connor Cuffe, 3rd Earl of Desart was born on 17th October 1818. As a young infant, he was styled Viscount Castle-Cuffe, until his father's death on 23rd November 1820, at which time he succeeded to Desart Court and the Earldom at the age of two years.

In 1830 John followed in his father's footsteps and went to Eton where he stayed until 1834.[251] He would thus have been far away from Kilkenny when "distressing riots" broke out over the payment of tithes in the early 1830s.

The 3rd Earl of Desart married Lady Elizabeth Campbell, third daughter of the Earl of Cawdor and granddaughter of the 2nd Marquess of Bath.

In marrying Lady Elizabeth Campbell, the Earl of Desart brought his family into close contact with the leading Society figures during a time when Great Britain was establishing itself as the most powerful empire on the planet. His wife was closely related - if not by blood, then by marriage - to the Dukes of Abercorn, Bedford, Bridgewater, Buccleuch, Devonshire and Rutland, the Marquess of Bath, the Earls of Cawdor, Carlisle, Ellesmere, Galloway and Harewood, and the Viscounts Torrington and Weymouth.

The young couple enjoyed the Queen's patronage. In 1845 the young wife was invited to be a Lady of the Bedchamber to Victoria, a position she retained until 1864.[252] The 3rd Earl must have been delighted with the appointment for it gave him an excuse to join his wife when she was in attendance upon Her Majesty at the Royal retreat of Osborne House in the Isle of Wight. A keen yachtsman, the 3rd Earl spent much time at Cowes where he and his young sons sailed and boated with the Royal family.

During the 1850s, the 3rd Earl began to pay close heed to the goings on at Desart, and it is there, in Kilkenny that his four children had their most powerful childhood memories. A daughter, Alice, was born in 1844. A son and heir, William Ulick O'Connor Cuffe, was born at Grosvenor Crescent on 10th July 1845. A "spare heir", Hamilton Cuffe, followed on 30th August 1848[253] and a "spare spare", Otway Cuffe, concluded the batch in 1853. The second son, Hamilton, recalled his childhood at Desart as "a permanent delight".

---

[251] Among his classmates at Eton was the future Crimean war soldier Colonel Lord Henry Percy (1817-1877) who won a VC at Inkerman in 1854.
[252] Ladies-in-Waiting, From the Tudors to the Present Day, by Anne Somerset (1984)
[253] In 1848 the 3rd Earl commissioned Henry Richard Graves (1818-1882) to paint his portrait. This was yet another of the family portraits destroyed in the 1922 fire.

The year of William's birth coincided with the first year of the potato blight in Ireland, an event that heralded the worst famine to hit Western Europe for several centuries, and which reduced the population of Ireland by over two million in less than a decade.[254] Like many of his peers the Earl was largely absent from Ireland during the famine years and like most of them he gave generously to the various Relief Committees set up to alleviate the sufferings of the poor. As already mentioned Kilkenny people were not so badly affected by the famine. Landlords were affected in that they had to forego or reduce rents in certain circumstances.

By the time that William joined the Grenadier Guards in 1862, tensions between the Federal States of America and Great Britain had been escalating for several years. The regiment was duly dispatched, along with the Scots Fusiliers, to shore up British defenses in Canada. William's younger brother and eventual heir Ham Cuffe also headed across the Atlantic at this time, as a Midshipman on board the wooden frigate, Orlando. The Grenadiers remained in Canada after the outbreak of the American Civil War later that year. William had attained the rank of Captain when, in the early spring of 1865, he was summoned back to London to attend upon his dying father. The 3rd Earl had been out hunting with the Kilkenny Hounds when he took a serious fall, compounding a spinal injury he had earlier sustained yachting in Greece. His wife, Lady Elizabeth, rushed him back to the doctors in London but a fatal paralysis had already set in and, on 1st April the 46-year-old died at his residence on Eaton Square.

William "Willie" Ulick O'Connor Cuffe lived for 53 years and was 4th Earl of Desart for 33 of them. In public life, he appears to have been much given to the leisurely pursuits of yachting and hunting so popular with the upper class in the late Victorian age, complimented by a penchant for writing mystery thrillers. His private life was a more complex affair, involving two very different marriages - the first to a great-granddaughter of Lord Edward Fitzgerald, the second to the Jewish heiress, Ellen Bischoffsheim.

The 4th Earl's first marriage of 1871 was an unhappy affair. His bride, Maria Emma Preston, was of a flighty disposition. Her grandmother was "Little Pam", daughter of Lord Edward Fitzgerald, the Irish revolutionary killed in the early days of the 1798 struggle, and the beautiful Pamela Fitzgerald, reputed daughter of the egalitarian Duke of Orleans. Her grandfather, Major General Sir Guy Campbell

---

[254] One of the more uplifting examples set by the landed gentry during the Famine was set by the 3rd Earl's half-sister, Maria, and her new husband, John la Touche. They culled their herd of deer at Harristown and fed the venison to their tenants.

(1786 - 1849) was one of the great heroes of Waterloo and later commanded the 3rd West India Regiment.[255]

Maria gave birth to the 4th Earl's only child, a daughter, Lady Kathleen Mary Alexina Cuffe the year following the wedding. The marriage came asunder in the early months of 1878 when the young Countess of Desart was revealed to have indulged in an affair with the Shakespearean stage actor, Charles Sugden.[256] The Desarts were divorced in May 1878, and Maria married her lover at the British Embassy in Paris the following 26th December. That same year, Prime Minister Disraeli appointed the 4th Earl's brother, Hamilton Cuffe, Assistant Solicitor to the Treasury.

Although the 4th Earl's second marriage to Ellen Bischoffsheim produced no children, the marriage was an infinitely more satisfactory affair, bringing the House of Desart into intimate contact with one of the richest families in Europe.

It was hailed as the wedding of the Season. Rumours abounded that the Jewish bride brought a dowry of £150,000 with her, a similar sum being due on the death of her father. Before the year was out, the 4th Earl was appointed Master of the Kilkenny Foxhounds.

---

[255] A contemporary recalled the courtship of Sir Guy and Little Pam thus: "Sir Guy, when a young officer, was at a fete where Pamela's daughter was present. A young man, one of the guests, called out to the band to play "Croppies Lie Down". Campbell conceiving the request to be intended as an insult to Miss Fitzgerald demanded an immediate apology from the young man. I remember, so far, the story, but whether an apology was made or a duel ensued I cannot recollect, but I often heard that Miss Fitzgerald was so pleased with the action of the young officer that she said if ever she got married it would be to the gentleman who championed her on that occasion". Reminiscences of Sir Charles Cameron, CB, Dublin; Hodges, Figgis & Co., Ltd. (1913).

[256] Charles Sudgen was born circa 1851 and died on the 3rd August 1921. He was perhaps an awkward man for, on 1st May 1891, his wife, the former Countess of Desart, was obliged to obtain a decree nisi against him. He performed as Bernardo in "Hamlet" (London Adelphi, June 1868), as Touchstone to Lily Langtry's Rosalind in "As You Like It" (St. James's Theatre, Feb - April 1890) and as Cardinal Mazarin in "The Man in the Iron Mask" (London Adelphi, March - May 1899). A Charles Sugden was living in Bradford in the 1890s. He may be something to Edward Buttenshaw Sugden, 1st Baron St Leonards.

Ceiling detail from Desart Court

On 4th October 1882, Ellen's sister Amelia married another Anglo-Irish noble, Sir Maurice Fitzgerald (1844 - 1916), the 20th Knight of Kerry. His father, Sir Peter Fitzgerald (1808 - 1880), the 19th Knight, had been closely involved with the banking house of La Touche.

It is not clear how much time the 4th Earl and the Countess Ellen spent at Desart. Like his father, the 4th Earl was a man who preferred the country pursuits of shooting and fox-hunting, or indeed, of yachting, to the more mundane business of running an Irish country estate. Indeed Ellen described her husband as "a reckless horseman". At this time, the Desart family estates consisted of approximately 8000 acres in Kilkenny and just under 1000 acres in Tipperary, which yielded £8,932 in 1883. Despite this, the 4th Earl played an active part in introducing the first show of the Royal Agricultural Society to Kilkenny in 1884, and was Master of the Kilkenny Foxhounds from 1882 to 1884. However, shortly after his second marriage the outbreak of the Irish Land Wars once again raised the spectre of politically motivated agrarian violence, and the 4th Earl felt compelled to close up Desart in the winter of 1884 when the family relocated to England for the next 14 years.[257]

On 15th September 1898, less than six months after the death of his mother, the 4th Earl died at the relatively young age of 53-years, after a short illness, on board his yacht off Falmouth.[258] The life of the 4th Earl may have been relatively short but his impact on the family was certainly useful, not least with his acquisition of part of the Bischoffsheim fortunes.

William Ulick O'Connor Cuffe was also a literary man and wrote some fifteen novels during his life. Beginning in 1869 with "Only a Woman's Love", his most successful works were the mystery thrillers *Herne Lodge* (1888) and *The Little Chatelaine* (1889), while his novel *Beyond These Voices* (1870) was a sweeping saga of seduction and revenge set against the background of the Fenian Rising. Other titles included *Children of Nature: A Story of Modern London* (1878), *The Honourable Ella* (1879) and *Lord and Lady Piccadilly* (1887).[259]

His widow, Ellen, Countess of Desart, retired to live with her family at Ascot. Following the death of her brother-in-law, Captain Otway Cuffe, in 1911, she returned to live at Aut Even, near Talbot's Inch, in Kilkenny, where she continued the Captain's good works in the community[260]. She went on to become the first woman Senator in the first Senate of the Irish Free State, and was the first Jewish woman accorded such honours anywhere in the world. She died in 1933 at the age of 75 and was laid to rest by the side of her husband in Falmouth Cemetery.

The life of "Ham" Cuffe, 5th Earl of Desart, is succinctly explained in his autobiographical contribution to his daughter's memoirs, *A Page from the Past*, published by Jonathan Cape in 1940. His granddaughter Iris Origo also provides a charming account of her relationship with him in her own memoirs, *Images and Shadows*, published by John Murray in 1970.

The three sons of the 3rd Earl of Desart were somewhat different in outlook. Where the eldest son, William, enjoyed the leisurely life of a country squire from his youth until his death, Ham Cuffe had a more sober career as one of the leading solicitors in Edwardian England while the youngest brother, Otway Cuffe, was of a

---

[257] Another casualty was the 4th Earl's cousin, the Marquess of Waterford, who awoke at Curraghmore one morning to find his hounds, had been poisoned; the house was closed down and the Marquess moved to England.

[258] GEC, The Complete Peerage Vol. IV (1913) pp. 227 - 231.

[259] John Sutherland, *The Longman Companion to Victoria* Fiction, Longmans (1988).

[260] Ellen and Otway Cuffe, between them had begun a huge number of enterprises namely – they built a theatre, a hospital, a model village with a Woodworkers' factory at Talbot's Inch, a public library, a recreation hall, a woollen mill, a tobacco farm and other co-operative ventures. (*Escape from the Anthill* by Hubert Butler)

decidedly more Celtic temperament and dedicated much of his life to the promotion of the ideals of W. B. Yeats and others, as envisioned by the Gaelic League.

Captain Otway Cuffe (courtesy College Books)

Their early life coincided with a period in which the country houses of the British Isles were in all their glory and, as well-connected young men, they enjoyed every privilege. Shooting weekends with the Duke of Rutland at Belvoir, visits to Paris with Randolph Churchill, dancing to quadrilles and polkas with the Bristols at Ickworth, smoking fat cigars and strolling the sumptuous gardens of Chatsworth with the Devonshires, flirtatious water-parties and archery contests at Longleat were the order of the day.

Ham Cuffe remembered the 1860s as a "very carefree society" in which nobody cared whether one arrived at a garden party "in a donkey-cart or a carriage-and-four". However, following the ill-fated marriage of his brother, the 4th Earl, to Maria Preston in 1871, he does not seem to have visited his childhood home again until he inherited the property in 1898.

He married Lady Margaret Lascelles the second daughter of the Earl of Harewood and they had two daughters but ill-health precluded Margaret Cuffe,

Ham's wife from having any further children and so Ham Cuffe would be the 5th and last Earl. His daughters were Joan and Sybil.

The months immediately following the death of the 4th Earl involved a legal dispute with Ellen, the newly widowed Countess of Desart, who initially sought to remain at Desart and run her late husband's estate herself. Ham Cuffe, now 5th Earl of Desart, was equally insistent on returning to his childhood home. In the end Ellen vacated the premises and went to live with her family in Berkshire. Ham Cuffe, his wife and youngest daughter returned to Desart in August 1899. His elder daughter, Joan had married in that year. Her husband was Sir Harry Lloyd –Verney. They had a son who was later to become Major General Gerald Lloyd-Verney and who commanded the 2nd Irish Battalion of the Irish Guards in Italy during the Second World War for which he was awarded the DSO.

The 5th Earl of Desart undertook a major renovation of his family home in County Kilkenny. For the next two decades Ham Cuffe, his wife and their employees were almost perpetually restoring and renovating both house and land, clearing woods and garden borders, fixing new windows, re-hinging gates, attending to dry rot and cracked walls.

Perhaps things became somewhat more manageable when, in accordance with the 1903 Land Act, the 5th Earl sold the bulk of his estate off to his former tenants, retaining just the immediate demesne for himself and his family circle. Nonetheless, his daughter, Lady Sybil, maintained that Ham Cuffe's time at Desart was probably the happiest period of his life and more than compensated for the stresses he had undergone during his time with the Treasury and Department of Public Prosecutions. He adored his new role as country squire, strutting the fields and woods with loyal Spaniel to heel. It was a world Sybil couldn't help comparing to that of The Irish RM - a time of croquet, tennis, picnics and hunting where the Kilkenny people gathered themselves into "a cheerful little company ... farmers on their home-bred hunters, boys on foot or on a donkey's back, a few gentlefolk, a priest or two ... with all that friendly gaiety, could there really be ill-feeling between the races or the classes represented there".[261]

In 1901, Ham's younger daughter, Lady Sybil Cuffe, married a charismatic young American, William Cutting who died young.[262]

In 1917 Sybil married secondly Geoffrey Scott (1884-1929), a young architect and writer then working as secretary to Bernard Berenson, the American art historian, at his villa in Settignano. Sybil's marriage to Geoffrey Scott did not last, and the couple divorced.

---

[261] A Page from the Past, p. 208.
[262] He died on the banks of the Nile in March 1910 with Sybil and 8-year-old Iris in tow.

She remained in Italy, and married thirdly, an old friend Percy Lubbock. Shortly before the outbreak of the Second World War, the couple relocated to a hotel in Vevey, Switzerland and lived amongst the Swiss whom Iris rather bitterly described as "the scavengers of War, more belligerent than any combatant". Sybil was plagued by ill-health, and gradually lost the will to eat. She died on 26th December 1942.

de Montmorency of Castle Morres

One of the most extraordinary characters of the 'old' family of the Morres/de Montmorency must surely have been Hervey Morres who was born c.1743. He was the son of Hervey the 1st Viscount and his mother was a daughter of Brabazon Ponsonby the 1st Earl of Bessborough. Politics was in his blood from both sides as his father had been an M.P. for many years and the parliamentary exploits of the Ponsonbys are legendary. John Ponsonby, the Speaker, was his uncle. Hervey was educated at Oxford and entered politics shortly afterwards. He was a strong Ponsonby supporter. Some quite amusing stories are told of him. One, in particular, concerned his duel with the Hon. Francis Hely Hutchinson. The cause of the quarrel has been quite forgotten, as so often happens with quarrels, but the duel did place at Donnybrook, in Dublin, a favourite venue for 'Affairs of Honour'. After taking their places the order to fire was given and Hutchinson was fastest with his shot. de Montmorency fell to the ground but after some time was able to rise to his feet. The protagonists bowed to each other and de Montmorency, helped by his second, was brought to his lodgings in Dublin.

Barrington, writing about the affair said that 'never did a person enjoy a wound more sincerely! He kept his chamber a month and was inconceivably gratified by the number of enquiries made daily respecting his health – boasting ever after of the profusion of friends who thus proved their solicitude. "No better", was his answer from first to last.'

Hervey was very well informed, but ostentatious and eccentric. He considered himself the greatest orator and politician in Europe. On one occasion he composed a lengthy speech which he intended to deliver the next day in the House of Lords. He sent the completed speech to the Press so that it would be printed verbatim, with all the suppositious cheering etc. in place. However, much to his dismay the debate did not occur at all and despite his efforts to notify the Press to omit his speech, it was printed the next day in the papers.

He inherited an estate of about 5000 acres but by that time it had become encumbered. He was it seems, on the look out for an heiress, but was, if methodical, slightly clumsy in his approach. It was said that 'when paying his addresses to a lady of large fortune he spent several days in the neighbourhood making enquiries as to the extent and value of her property, measuring trees with his eyes and was at last found in the act of boring the marle'[263] He never did find the right lady.

Hervey committed suicide by shooting himself in the head at his lodgings in York Street, St. James's Square, London, in 1797. It was said that he had become depressed by the state of Ireland at this time just prior to the rebellion of 1798.

Hervey's obituary in the Gentleman's Magazine describes him as 'a good natured, intelligent man, fond of talking, but more from the prevalence of strong animal spirits than vanity'.

Another writer of the period said that 'no man seems to have been more highly esteemed by his tenantry that the late Lord Mountmorres; he renewed his leases on much lower terms to the resident tenants than he might have obtained from others and made liberal allowances for all improvements.'

According to Lodge the family descended from Hervey de Monte Marisco, who accompanied Strongbow into Ireland in 1170. They received grants of land in Wexford, Tipperary and Kerry. Many of these lands were later conveyed to the Ormondes through marriage connections.

The family, however seems to have persisted in Tipperary where the name had become Morres. The Kilkenny family descended from Hervey the second son of John Morres of Knockagh in Tipperary. This John was the grandson of Sir John

---

[263] The Complete Peerage

Morres who was created a baronet in 1632. Harvey who was born in 1625 saw few prospects at home and probably in a spirit of adventure left and joined Cromwell's army.

The Morres family had always been a Catholic family but Hervey, being an astute man, saw the writing was on the wall for Catholics and promptly changed his religion. He backed the Parliamentary party and campaigned with Cromwell as a Captain of Horse during the War in Ireland. It is unclear how he came to be the owner of Castle Morres but in 1667 a Mathias Westmerland had a grant of "Deerelegh" the estate of Thomas Comerford to be called 'Castle Morres' and the estate of David Rothe to be called 'Westmerland' to have and to hold 'to himself and his heirs to the only use and behoof of Harvey Morres.'

In 1684 the Castle, manor, town and lands of Castle Morres and many other lands were granted to Hervey Morres Esq. 'the premises created and erected into the manor of Castle Morres; to keep apart 300 acres more or less for ye demesne lands, to hold courts baron, to appoint seneschals, to hold a law court of record to receive ye fines, issues etc. of the said manor, to erect a prison within the bounds thereof, to receive all wayfes, strays, felons, goods etc., to impark 500 acres, more or less, at pleasure, with free warren and chase and to appoint a clerk of the market. This grant was given to him at the King's Inns in Dublin and signed by the Lord Lieutenant and other commissioners.

He was very active locally and High Sheriff of the county in 1668. He was also a J.P. for the county and was Portrieve of Knocktopher in 1688. The following year he was elected an M.P. and was one of only five Protestants in the Parliament of King James.

Hervey's third wife was Frances Butler, the daughter of Pierce Butler of Barrowmount. By her he had an only surviving son, Francis, who it would appear was born c.1680. It is unclear how Hervey managed to weather the storm of 1689-90 when King James and his Catholic supporters began taking the Protestant lands in many counties, including Kilkenny. He seems to have been a gifted and intelligent man and presumably by this time he had friends in both camps. Hervey lived a very long and productive life and was almost 100 when he died in 1724.

Francis got married in 1706. His wife was Catherine Evans the daughter of Sir William Evans of Kilcreene, Co. Kilkenny. They had three sons, Hervey, William and Redmond.

William was created a baronet, in his own right, in 1758. Sir William married Margaret Haydock of Kilkenny city and of Buolick, Co. Tipperary.[264] By

---

[264] Margaret was the daughter of an apothecary who was an alderman and Mayor of Kilkenny in 1702.

her he had one son, Haydock-Evans and two daughters, Isabella and Mary. His wife died in 1753 and he married again. His second wife was Maria, an heiress, the daughter of William Ryves of Uppercourt, Co. Kilkenny. Sir William and Maria had one son, William-Ryves. Sir William's heir was his eldest son, Haydock-Evans who married the heiress, Miss Gore of Barrowmount. Sir Haydock had no children and when he died he was succeeded by his half brother, William Ryves. Sir William Ryves Morres died in 1829. He had never married and left his estate, Uppercourt, Freshford, Co Kilkenny to his natural son William de Montmorency who was married to Harriet-Ursula, youngest daughter of Eland Mossom, M.P. for Kilkenny City 1777-83. Their son William, married to Sarah Proctor, had to sell Uppercourt under the Encumbered Estate Act in 1849. They continued to live in the Freshford area but subsequently all of their large family emigrated to Canada where a number still reside in the Toronto area.

The third son of Francis was Redmond Morres who was also active in politics. He was M.P. for Dublin city from 1761-68 and from 1773-76. He married an heiress, the daughter of Francis Lodge of Dublin. Their son, Lodge Evans Morres, who was Chief Secretary to Lord Fitzwilliam and was created Viscount Frankfort de Montmorency in 1816 having been created Baron Frankfort of Galmoy in 1800. The 1st Viscount died in 1822 and was succeeded by his sixteen year old son.

The second Viscount Frankfort (1806 – 89), Lodge Raymond de Montmorency, had estates in Cavan, Carlow and Kilkenny[265]. His land agents were Stewart & Kincaid, a Dublin firm that specialised in managing estates for the gentry. Lodge Raymond acquired the Kilkenny lands through his marriage in 1835 to Georgiana Henchy an heiress. His largest Kilkenny property was in Coolcullen, a townland on the Carlow border, south east of Castlecomer.[266] He was an absentee landlord, but he was kept well informed about matters relating to his properties. As an absentee he did not play any significant role in famine relief but the fact that he gave an annuity of £20 per annum to Jane Tyndall, of Leighlinbridge, the widow of one of his tenants indicates that he was a compassionate landlord. In addition Frankfort paid for the passage of the widow's son and his family to Quebec, in 1846 after Mrs. Tyndall's death[267]. Lord and Lady Frankfort were divorced in 1844. Thereafter he appears to have lived in England whilst she continued to reside in Dublin. Lady Frankfort died in 1885.

---

[265] He had about 600 acres in Carlow, over 1000 in Cavan and almost 5000 in Kilkenny.
[266] The grandfather of John Tyndall, the famous scientist (1820-93), lived in Coolcullen.
[267] Desmond Norton (in an unpublished article based on the Stewart & Kincaid correspondence).

Viscount Frankfort

Lord Frankfort died in 1889. His grandson, the Hon. Capt. Raymond Hervey Lodge Joseph of the 17th Lancers won a V.C. at the battle of Omdurman but was killed in action at Molteno during the Boer War. The title became extinct on the death of the 4th Vt in 1917. The Frankforts never had a mansion on any of their landholdings in Ireland and therefore were not resident landlords but lived in Dublin or England.

Hervey the eldest son of Francis mentioned above was educated at Trinity College, Dublin, where he was admitted in 1721 aged 15[268]. He was an M.P. for

---

[268] *The Complete Peerage*

Irishtown from 1734-1756 and was Mayor of Kilkenny from 1752-53. He was created Baron Mountmorres in 1756 and moved into the House of Lords. Seven years later he was created Viscount Mountmorres of Castle Morres. He was married twice and his first wife was Laetitia the daughter of the 1st Earl of Bessborough. This liaison was probably the reason Hervey found it relatively easy to progress in the Honours league. They had one son, Hervey, and two daughters the younger of whom, Sarah, inherited Castle Morres from her brother. Laetitia died at the very young age of 34. Harvey, the year following Laetitia's death, married a widow. She was Mary Baldwin, the daughter of William Wall of Coolnamuck Castle, Co. Waterford. Mary and Hervey had two further sons and Harvey died in 1766.

He was succeeded by his eldest son, Hervey, already mentioned above, who committed suicide in 1797. When Hervey the 2nd Viscount took over the estates they were already in deep financial difficulties. One reason may have been the building of Castle Morres which seems to have taken place in the mid 1700s. The house was reputedly designed by Francis Bindon the celebrated architect of the period who designed such notable houses as Bessborough and Woodstock in Co. Kilkenny and in conjunction with Richard Castle, Russborough in Co. Wicklow.[269]

In his will, Hervey, who tragically took his own life in London, left the estate to his two sisters Laetitia, (who had married the 6th Marquess of Antrim in 1774) and Sarah in 1797. He left the title to his half-brother, Francis Hervey. This branch of the family remained living in Ireland, mostly in Dublin, until the murder of the 5th Lord Montmorecny (Mountmorres) near Clonbur, Co Galway in 1880. His widow then took her family to England. The title of Viscount became extinct in the mid-twentieth century. The last Baronet Sir Arnold de Montmorency died in December 2003 leaving no heir.[270]

Sarah, who inherited half the estate, married the Rev. Joseph Pratt of Cabra Castle, Co. Cavan in 1770 and they had three sons and two daughters, Mary and Letitia, neither of whom had a family.

---

[269] Bindon (1700 – 1765) was born in Co. Clare and started out in life as a portrait painter, having studied under Kneller, in London. His best known portraits are those of Dean Swift and one of O'Carolan the blind harper, which is currently on display in the National Gallery in Dublin. He travelled widely and became interested in architecture because of his family relationship with Sir Edward Lovatt Pierce.

[270] Mrs. Jane de Montmorency Wright.

Castle Morres (courtesy College Books)

The Pratts descended from Joseph Pratt, formerly of Leicestershire, who, with his brother, Benjamin came to Ireland with Cromwell. They got grants of lands in Ireland and Joseph, High Sheriff of Co. Meath in 1698, married Frances, an heiress, the sister of Colonel Thomas Cooch of Cabra Castle, Co. Cavan. His first wife had no children and he married again after her death. His second wife was Elizabeth, a widow, the daughter of Sir Audley Mervyn and they had five sons, the youngest of whom, Mervyn of Cabra Castle, an M.P. for Cavan and High Sheriff was the grandfather of the Rev. Joseph Pratt who married Sarah Morres.

Rev. Joseph's sons were Joseph of Cabra Castle, Rev. Mervyn and Harvey[271]. Joseph remained in Cabra Castle and Sarah's considerable estates[272] were managed by her son Harvey. Harvey joined the Army where he rose to the rank of Major. In 1831 after his mother's death he succeeded to the entire estate and assumed, by Royal Licence, the name and arms of de Montmorency. He married Rose Kearney, the daughter of the Bishop of Ossory. They had four sons and six

---

[271] According to Mrs. de Montmorency Wright the name Harvey was spelt with an 'a' rather than an 'e' from this time onwards.
[272] Sarah inherited an estate of 4,840 acres.

daughters[273]. The fact that five of the daughters married, followed by the Famine disaster, must have put considerable strain on the family finances.

The sons were John, Joseph, Harvey and Raymond. Joseph, an Army officer rose to the rank of Major General and although married had no children. He died in 1889. There is a memorial tablet in St. Nicholas Collegiate Churhc in Galway city erected by his grieving widow. Raymond, also an Officer, remained a bachelor. He died in 1916.

Harvey Mervyn married Louisa, daughter of their neighbour William Morris-Reade of Rossenara, Kilmoganny, county Kilkenny. They lived at Kilcoran, near Callan and later at Tennypark House near Kilkenny. They had two sons Harvey William who died unmarried in 1887 and Mervyn, born 1863, an army officer who served in the Burma campaigns 1885-92 and in South Africa during the Boer War. His wife whom he married in 1894 was Mona Jeffreys, daughter of Capt Richard Jeffreys. They lived at Inch House Kilkenny. Their only daughter Norah, born 1902 married her cousin John Pratt de Montmorency in 1936 (see below). Harvey Mervyn died in 1889 and his widow, Louisa who lived until 1918 retired to live in Delgany, county Wicklow.

John Pratt de Montmorency, of Castle Morres, the eldest son, married the Hon. Henrietta O'Grady, daughter of Viscount Guillamore and they had four sons and two daughters.[274] The sons were Harvey John, Waller, Mervyn Standish and Raymond Oliver. Both Mervyn Standish and Raymond Oliver were married[275] but neither had a family. Mervyn, an Oxford graduate, became a distinguished barrister and Raymond Oliver rose to the rank of Colonel in the Army.

Harvey John the eldest son, a J.P. and High Sheriff and an officer in the Dragoon Guards in his youth, married Lady Grace Fraser Grove and they had one

---

[273] The daughters were Anne, Letitia, Rose, Elizabeth, Sarah and Fanny. Five of the ladies married. Anne's husband was John Congreve Fleming, Letitia married John Armstrong from Co. Laois, William Blacker from Woodbrook, Co. Wexford was Elizabeth's husband, Sarah married Thomas Browne from Co. Tyrone and Fanny's husband was Captain Thomas Bookey from Doninga, Co. Kilkenny. Only Anne and Sarah had families. The Fleming descendants from Barrachore, Goresbridge sold that estate in the 1930s. The Armstrongs moved to Galway and their eldest son, William who married Kathleen Lushington, spent the early years of his married life, ranching in Wyoming with Moreton Frewen and others. After several exciting years during which their daughter Edna was born, they returned to Connemara and their descendants still live there today. Edna died in Enland in 1983 aged 101.

[274] They were Katherine and Rose Emily. Rose Emily married Captain Frederic Bertie, the son of the Rev. Hon. Frederic Bertie whose brother was an Earl. They had a family.

[275] Raymond's wife was an heiress. She was Ada, the daughter of Captain Hon. John Bury.

daughter Henrietta[276]. Harvey John died in 1873 at the young age of 33. He died from complications following an accident some years earlier while pig-sticking during Army service in India. He left a young widow who many years later, in 1896 married a distinguished soldier General Frank Hamilton, and a small daughter Henrietta. Henrietta, born in 1868 married George Mauger of St Claire, Jersey. He died 1917. They had one daughter Joan who married Captain Raufe Grosvenor Taunton. Henrietta's descendants still live in Jersey.

Venerable Waller de Montmorency

Venerable Waller, a Cambridge graduate, succeeded to Castle Morres and the estate in 1873. He was a J.P. and was Archdeacon of Ossory. He married Mary, the daughter of Thomas O'Brien, the Bishop of Ossory, Ferns and Leighlin. They

---

[276] Henrietta married Captain George Mauger from Jersey and after her death in 1958 she was succeeded by her daughter.

had two sons John Pratt and Geoffrey Fitz Hervey. Whilst continuing to carry out church duties (Waller became archdeacon of Ossory in 1911) he lived and farmed extensively at Castle Morres, later to be assisted by his eldest son John Pratt, born in 1873. On his death in October 1924 the Castle Morres estate was acquired by the Land Commission. His widow Mary only survived by a few months dying in July 1925.

Sir Geoffrey FitzHervey de Montmorency was a gifted Cambridge graduate who became a very distinguished Civil Servant. He was Chief Secretary to the Prince of Wales during his Indian Tour in 1921-22. He remained in India and was Secretary to the Viceroy from 1922- 26, member of the Punjab Executive Council from 1926-28 and was Governor of the Punjab from 1928-33 when he retired early due to ill-health. He went to live in Cambridge, becoming an Hon. Fellow of His old college Pembroke. He continued to write and lecture on Indian affairs. He died unmarried in 1955.

Shooting Party at Burnchurch

The elder son John Pratt entered the Royal Navy training ship H.M.S. Britannia in 1886 going to sea as a midshipman on H.M.S. Bellerophon in 1888 aged 15 years. He retired in 1910 and returned to assist his father running Castle Morres with his wife Margaret, daughter of Col Samuel Pym R.A., who he had married in 1908. At the start of W.W.I, he rejoined the Navy finally retiring in 1919. He had received C.M.G. in 1916 and the *Legion d'Honneur* in 1917. He and his wife moved to live in England after the sale of Castle Morres in 1924. She died in 1932.[277]

Captain de Montmorency married his 2nd cousin Norah de Montmorency (see above) in 1934. They had two daughters, Jane Avril and Sarah Anne. The family returned to live in County Kilkenny, purchasing Burnchurch House, Bennettsbridge, in 1949. The Captain died in November 1960. His widow continued to live in Burnchurch House until 1981 when she moved to a smaller house nearby. She was a keen supporter of the Kilkenny Hunt which she followed by car until well into her eighties. She was a founder member of Kilkenny Country Markets, and that and the I.C.A. were her two great interest. Norah died in November 1987.

Sarah Anne (Sally) born in 1943 married Brian FitzMaurice of Laurel Lodge, Carlow in 1963. They lived in Carlow and had two sons John and Christopher. John, born in 1965, is a minister in the Church of England and he has a son and a daughter. Christopher, born in 1969 is married and lives and works in Waterford. He also has a son and daughter. Sally died in 1997 and her husband in 2000.[278]

The older daughter Jane Avril, who returned to live at Burnchurch House in 1981 was born in 1936. She married Beverley Wright in 1960 (divorced in 1979). They have a son Jasper John de Montmorency who was born in 1967 and two daughters, Caroline Lucy and Petronella Kate. Jasper John is married and has two daughters, Charlotte and Rose, and lives in County Down. Caroline Lucy who was born in 1964 is married to Adrian Sutherland. They live and work in County Kilkenny and have a daughter Kate and two sons Luke and Kirk. The youngest of Jane Avril's daughters, Petronella Kate (known always as Nell), is married to Richard Duffin. They also still live and work in County Kilkenny.

---

[277] Mrs. Jane de Montmorency Wright
[278] Ibid.

Flood of Farmley

Henry Flood the great Irish politician and statesman was the most high profile man of his family. The circumstances surrounding his birth were somewhat out of the ordinary and the circumstances arising from his death were quite extraordinary.

His father, Warden Flood who later became a very eminent lawyer, met his future wife while studying in the Temple, in London. She was Isabelle Whiteside. Like many a young couple before them they fell in love and Isabelle became pregnant. Warden[279], being the gentleman he was, proposed marriage and the date

---

[279] Warden was approached by James Agar of Gowran with a view to making a match between his daughter Ellis Agar and the young Flood. A substantial dowry was mentioned but Warden, being in love with his London mistress turned down the offer. Twenty five years later the jilted Ellis egged on her brother James to quarrel with Henry Flood, Warden's son. A duel ensued.

was set. Young Henry to be, not being privy to their plans arrived early and so had to bear the stigma of illegitimacy that bedevilled many a good man before and after him.

Henry was, of course, treated just like a lord and was provided with an excellent education that enabled him to rise to the highest ranks in the political world of his time and in the process amassed a considerable fortune in money and property. When his time came to leave this world he made a most controversial will. He left some money to provide for his wife, made a few other bequests and left the bulk of his estate to Trinity College for the advancement of the study of the Irish language. Naturally there was consternation among the Floods in waiting and legal proceedings were instigated. These were protracted and probably painful to the pockets of all. In the end the will was overturned on the grounds of Henry's early arrival into the world which made him illegitimate.

According to Burke's Landed Gentry of 1879 Francis Flood 'was a Major of a body of horse in the army of Oliver Cromwell.' Warden Flood the family biographer does not agree however and states that Major Francis Flood of the Royal Cavalry Regiment came to Kilkenny and married Anne Warden the heiress of Burnchurch in 1692. If Major Francis was indeed a Major in Cromwell's army he must have been quite elderly when he married Anne Warden. Assuming that he was in Cromwell's army then he must have been born c. 1730 or earlier. That would mean that he was at least sixty two when he married. We are told that Anne was only about sixteen at the time of her wedding. Francis was a member of Parliament for Callan in 1713 and continued to sit until the dissolution of that parliament. This would mean that he was in his late seventies or early eighties when that event occurred. It is more likely that Francis was a Major in the army of William of Orange.

Regardless of the exact origin of the Major or the speculation about his age, or in what Army he served, we are sure that by marrying young Anne Warden, who successfully claimed her inheritance, he became the owner of a very large estate in a beautiful area of Co. Kilkenny. Apart from the natural scenery of the district, an even more delightful attraction must have been the fine rental roll that accrued each year from the lettings to the numerous tenants.

The 4,629 acre estate was forfeited by a family of Fitzgeralds[280] after the Cromwellian Wars and granted to William Warden, a Colonel in the

---

[280] According to Carrigan they were a branch of the original Fitzgerald dynasty that settled in Ireland after the Norman invasion. They in turn were settled on the lands of the Mac Giolla Padraigs or Fitzpatricks. The Fitzgeralds were a very highly regarded family many of whom were Sheriffs of Co. Kilkenny. The last of them in Burnchurch was Richard Fitzgerald

Parliamentarian Army. The Colonel was more avaricious than most and 'grabbed' more land. This is what was said of him in Prendergast's *The Cromwellian Settlement of Ireland* 'Colonel Warden, having obtained an order from the Council Board to be satisfied his arrears in the barony of Gowran, in the county of Kilkenny, the lands of Jackstown, Kilbeg and Kilmarry were assigned to him by the Commissioners for setting out lands; but by leaving out all the coarse lands in his lot he encroached into Columkill, and made up his pretended want out the best part of Columkill, in the lot of Quartermaster Hugh Farr.'[281]

The Colonel had a son John, who married a daughter[282] of Sir John Otway of Cumberland and it was their daughter, Anne, who married Major Flood.

It is unclear what actually happened to the Warden lands after John Warden died. It is known that the Warden lands were declared forfeit in 1689 but upon the victory of the Williamites the lands were restored. Burnchurch was apparently claimed by his widow when she married Agmondisham Cuffe and the Cuffes took up residence there for a period. However at some stage young Anne, John's daughter succeeded in having the lands restored to her and her husband Major Francis Flood. There must have been some acrimony as Agmondisham Cuffe petitioned to have Francis removed from Parliament in 1702 and Francis was in fact expelled. The charges brought by Agmondisham Cuffe were vexatious to say the least. The following is a sample. The Major had; billeted his troops on the Cuffe tenants; imprisoned English inhabitants of the area in the stocks in the dungeon of Burnchurch castle because they refused to 'give him a day's attendance to entitle him to his pay'; he dragged a sick man from his bed to the prison for the same reason but released him after two days when the man then died.[283]

Francis was undeterred by this hostility and when the next election came about he was elected for Callan and continued to sit until the dissolution of that Parliament.

Anne performed her duty too in an exemplary fashion and produced eight sons and one daughter, predictably called Anne, who married Venerable Henry Candler, Archdeacon of the diocese of Ossory.[284] The eight sons were Warden of

---

who joined the Confederates and so forfeited his lands. His children sought to claim back the lands later, as innocents, but were unsuccessful.

[281] *The Cromwellian Settlement of Ireland* by Prendergast pg. 111

[282] She was Anne Otway and when John Warden died she married Agmondisham Cuffe (see that family) whose son became the first Lord Desart. In this way the name Otway was introduced into the Cuffe family.

[283] Mary Kenealy in Old Kilkenny Review 1983 pg. 518

[284] He was one of the Candlers of Callan whose most famous son was Asa Candler the man who made Coca Cola famous (and successful) in the early 1900s.

Burnchurch, John of Flood Hall, Francis of Paulstown,[285] Charles of Ballymack, Rev. Henry, Rev. George (Rector of Rathdowney) and Richard and William who both died young.

Warden was the father of the great Henry Flood already mentioned in the introduction. Warden was a very able man and the fact that he was able to become the Lord Chief Justice of Ireland[286] is proof not alone of his keen legal mind but also of his innate ability to network successfully with his peers.

Warden had another son, Warden, who died young in 1767 and a daughter Isabella, who also appears to have died unmarried. This left Henry Flood as his heir.

Henry's illustrious political career has been widely acclaimed in various publications but an attempt will be made to summarize his achievements here. Unlike his father, Henry did not attend the Temple but instead he was sent to Trinity College[287] and later Oxford before completing his legal studies at the Inns of Court in London. It was in the latter establishment that he formed a very valuable friendship with the man who was to become Lord Charlemont, James Caulfield.[288]

In his early years, it was said, Henry was handsome, witty, good-tempered, and a brilliant conversationalist. His judgment was sound, and he had a native gift of eloquence which had been cultivated and developed by the study of classical oratory and the practice of elocution.

He got married in 1761 to a lady whose family launched his political career, Frances Beresford, the sister of the 1st Marquess of Waterford.[289] They went to live in Farmley, a house on the Burnchurch estate that was built by Henry's father. Unfortunately his political career was beset by much turmoil and he made many bitter enemies.[290] According to Hubert Butler, Henry regarded his substantial estate

---

[285] See the last paragraph of this article for the details of the Floods of Paulstown.

[286] He was the first Anglo Irishman to hold this position. Prior to this the post was always held by Englishmen.

[287] According to one commentator 'his career in college was marked more by dissipation than literary faculty; but he soon grew weary of the orgies then so freely indulged in by the fast youth of the Irish metropolis, and he resolved, by severe toil, to make amends for hours of folly.'

[288] Lord Charlemont was the man accredited with founding the Volunteer movement. He built Charlemont House in Parnell Square and the 'Casino' in his villa in Marino.

[289] The Beresfords were a hugely important Waterford based political family in the 18th and 19th centuries. As well as benefiting politically and socially Henry received a considerable dowry with his bride.

[290] He was closely associated with what came to be known as 'the Patriot Party' until his perceived defection in 1775 when he accepted the government post of Vice Treasurer. He later became closely associated with the Volunteer movement and was in fact a Colonel in the Volunteers. He resigned his post in the government but was superceded by Grattan in

Flood of Farmley

of Farmley as his 'Tusculum', where he relaxed from toil. He had amateur theatricals performed in the house and lent his support to the revival of interest in the Celtic past.[291]

In the case of the borough of Callan, Flood's claim to this borough brought him into direct conflict with the Agars (later Viscounts Clifden).[292] He was forced into an uncompromising position[293] that resulted in his having to fight a duel against James Agar of Ringwood.[294] The duel proved fatal for Agar.[295] It took place in Dumore, in Co. Kilkenny and there James Agar received a fatal wound. Flood was devastated by the result. He was arrested, freed on bail and later tried for murder, the following year in 1770, but was acquitted on the grounds that his actions during the duel were fair and honourable.[296] The family seems to have had a penchant for aggressive behaviour. Hubert Butler in his fine book *Independent Spirit* said that

---

the Patriot Party. In his thinking he might best be described as the forerunner of the United Irishmen, insofar as his main aim was an independent Ireland.

[291] *Escape from the Anthill* by Hubert Butler

[292] The town of Callan was originally part of the Ormonde estate but after the attainder of the Duke in 1714 and the absence of the Ormondes from the area the Floods acquired the borough interest. When the Agars bought out the interests of the house of Ormonde, in Callan, they claimed the right to the parliamentary representation, but this was fiercely disputed by the Floods.

[293] A woman named Bridget Knapp whose husband, a tenant of the Floods, was a burgess of Callan and had a vote, offered the vote to Agar on condition her husband would get money and a farm on the Agar property. She invited Agar to accompany her to her husband's house to seal the bargain. They had met Agar at a public house in Kilkenny. The landlord of the house a man called Keogh, advised Agar that it might not be safe for him to go 'into enemy territory' but said he himself would go on his behalf. Keogh set out with Mrs. Knapp. Before they departed Agar gave Keogh his pistols in case they encountered any hostile forces. This proved to be the case and at Burnchurch, when Mrs. Knapp had left the carriage it was attacked by a crowd of Flood supporters who had got wind of the word of what was afoot. The carriage was smashed and the driver assaulted. Keogh fired the pistols in the air, to no avail. They were snatched from his grasp and he ran for safety.

[294] Agar demanded the return of his pistols, but Flood denied he knew anything about the pistols. Agar was very persistent and finally sent a message to Flood to hand over the pistols or fight him. Flood replied in writing that he did not know where the pistols were and if they came into his possession he would immediately hand them over. Agar was still not satisfied and demanded satisfaction.

[295] They met in the 'Triangle Field' at Dumore and Agar fired first. He missed his target. He stooped to pick up his second pistol and as he faced Flood the latter fired and Agar was mortally wounded. Richard Rothe was Agar's second and Gervase Parker Bushe of Kilfane was Flood's second.

[296] *An Affair of Honour* by Michael Barry

'the Cuffes only rivals were the Floods of Farmley. With them they had a feud which led to duels and lawsuits and even murders about the political representation of Callan.'[297]

Henry Grattan had this to say about Henry Flood after his death in 1791 - "Mr. Flood, my rival as he is called, and I should be unworthy of the character of his rival, if, in his grave, I did not do him justice. He had his faults, but he had great powers, great public effect. He persuaded the old, he inspired the young; the castle vanished before him. On a small subject he was miserable; put into his hand a distaff, and, like Hercules, he made sad work of it; but give him a thunderbolt, and he had the arm of a Jupiter. He misjudged when he transferred himself to the English Parliament. He forgot that he was a tree of the forest, too old and too great to be transplanted at 50; and his seat in the British Parliament is a caution to the friends of union to stay at home[298] and make the country of their birth the seat of their action."

This is what Lecky the historian had to say about him – 'Though he was regarded as the greatest intellect that ever adorned the Irish parliament, yet his career presents one long series of disappointments and reverses. The party he had formed discarded him as its leader, the reputation he so dearly prized was clouded and assailed; the principles he had sown germinated and fructified indeed, but others reaped their fruit.'

Henry had no children and the unusual complexities surrounding his will have already been the subject of the opening paragraphs. His beneficiary was John Flood of Flood Hall, his cousin, who received the remainder of the estate including Farmley House. John Flood's eldest son, also called John, led a relatively sedentary life.

His second son was Frederick, who as well as being a lawyer was an M.P. for Wexford and was knighted in 1780. He was born in 1741 and was educated at Trinity College, Dublin, where he pursued legal studies. He was called to the Irish Bar in 1763, and soon attained considerable success both in legal practice and in the

---

[297] Henry Flood almost had a duel with Grattan also. After a particularly acrimonius debate in the House both men resolved to settle their differences by fighting a duel. Many of their peers remonstrated with them and the authorities were alerted. Despite the efforts being made to reconcile the parties they went ahead with preparations for the encounter. The government officials were, however, very vigilant and managed to apprehend the two would-be-combatants on their way to the venue. Both were brought before the magistrates and fined £2,000 each and bound to the peace. This sobering action by the government settled the dispute.

[298] This was a reference to Henry Flood's action of buying a seat in the English Parliament in 1790.

social circles of Dublin, in which he was immensely popular because of his wit and oddity. He succeeded to large estates both from his father and his mother, and, in 1776 he was elected to the Irish House of Commons as member for Co. Wexford. In 1778 be was called to the bar and in 1780 he was knighted as a baronet 'of Newton Ormonde, Co. Kilkenny, and Banna Lodge, Co. Wexford'. He took a prominent part in the Volunteer movement, and was Colonel of the Wexford Regiment.

Writing of Sir Frederick, Jonah Barrington said that he was a man "whose exhibitions in the Imperial Parliament have made him tolerably well known in England, and who had a love of money and ostentation which he never lost during his lifetime." Barrington went on to say "he was a pretty, dapper man, and very good-tempered; and he had a droll habit. Whenever a person behind him whispered anything to him while he was speaking in public, he invariably repeated the suggestion in its original form. Once he was making a speech in the Irish Parliament praising the merits of the Wexford magistrates while making a case to extend more power to them, to keep down the disaffected. He was in process of concluding his speech and was saying 'the magistracy should receive some mark of the Lord Lieutenant's favour' when John Egan, sitting behind him whispered jokingly 'and be whipped at the cart's tail'. 'And be whipped at the cart's tail' repeated Sir Frederick, unconsciously, giving rise to uproars of uncontrollable laughter."[299]

Sir Frederick's 2nd wife was Frances Cavendish[300] and they had an only child, a daughter named Frances. She married a man called Solly and her children adopted the name Flood in addition to Solly and became the Solly Floods of Ballynaslaney, Co. Wexford.

John Flood II, Frederick's elder brother, was married to a Miss Aldworth and they had two sons John III and Robert and a daughter Elizabeth who does not appear to have married. Farmley was given to Robert and he died unmarried in 1836. Farmley then reverted to John III.

John III was a bit of a rake and had an affair with a blacksmith's daughter named Lloyd. The affair lasted a number of years and resulted in John III fathering two illegitimate children William and Anne. These children were reared in the Flood family home and were regarded as adopted children. John III later married Sarah Saurin the daughter of Sir William Saurin who was Attorney General of Ireland. When John III died his estates passed to his illegitimate son William as he had no family with Sarah Saurin.

---

[299] *Personal Sketches* - Barrington
[300] Frances Cavendish was the daughter of Sir Henry Cavendish from England. Frederick's first wife was Lady Juliana Annesley the daughter of the 6th Earl of Anglesey.

Flood of Farmley

William, after his father's death, went to live in Farmley, as Sarah his stepmother was still in Flood Hall. William was lucky and managed to find himself an heiress, Frances Handford, who inherited valuable estates in England. William and his wife spent half their time in England and the remainder in Ireland at their Kilkenny estates. They had three sons and five daughters. One of these daughters, a Mrs. Mary Harvey, eventually inherited what remained of the estate (after the Land Commission had sold off most of the lands) and came to live in Flood Hall in 1925, with her husband who was quite elderly at the time. She died in 1937 and the rest of the estate was sold off and Flood Hall was later demolished.

Farmley is still in existence and is lovingly cared for by the present owners, the Woodcock family, and it is gratifying to know that Henry Flood's residence continues to be the fine country house it was in his day.

The Flood arms consist of a green shield with a chevron between three wolves heads. The crest is a Wolf's head and the motto is Vis Unita Fortier.

Langrishe of Knocktopher

Possibly the most colourful Langrishe of all was Hercules Langrishe the 5th Baronet. He was known as Herky to his friends. He was born in 1859 and during his lifetime the death knell of the large estates was sounded.

A dashing, handsome young man, Herky was enthusiastic about all his pursuits and on the one day in 1879 he won a tennis tournament and a prestigious bicycle race.[301] His sister Mary was Irish Lawn Tennis Ladies Champion on three occasions in the 1880s. Herky's other pursuits included horse riding at which he was quite adept, winning two races on the one day in the Kilkenny Hunt point to point meeting in the early 1880s and yachting. He also had a passion for motor cars and was one of the first men in Ireland to own one. But like many of his ilk his first love was horses. He was later to become the Master of the Kilkenny Hunt.

When he married his beautiful bride, Helen Hume Dick, her father very generously provided a dowry of £100,000 which helped Herky to live in the style

---

[301] *Twilight of the Ascendancy* – Mark Bence Jones

to which he had become accustomed. This happy event occurred in 1887 and while the estate was nominally still intact it was heavily mortgaged. Bence Jones states that it was mortgaged seven times over![302]

Herky was nothing if not a sociable person and he knew most of his peers in Ireland and quite a number in England also from King Edward VII down.[303] When the Kilkenny Hunt balls were held Herky and his wife were the host and hostess. Invariably the Marquess and Countess of Ormonde were the guests of honour. Those balls were attended by the gentry from Kilkenny and much further afield. Such functions went on all night and supper was not served until midnight.

Herky was a noted wit and was given to mimicry, a talent that backfired on him in 1904. King Edward VII and Queen Alexandra visited Kilkenny in that year and stayed in the Castle where they were entertained by the Marquess and Duchess of Ormonde. A banquet was organised in their honour to which all the local aristocrats and gentry were invited. As was customary the King entered the hall with the Countess on his arm, followed by the Marquess escorting the Queen, in a small procession. Hot on their heels came Herky, imitating the walk of the King much to the amusement of the onlookers gathered in the great hall.

The King and Queen were scheduled to visit the Langrishe home in Knocktopher the following day and Herky and his wife had spent a considerable sum refurbishing for the occasion and in preparing for the regal supper and entertainments. They stood proudly outside on the steps of Knocktopher, with their family, waiting. They waited and waited. The royal guests never arrived.

The Langrishe connection with Kilkenny began with John Langrishe, the son of Hercules Langrishe. Hercules was living, in Drogheda in the 1660s, according to the Ormonde papers. Burke's Peerage and Baronetage states that he was a Captain in the 44th troop, in the Earl of Bedford's regiment. If he stayed in the Earl's regiment then he would have been a royalist in the Civil War, since the Earl, while at first siding with the Parliament, changed his allegiance in their war with Charles I.

There is no record of any Langrishe in Prendergast's *Cromwellian Settlement* so we can assume that the Hercules living in Drogheda in 1660 may well have been a supporter of Charles II. John, a son of Hercules, was the first of the family to have any connection with Kilkenny.

It was thanks to a couple of fortuitous marriages that John (1660 – 1735) came into the possession of Knocktopher. His first wife was Sarah Sandford who passed away quite soon after their marriage in 1684. His second wife was the Hon.

---

[302] Ibid pg.93
[303] Ibid

Alice Blaney, the daughter of Harry the 2nd Lord Blaney and widow of Thomas Sandford. Thomas was the owner of Knocktopher. However, when Thomas died in 1679 he left his property to his wife Alice for her lifetime and thereafter to their son Blaney Sandford.[304] Blaney was a minor when his mother married John Langrishe and Knocktopher was leased to John 'for three lives renewable forever'.[305] It is probable that the family lived in the Abbey, south of Thomastown and John must have been very pleased with the magnificent estate set in lush countryside with tenants already *in situ*.

The Hon. Alice did not live very long and after her death he married for a third time in 1695. His third wife was Mary Grace of Courtstown and they had one son Robert Langrishe who succeeded his father in Knocktopher when that man died in 1735.

Knocktopher Abbey

---

[304] Blaney Sandford, an M.P. for Knocktopher 1695-99, was the ancestor of Lord Mountsandford whose name is remembered in many parts of Dublin – e.g. Sandford and Sandford Park.
[305] Monica Brennan in *Kilkenny History & Society* – Ed. Wm. Nolan pg. 185

John of course must hold the record as the most married man in the 18th century as he was married no less than five times. His fourth wife was Frances Plowden, a lady who inherited a considerable legacy from her uncle, Sir Algernon May.[306] John's fifth wife was Anne Newport of Waterford. Despite his many marriages he had only one child, his son Robert.

Robert Langrishe (1706 – 1770) was High Sheriff of Co. Kilkenny in 1640. He was also a Gentleman Usher of the Black Rod in the House of Lords, in Ireland. This interesting post was first introduced into the House of Lords in England in 1522. The Gentleman Usher had a number of duties to perform including keeping order in the house, meeting the King and other members of the royal party and showing them to their seats and summoning the members of the House of Commons to open their door by knocking three times on their door with his rod. The rod itself was an ebony cane with a gold lion's head on top.

Robert didn't even attempt to tackle his father's record and was content to settle for two wives. His first wife was Anne Whitby and they had two sons and three daughters. The eldest son died young and the second son, Hercules, became the heir. He was by far the most famous man of his family – a Hercules by name and by nature.

One of the three daughters died young and the other two married into very respectable landed gentry families from Kilkenny and Tipperary. Mary's husband was William Nicholson of Wilmar, Co. Tipperary with whom she had a family. Olympia kept up the family tradition of multiple marriages and had two husbands. Her first marriage was to George Birch of Birchfield, Co. Kilkenny and her second husband was John Greene of Greeneville, also in the county.

Robert's second wife was his sister-in-law, Elizabeth, who was widowed. Her husband was William Christian of Oldgrange in Co. Waterford. They had no children and Robert died in 1770 when he was succeeded in Knocktopher by his only surviving son Hercules.

Hercules (1731-1811) was a political colossus in his time. Like his grandfather he was a record setter. He was an M.P. for Knocktopher for almost forty continuous years from 1761 until the Act of Union in 1800. No other Kilkenny politician of his era accomplished this feat with the possible exception of Nicholas Alyward who represented Thomastown from 1717 until 1756. He was able to

---

[306] Sir Algernon May was a Cromwellian grantee. He was given Rockett's Castle on the Suir, near Portlaw and the area subsequently became known as Mayfield. The May family died out c. 1790.

accomplish this by buying up all the property in the town of Knocktopher and leasing it to Catholics.[307]

He graduated from Trinity College, Dublin, in 1753 and was made a freeman of Kilkenny on 3 November 1750[308]. Whether or not he was the actual author of the political satire 'Baraterania' is debatable but his name has generally been associated with that publication.[309] He held posts as Commissioner of Revenue 1774–1801 and of Excise 1780–1801. These were very lucrative posts and combined with his rent roll from his Kilkenny estate[310] they made him a reasonably wealthy man. Like many public men of his time he was honoured by being created a Baronet in 1777 and a privy councillor in 1786. Despite being quite well off he had to mortgage his Knocktopher property on three different occasions for sums in excess of £1000.

The fact that he had three daughters who got married might account for his need of extra money, since dowries had to be found for those ladies. Under the circumstances it was small wonder that he succumbed on occasion to visiting the hazy depths of alcoholic release as this anecdote illustrates. One evening a friend, amazed that Sir Hercules had allegedly managed to consume three bottles of port at a single sitting, asked the noted drinker whether he had had any assistance. "None," Langrishe replied, "save that of a bottle of Madeira."

Barrington told another tale about Sir Hercules and a Mr. Dundas 'Mr. Dundas, himself a keen sarcastic man, who loved his bottle nearly as well as Sir Hercules, invited the baronet to a grand dinner in London, where the wine circulated freely and wit kept pace with it. Mr. Dundas wishing to procure a laugh at Sir Hercules said "Why Sir Hercules, is it true that we Scotch formerly transported all our criminals and felons to Ireland?"

"I dare say", replied Sir Hercules, "but did you ever hear, Mr. Dundas, of any of your countrymen returning to Scotland from their transportation?"

---

[307] The significance of this seems to be that all Protestant residents of Knocktopher had a vote. If there was a strong Protestant community in the town Langrishe had no guarantee that he would be elected on a continuous basis. In point of fact he had only one Protestant voter in the town and he was a paid employee who had the duty to return the votes for the borough.

[308] Thomas Gregory Fewer in an article due for publication in *The Oxford Dictionary of National Biography*

[309] This book was a satire on Lord Townshend's period of government in Ireland (1767-1772).

[310] The estate was about 1300 acres in extent and the rent from the tenants amounted to a little over £500.

Langrishe of Knocktopher

Sir Hercules is best remembered for his pro Catholic relief stance and for the fact that he was a friend of Edmund Burke. Burke wrote him a very long and complex letter which is quite famous in its own right, dealing with the issues of Catholic Relief. As a result of that particular communication Sir Hercules introduced the Catholic Relief Bill of 1792, a landmark in the fight for justice for the Catholics. He said 'he wished that Catholic and Protestant should become one people, which they would do in time, unless intemperance retarded their progress, and revised the prejudices which so long kept them asunder'

The Baronet Langrishe seconded the Catholic Relief Bill of 1793 because he felt (as did the British government) that the Catholics of Ireland would be useful allies against the spread of 'foreign principles more dangerous than armies, more cruel than the sword' This bill, passed as the Catholic Enfranchisement Act, gave the parliamentary vote to all Catholics holding property of at least forty shillings in value.[311]

When the Act of Union was proposed in 1800 he voted with the government for the abolition of the Irish Parliament. His decision, however, was not just a matter of accepting a bribe. He had in fact been an advocate of the Union for ten years previous to that. He was paid handsomely for his loyalty and received in excess of £13,000.

Sir Hercules's wife was Sarah Myhill[312] from Killarney, Co. Kilkenny, an heiress. They had three sons and three daughters, Mary, Elizabeth and Hanna.[313] Their sons were Robert, John and James.

John Langrishe who was born in 1760 followed a brief career in the army where he attained the rank of lieutenant. Unfortunately his career was cut short when he was challenged (or challenged his opponent) to a duel. Young men of that period were quite hot-headed and duelling was quite common and socially acceptable. The first two questions asked of a young man, seeking a wife, so as to ascertain his respectability were 'What family is he of?' and 'Did he ever blaze?' Young John, sadly, came off second best in the duel and lost his life. He was only twenty years old.

James, the third son, entered the Church and became in time, the Very Rev. James Langrishe, dean of Achonry and Archdeacon of Glendalough. He married

---

[311] Fewer

[312] Her sister Jane was married to Charles Tottenham Loftus the 1st Marquess Ely. (For details of that family see *The Wexford Gentry II* by Art Kavanagh & Rory Murphy.

[313] Mary married James Wilson of Parsonstown, Co. Meath. Elizabeth married the Rev. C. Robinson from Granard (their sons were Admiral Hercules Robinson and Sir Bryan Robinson, a Supreme Court Judge in Newfoundland). Hannah's husband was Thomas St. George of Woodsgift, Co. Kilkenny.

Mary Mitchel and they had four sons and six daughters.[314] His sons, who followed careers in the Army and the Church, though married, had no children and so the line of James died out.

Robert (born in 1756) the eldest son of Sir Hercules also became an M.P. for Knocktopher (1783-1796) and both father and son sat in the houses of Parliament simultaneously. Robert, a Barrister, who had graduated from King's Inns, also became a revenue commissioner in 1796. Robert was married in 1782 to Anne Boyle, an heiress, who was the granddaughter of the Archbishop of Armagh. When Sir Hercules died in 1811, Robert became the 2nd baronet as Sir Robert Langrishe. Robert was very much associated with the theatrical productions that were a feature of the early 19th century in Kilkenny.[315]

The Hunt at Knocktopher

Sir Robert and Anne had two sons and six daughters. Four of these ladies married and the provision of dowries must have been a serious drain on the Langrishe finances. These marriages meant that the Langrishes became in-laws of the Hills, Monck Masons, St. Georges and the Henrys.[316] Robert the second son never married and lived until 1858. The eldest son was Hercules Richard and he

---

[314] Only three of the daughters married and of those only Margaret the eldest had any family. She was married to Lt. Gen. Wm. Loftus of Kilbride and Ballcummin and Oldtown Co. Dublin, a descendant of Adam Loftus, ancestor of the Earls of Ely.

[315] For more detail on the Kilkenny theatricals see the chapter in this book about the Powers of Kilfane.

[316] They were already connected with the St. Georges (see note 13 above).

entered the Church, becoming the prebendary and rector of Lockeen[317]. There was some unrest in the Lockeen/Shinrone area of Offaly during the period of the Tithe agitation and sad case of the Tithe Martyr from Shinrone occurred only two years after the departure of Rev. Sir Hercules from Lockeen.[318]

When his father died in 1835 he became Rev. Sir Hercules Langrishe the 3rd Baronet. His wife was Maria Cottingham from Co. Cavan and they had five sons and four daughters. Anne Maria married Peter Connellan of Coolmore, Thomastown and Rose married William Williams of Surrey. Both ladies had families.

Rev. Sir Hercules Langrishe

---

[317] Lockeen in Co. Offaly.
[318] Thomas Tyquin, a prominent businessman from the area refused to pay the Tithe to the agent of Rev. William Savage in 1837. He was arrested and confined in Kilmainham Gaol. A fine strapping young man in his twenties he died in the Gaol within a couple of days of his incarceration. His death led to a massive outburst of public anger that manifested itself in the vast numbers that attended his funeral.

The sons of Rev. Sir Hercules were John, Robert, James, Hercules and Richard. Three of the sons died young and only James and Richard survived to adulthood and both married.

Richard Langrishe an uncle of Herky who died in 1922 was a distinguished scholar and author. He was born in 1834. His father was Rev. Sir Hercules the 3rd Baronet. Sent to school in Fleetwood in England he was brought home again as family finances suffered at the time of the famine. The estate suffered a severe setback because of the inability of the tenants to pay rent. He was sent to Kilkenny College as a boarder in 1847. The family finances took a further turn for the worse when Knocktopher was accidentally destroyed by fire in 1850. Richard was to go to Trinity but his seventy year old father wished to keep him at home ostensibly to run the estate, but more likely because he was cash strapped following the necessary rebuilding of the house after the fire. Richard's older brother, James, ten years his senior, had bought a commission in the Army in the Royal Irish Regiment and rose to the rank of Lieutenant General before his retirement in 1862 (when his father died).

Richard however decided not to become estate manager and turned to engineering. It took him almost ten years to become an accredited engineer, having got his training and practical experience in counties Galway and Down. He got married in 1863 and he began mining in France as a partner in a mining company but the mine proved to be unfruitful and had to close. He and his wife Frances (nee Chaine) spent some time in Italy and later moved back to England. Frances developed tuberculosis and died in 1867.

Richard went back to Ireland in due course became the Clerk of the Peace for Co. Kilkenny, a post with a salary and status. He married his second wife Sarah Moore[319] in 1871. His civic post carried with it the permission to appoint a Deputy who could perform all the duties of the office and this left Richard in the position that he had ample time to pursue his leanings towards architecture. He was appointed diocesan architect for Ossory. He developed an interest in history and wrote a handbook about St. Canice's Cathedral. He carried out many renovations and repairs to churches in the both Ossory and Ferns and his reputation as an architect grew. He was accepted into the R.I.A.I. in 1868.

Sarah died after childbirth in 1873. Following reorganisation in the Church of Ireland Richard was given a post as diocesan architect in the mid west and the family moved to Athlone. Richard then married his third wife, Amitia Brown, in 1882. She was twenty years younger than he. She had five children while she lived in Athlone and according to family lore she didn't really enjoy the midland town.

---

[319] Daughter of the Dean of Clogher

Langrishe of Knocktopher

In 1892 after the death of his deputy in Kilkenny Richard had to return and it was during the next ten years of his life that his finest work was carried out on St. Canice's.

The work he did then is still in place now, including the marble sanctuary floor, the choir stalls and the oak screens in the entrance arches. His dedication was duly recognised by his fellow citizens as he was elected a J.P. for the city in 1893 and in 1894 he was made a freeman of the city. The family moved to Dublin where they lived for the next fourteen years before finally returning to Kilkenny.

Sir James Langrishe the 4th Baronet, succeeded to the title and estate in 1862. An Army officer, Sir James attained the rank of Lt. Col. before he retired to Kilkenny. There he was High Sheriff in 1866 and also a J.P. and Deputy Lieutenant. He was married twice.[320] His first wife was Adela de Blois Eccles and they had one son and five daughters. The 4th Baronet died in 1910.

His son was Sir Hercules the 5th Baronet already mentioned at the start of this chapter. Like his father Hercules (Herky) did his stint in the Army and saw service in Russia and on the Mediterranean. He was a High Sheriff in 1891 and was also a J.P. and a Deputy Lieutenant. He led the life of a dashing young aristocrat as already mentioned and was Master of the Kilkenny Hounds for a number of years. He married Lady Helen Hume Dick and they had two sons Hercules (Heck) and Terence (Pingo).

Heck, who was born in 1888, was educated at Eton and then entered the Army. He was a Lieutenant in the First World War and was killed in a flying accident in 1917.

Pingo, like his brother, an Eton graduate, also served in World War I but was fortunate to survive. He went on to see active service in World War II in the intelligence corps. After the War he became a Lloyd's name. The 5th Baronet died in 1943 and Pingo became Sir Terence the 6th Bt. He married Joan Grigg the daughter of an Army officer[321] and they had three sons Hercules, Patrick and Robin. Prior to his marriage to Joan, Pingo was engaged to Barbara Cartland. Robin, an Army officer and old Etonian, married Barbara Lygon and they have one son Robin. Robert senior died in 1982.

Patrick, another old Etonian became a Major in the Army, served in Malaya, and was later a member of Lloyds. He married Penelope Horley and they have two daughters, Caroline and Marianne. Marianne and her husband Nicholas Di Biasio have three sons Adam, Jamie and George.

---

[320] His first wife died in 1901 after almost fifty years of marriage. He remarried in 1906. His second wife was Algitha Gooch.
[321] Joan's father was the man who started Carmart in Picadilly and became very wealthy.

Caroline went on to become a celebrated actress of both stage and screen. She married Patrick Drury and has two daughters Leonie and Rosalind.

Pingo in uniform

Sir Hercules (Heck) Langrishe the 7th Baronet attended Eton and then pursued a career in the Army. He married Lady Grania Wingfield the only daughter of the 9th Viscount Powerscourt and they have one son, James Hercules and three daughters, Miranda, Georgina and Atalanta.

The three daughters are married. Miranda's husband is John Markes formerly of Recess, Co. Galway and they have three children, Alice, Louisa and Julia. Georgina married Dr. S. Ross Wallace from Australia and they have two sons and Oliver and Sam. Atalanta's husband is J. Arthur Pollock and they have one son, John, and two daughters Marina and Josephine.

Heck died in 1998 and was succeeded by his son Sir James Hercules Langrishe the 8th Baronet. Sir James married Gemma O'Daly from Dunsany Co. Meath and they have one son Richard James Hercules and one daughter Victoria both born in the 1980s.

Lady Langrishe (Heck's widow) was associated with films in her youth and played a minor part in the film *Captain Lightfoot* which starred Rock Hudson and Barbara Rush. Lady Langrishe is currently a prominent member of the Watercolour Society of Ireland and has already illustrated one book entitled *Irish Trees, Myths, Legends and Folklore*.[322] This active Lady is presently engaged in preparing illustrations for another book about the Flora of Ireland.

Lady Langrishe getting ready for her role in *Captain Lightfoot*

---

[322] By Niall MacCoitir

Loftus of Mount Loftus

It is reputed that the Mount Loftus estate or Mount Eaton as it was then known was won in a card game. The then owner was Mr. John Eaton, a grandson of the original grantee of the same name. It would appear that the winner of the game was Rt. Hon. Nicholas Lord Loftus, first Viscount Ely. The difficulty encountered by the Rt. Hon. Nicholas in getting actual possession would lead one to believe that the story of the card game was very probably true.[323]

Mr. Eaton was not overly anxious to give up his ancestral home easily. Lord Loftus was compelled to seek legal redress and obtained a Chancery suit. Eaton refused to quit. He had two bodyguards, prize-fighters, one armed with a pike and the other with a blunderbuss to prevent the Chancery suit being served. He also had two men to guard the demesne to prevent the Sheriff's officers from entering.

John Eaton, the son of Theophilus Eaton and grandson of John who got the original estate in 1703, which was called Mount Eaton, was still embroiled in the

---

[323] Bettina (Loftus) Grattan-Bellew in Old Kilkenny Review no. 23

legal wrangle over the ownership of the estate in 1763. Garret Drake in an affidavit in the case of Eaton V Loftus – Drake was employed as a process server- said Eaton never left his house for fear of being served a process; that he (Drake) was kept out of the house by two persons armed one with a gun and the other with a hanger who told him that 'if he were a bailiff or person who came from Lord Loftus... this deponent .should never go back alive... and that Eaton gave out and declared he would destroy any person who should come upon such business.[324]

In this same year the affair seems to have been settled when Lord Loftus granted a lease for lives to John Eaton and his sons James and Henry for some of the lands in the area.[325] According to Mrs. Grattan Bellew, Loftus eventually got possession with the help of the notorious Freney the robber.[326]

The townland of Drumroe with other lands were granted to John Eaton after the Williamite Wars of the 1690s. The nucleus of this 2000 acre estate was the village of Powerstown where there was a church and a burial ground. Powerstown Church is very ancient[327]. Inside the church there was an early fluted font, similar to those in St Canice's Cathedral and St Mary's Church, Kilkenny. The font was removed to the new Protestant Church at Goresbridge about the year 1812. The fine Kilkenny marble altar which is now at Grange Sylvae Church was presented to Powerstown Church by Ralph Gore of Barrowmount in 1766. The Loftus vault is in the south west corner of the churchyard. In it are buried Sir Edward Loftus, 1st. Bart, his sons Sir Nicholas Loftus and Sir Francis Loftus. The last of that family to be buried there was Marie Loftus Murphy in 1916. Some of the Eatons are also interred in a vault near the church.

The lands granted to John Eaton were part of the great estate of Viscount Galmoy, one of the Butlers, who supported the Jacobite cause and was subsequently dispossessed. It would seem that the Earl of Ormonde recovered these lands and then leased them to John Eaton as the Fee Farm Lease was enrolled in the Bills

---

[324] Loftus Papers
[325] Ibid.
[326] Freney was said to have been descended from the ancient Norman family of de Freyne, landowners in the Rosbercon area, near New Ross. He began his career as a robber in the mid 1700s. He was very wily and somewhat lucky and while many of his companions in crime were caught and transported he managed to elude capture. He seemed to be something of Robin Hood and robbed only the rich. It would appear that he cut a deal with Lord Carrick and betrayed his companions who were executed. His autobiography was written in 1754 and he disappeared from public view until 1776. He was given a post at New Ross where he died in 1788.
[327] According to James Robertson, architect, writing in the Journal of the Royal Historical and Archaeological Society of Ireland.

Office in the Court of Chancery, in Ireland in 1712. The place became known as Mount Eaton. John Eaton's grandson was the unlucky card player who risked his birthright on a hand of cards in 1754.

Sir Edward Loftus, an illegitimate son of Sir Nicholas, by his Irish housekeeper, Mary Hernon, became the beneficiary of John Eaton's largesse. At a later stage a fine house was built and the name was changed to Mount Loftus.

Adam Loftus

The Loftus story in Ireland began with Rev. Adam Loftus, private chaplain to the viceroy, Thomas, Earl of Sussex, when he came with him to Ireland. Rev. Adam was advanced to the See of Armagh and was consecrated Archbishop of Armagh in 1562. He was one of the founders of Trinity College, Dublin and was its first provost. He resigned that post in 1594. In 1578 he was appointed Lord Chancellor of Ireland, a position he held until his death in 1605. He was granted the lands of Rathfarnham in the late 16th century and built Rathfarnham Castle. This castle was one of a ring of fortresses defending Dublin from the Irish clans in the Wicklow Mountains. The Castle and lands descended through the Loftus family and through a Loftus heiress to the Wharton family who were so profligate that the estate had to be sold in 1723. It was eventually bought back in 1767 by Nicholas Loftus Hume, 2nd Earl of Ely, whose uncle and heir, Henry Loftus, set about remodelling the Castle on a scale of 'regal magnificence', employing the most talented artists and craftsmen including Angelica Kauffman.

Henry Loftus succeeded his nephew as Earl of Ely but died childless in 1783, when the Castle and lands passed to his brother-in-law Charles Tottenham, who became the first Marquess of Ely assuming the name Loftus. The castle was sold in 1837 and the Loftus Elys lived from then on in Loftus Hall in Wexford. [328] All that remains of the Rathfarnham estate now, is the beautiful Castle Golf Course. Rathfarnham Castle itself has been recently opened to the public.

During the latter half of the 16th century Archbishop Loftus was one of the most powerful men in Ireland. When the lands of Ferns were granted on lease to Thomas Masterson, it was to the Archbishop that the Queen wrote to confirm the grant.[329] Earlier in 1566 the Queen sought his opinion as to the fitness of Sir John Devereux to be appointed to the vacant See of Ferns. He was highly recommended by the Bishop of Meath, but the scathing reply sent by Loftus deserves mention: 'the Bishoprick of Ferns is presently void, and I fear laboured for by one Devereux, an unfitter man can not be, he is now of late deprived of his Deanery for confessed licentiousness'.[330]

He was most concerned too with the subjugation of Feagh McHugh O'Byrne, the "Wolf of the Mountains". Following the capture and execution of Feagh he wrote a letter to Lord Burghley acquainting him with the details. Here is a transcript of part of his letter. "The 7th of this month, (May, 1597), the Lord Deputy having before appointed those Companys of Foot that lay at the fort of Rathdrum and Tullow to be in readiness, departed this City (Dublin), taking his journey towards the Mountains, and the next morning at 2 o'clock came to the wildest part of the glens, where the old traitor generally dwelt, which his Lordship caused to be entered by several ways, with such good planning that our men got through without any being injured. One of the Companys came upon the dwelling where Feagh was lying asleep, but he immediately seeing that he was surrounded tried to steal away. Fleeing from that house he was seen by

---

[328] 'The Tottenham family' by Charles Loftus Tottenham
[329] Hore's History of Wexford Vol. 6 pg. 78
[330] Ibid. pg. 231.

Captain Lee's company. He was pursued by the Sergeant and some of his men, who slew him. His head and quarters are now in their proper place here (in Dublin)".[331]

Archbishop Loftus was married to Jane Purdon of Co. Louth and they had twenty children, seven of whom died in infancy. Of the remaining thirteen most were married into the greatest families of the day, including three sons and seven daughters. Anne, for example, married three times. Her husbands were Sir Henry Colley, Captain George Blount and Baron Blayney. Alice's husband was Sir Henry Warren. Martha was married to Sir Thomas Colclough of Tintern.

The fourth son, Thomas, was the ancestor of the Loftus family of Killyon, Co. Meath. The eldest son and heir was Dudley Loftus, who was created Sir Dudley Loftus of Rathfarnham. Sir Dudley was born in 1561 and he married Anne, the daughter of Sir Nicholas Bagenal of Newry - (the Bagenals were later to found the town of Bagenalstown of Co. Carlow). Sir Nicholas himself was a very sinister figure. He received a pardon from Henry VIII 'of all murders and felonies by him committed'. He later bought the Barony of Idrone in Carlow (1585) for his second son.

Queen Elizabeth granted Kilcloggan, (in Co. Wexford) which was a preceptory of the Knight's Templars, and subsequently of the Knight's Hospitallers, to Sir Dudley, where he lived until his death in 1616. Kilcloggan, now known as Templetown was said to have been granted to the Knight's Templars by one Concubhair O'Mordha of Laois in the 12th century and is said to be the only Templar foundation in Ireland that resulted from Gaelic patronage.[332] After the dissolution the property was leased to James Sherlock of Waterford and later granted to Sir Dudley Loftus.

Sir Dudley had two sons that mattered (from the point of view of this dissertation), Sir Adam and Sir Nicholas. The Dublin and Wicklow lands seem to have been given to Sir Adam and the Wexford lands to Sir Nicholas. When Sir Adam's grandson and namesake died in 1690 the male heirs of that branch of the family died out, and the Rathfarnham estates passed to the infamous Marquis of Wharton, who had married the surviving heiress, Lucy Loftus. Sir Nicholas on the other hand had descendants who were more persistent and from him of course the Loftus family of Mount Loftus descended.

Sir Nicholas the second son of Sir Dudley was born in 1592 and he was given the high post of Clerk of the Pells and of the Treasury in Ireland in second decade of the 17th century. As well as having two sons by his wife Margaret Chetham, he also had a daughter who married John Cliffe, secretary to Ireton, Cromwell's son in law.

---

[331] Ibid. pg. 416
[332] The last preceptor was William Keating who was given a pension in 1541.

In 1641 Sir Nicholas acquired Fethard Castle, on the opposite side of the Hook to Kilcloggan, but had hardly moved in to his new home before he had to flee for safety to Dublin, with the outbreak of civil war. When the wars were over he was granted additional lands on the Hook and also purchased Redmond Hall and its estate from various Cromwellian soldiers, who had been granted the Redmond lands in settlement of their arrears of pay – but he never lived there, and died at Fethard in 1666.

He was succeeded by his son Sir Nicholas who had no heir and so his estates passed to his brother Henry of Dungulph Castle, who moved to Redmond's Hall, significantly remodelled the house and its grounds and renamed it Loftus Hall.[333] Henry's surviving son was another Nicholas, an able man who was an M.P. for Wexford in 1751. He was made Baron Loftus and in 1756 he was created Viscount Loftus of Ely. Nicholas proved to be truculent as well and threatened to extinguish the light of the Hook lighthouse unless he was paid more rent by the government. As a result of many petitions to the government by shipping and fishing interests it would appear that he got his rent increase and the light continued to act as a beacon right down to modern times. Nicholas married Anne Ponsonby the daughter of Sir William Ponsonby, of Bessborough, Viscount Duncannon (and following her death was married to Letitia, widow of his cousin Arthur Loftus, 3rd Viscount Ely).

When he died in 1763 he was succeeded by his son, Sir Nicholas, who was created 1st Earl of Ely in 1766. He died in the same year. Sir Nicholas (who died in 1766) took as his wife Mary the eldest daughter of Sir Gustavus Hume of Co. Fermanagh, and they had one son Nicholas who became the 2nd Earl of Ely on the death of his father in 1766.

In addition to his legitimate children, Nicolas Loftus, Viscount Ely, had two illegitimate sons by his Irish housekeeper, Mary Hernon, Edward and Nicholas. This latter Nicholas was an army officer and he fought under Clive in India. He came home from India, a very rich man, and eventually settled in England.

Nicholas the 2nd Earl died unmarried in 1769 when the earldom expired but the other titles reverted to his uncle Henry who became the 4th Viscount Loftus of Ely.

Henry the 4th Viscount, who was born in 1709, was advanced to an earldom as the Earl of Ely, Co. Wicklow, in 1771. While he had married twice he had no children and

---

[333] Dungulph Castle was the residence of the Whittys before it was granted to the Loftuses this castle later became the home of the celebrated Sean Cloney, a writer and scholar, who was embroiled with the Catholic Church in the controversy surrounding his stance to have his children educated in the Protestant school. The events of 1957 became known as 'The Fethard Boycott'.

when he died in 1783 the titles expired, but the estates were all left to his nephew, Charles Tottenham the grandson of "Tottenham in his boots".[334]

The Hon. Sir Nicholas Loftus

---

[334] Jonah Barrington recalls how Charles Tottenham got his sobriquet "Tottenham in his Boots" and it is well worth reproducing here. 'A very important constitutional question was debating between government and the opposition on how to appropriate a sum of £60,000 then lying unappropriated in the Irish Treasury. The numbers seemed to be equally poised though it had been supposed that a majority would incline to give it to the king, whilst the opposition would recommend laying it out upon the county; when the sergeant at arms reported that a member wanted to force into the House undressed, in dirty boots and splashed up to his shoulders.

The Speaker could not oppose custom to privilege and was necessitated to admit him. It proved to be Mr. Tottenham of Ballycarney, Co. Wexford, covered with mud and wearing a pair of huge jack-boots! Having heard that the question was likely to come on sooner than expected he had mounted his horse at Ballycarney, set off at night, ridden nearly sixty miles up to the Parliament House direct, and rushed in, without washing or cleaning himself, to vote for the country. He arrived just at the critical moment and critical it was. The numbers were in truth equal and his casting vote gave a majority of one to "the country" party. I recollect "Tottenham in his Boots" remaining, down to a very late period, a standing toast at certain patriotic tables.'

A commission was bought for Edward, the illegitimate son (born c.1730), in Conway's Regiment and he was created a baronet in 1768. He was High Sheriff of Tyrone in 1777 and High Sheriff of Co. Wexford in 1784. Edward fought in France at Flanders under Sir John Lignier against the French under Marshal Saxe and was promoted to Captain.

Sir Edward Loftus

Captain Loftus, later Sir Edward, married Anne Read and they had four sons, Sir Nicholas, Edward, Henry and Francis. Anne Read was an heiress and was 'rather a haughty lady' while Edward was the opposite. In later life she was sometimes taken for his mother when they travelled which annoyed her a lot.[335] Her mother died in 1763 and the couple came into the inheritance which consisted of lands and properties in counties Tyrone and Donegal.

There is some uncertainty, but it seems likely that Mount Loftus was known as Mount Eaton until after Lord Loftus's death[336], and it is thought that the new house was built by Sir Edward.

Edward and Anne lived partly in Dublin and partly at Mount Loftus. After the death of his half brother Henry, Sir Edward also came into possession of Richfield or Ballymagir[337] in Co. Wexford the former estate of the Devereux family and they spent some of their time living at Richfield. Their house in Dublin was initially in Sackville Street[338] but subsequently it seems that they moved to Gardiner Place.[339]

Sir Edward was Colonel of the Yeomanry in Wexford and was also much involved in the Volunteer movement, becoming Colonel of the Barrow Rangers in 1779. He was said to have been offered a Peerage but declined on the advice of his wife who said that they 'were well off as baronets but would make poor lords'! Sir Edward was a member of the Dublin Society and was known as an exceptionally good landlord, interested in agriculture, fair to his tenants and keen to give employment to all who needed it.[340] He and his wife had three surviving sons and two daughters, Elizabeth[341] and her older sister Mary, who married the Rev. Edward Carey of Munfin in Co. Wexford.[342]

---

[335] Old Kilkenny Review no. 23 – article by Bettina (Loftus) Grattan-Bellew.

[336] He died in 1763 at his house in Capel Street in Dublin and was buried in the family vault at Fethard.

[337] This was where the Earl of Essex and his army were entertained by his cousin Sir Nicholas Devereux in 1599 when Essex came to Ireland as Lord Deputy. It was said that Devereux had to sell an entire townsland to pay for the entertainment. – *The Kavanaghs Kings of Leinster* by Art Kavanagh.

[338] In a lease of the Powerstown lands made in 1766 Edward is noted as of Sackville St. – Loftus Papers

[339] Simon Loftus – family historian

[340] Tighe: *Statistical Observations relative to the County of Kilkenny [1802]*; Rev James Hall: *Tour through Ireland [1813]*.

[341] According to Bettina Grattan-Bellew, Elizabeth was the fiancé of Bagenal Harvey and was so traumatised by his untimely death that she never afterwards considered marrying another man. While this may have been the case it is known that Bagenal had several liaisons and was secretly married to a Miss Judith Dockrell – *Ireland 1798 The Battles* by Art Kavanagh.

[342] This was the Mrs Carey who saved the life of William Farrell, the Carlow rebel, in 1798. Following the start of the insurrection in Co. Wexford, the Careys fled to Carlow and went

Sir Nicholas, the eldest son, who succeeded in 1818, never married but had a succession of mistresses, and lived through the turbulent times of the French Revolution in 1789, the Rebellion of 1798[343] and the passing of the Act of Union in 1801.[344] He was active politically in Co. Kilkenny during the years of the Tithe War.

Sir Nicholas Loftus

Sir Nicholas was a magistrate and as such was consulted by both the authorities and the tithe objectors. It is on record that in 1831 he was quoted as being in opposition to the Tithe Composition and therefore his sympathies were with the tenants who opposed

---

to stay in Farrell's sister's house only to find that William had been implicated in the rising in Carlow. He had been tried and was to be executed the very next day at Leighlinbridge. Mrs. Carey, whose brother was an officer in Carlow rushed down to Leighlinbridge and persuaded the commanding officer, Mahon, to spare William's life.

[343] Mount Loftus did not escape the attentions of the rebels in 1798 and according to Bettina Grattan-Bellew a contingent arrived at the house and drank all the wine in the cellars and then stuck a pike in the portrait of Lord Loftus, where the hole can still be seen. The family had vacated the home at the time as a precaution.

[344] Sir Nicholas had his portrait painted by Gilbert Stuart the famous American portraitist who painted among others Jefferson, Washington and John Adams.

the tithes. This was stated by Rev. Martin Doyle, Parish Priest of Graiguenamanagh and formerly Parish Priest of Powerstown at an anti tithe meeting.[345] The 1830s were turbulent times in Kilkenny and adjoining counties as the vexed question of tithes came to a head.

Tithe Composition Acts were passed in various years giving the local Protestant rectors the power to agree with the landholders and tenants on a particular acceptable formula for the collection of tithes. In some areas such acceptable formulae were not forthcoming and this led to friction between the various interested parties.

In the case of Powerstown and Mount Loftus, Sir Nicholas, it would appear, could not agree a Composition with the local rector and he was supported by the Catholic priest Rev. Martin Doyle. At a meeting held in Graiguenamanagh in January of 1831 Rev. Doyle told the gathering that he had dined the previous day with Sir Nicholas at Mount Loftus and that Sir Nicholas had agreed to mediate between the rector and the parishioners. Sir Nicholas, however, was above all else a 'law and order man' and so when his attempts at mediation failed and when his fellow magistrates became increasingly alarmed by the activities of the anti-tithe protestors, he, along with his fellow magistrates signed a requisition which was sent to Colonel Harvey to send 400 men to the area to enforce the payment of tithes.

Sir Nicholas and his brother Francis lived the life of country squires and they had a very fine stable and a pack of Harriers which they hunted. He had the best racing stable in Ireland at the time. One of his finest horses was a stallion called Hollyhock that he had bought from a hawker of hollysticks, which in those days were used for making whip handles. He paid the hawker £5 for the young horse which turned out to be the finest race horse of his day in both England and Ireland. He won fifteen King's Plates as well as other very prestigious races. His progeny proved to be quite successful also.[346] In his younger days Sir Nicholas was an officer in the Kilkenny Militia and was present at the Battle of New Ross in 1798.

Sir Nicholas[347] died in 1832 and his title and estates passed to his youngest brother Sir Francis[348]. When the latter died the title became extinct, but the estate was

---

[345] *Kilkenny History & Society* pg.487 ed. Wm. Nolan
[346] Old Kilkenny Review no. 23 - Article by Bettina Grattan-Bellew.
[347] According to Bettina Grattan-Bellew, Sir Nicholas was a fun loving man who had an eye for the ladies. She recounts a story of how on an occasion in Carlow town he saw a soldier beating his wife, a very pretty woman. Sir Nicholas bought the woman on the spot and brought her to Mount Loftus where he had her ensconced in a house on the grounds. As a result of this action his sister Elizabeth left Mount Loftus bringing her niece Mary with her.
[348] Sir Francis was invalided for a number of years before his death. He was a noted musician. After the death of Sir Nicholas his sister Elizabeth came back to Mount Loftus with Mary.

left to his niece, Mary, who married Matthew Murphy, the estate agent, and so began the Murphy connection with Mount Loftus.

Sir Edward and Lady Anne's second son, Edward, an army lieutenant, died in 1795 at the age of 35. He was wounded in the French Wars and came home but died a short time later. Prior to going to war he had fallen in love with a Catholic girl named Mary Carroll and they got married. They had a daughter Mary. It was this girl, Edward's daughter, who eventually inherited the estates.

Edward Loftus, Mary's father

Colonel Loftus (Sir Edward) had offered to settle £10,000 on Mary on condition she was educated as a Protestant but her mother Mary Carroll refused. She was taken to Mount Loftus and raised there by her adored aunt Elizabeth. When she married Murphy they went to Dublin where they bought Diswellstown House in Castleknock, Dublin. Mary's grandmother, Lady Anne, was said to have been very annoyed since Murphy was the agent of the Mount Loftus estate.[349]

Mary Murphy (nee Loftus)

After the death of Sir Nicholas they came back to manage the place for Sir Francis who was an invalid. He was a talented musician Sir Edward's eldest daughter [Mary] and her husband the Rev. Edward Carey took exception to Sir Francis' will in favour of his niece Mary and they took a suit in Chancery on the

---

[349] According to Simon Loftus his grandfather Pierce Loftus said that Murphy may have been descended from another illegitimate branch of the Loftus family.

grounds that Mary was illegitimate, as her mother was Catholic and her father a Protestant but they lost the case and Mary retained the estates.[350]

Bonfires were lit on the hillsides and the carriage was pulled from Goresbridge by the delighted tenants, on the day Mary and her husband came back to Mount Loftus. Mary who was an angel of mercy during the famine was very popular. She won a landmark case in a fishery dispute which ruled in her favour and after that her popularity declined. She died in 1869. Matthew died in Diswellstown in 1876. They had three sons and two daughters the eldest of whom married Hyacinth Chevers Plunkett K.C., who was known as 'the Father of the Irish Bar'.

Mary's eldest son, John, born in 1822, was educated at home, by Sir Francis and was a very knowledgeable man. He was known as the walking encyclopedia. He was a D.L. and a J.P. for both Kilkenny and Wexford and was created Lord of the Manor of Ballymagir. He was High Sheriff of Kilkenny in 1873. His wife was Belinda Creagh the daughter of Pierse Creagh of Mount Elva and Bryan's castle Co. Clare.

John was an invalid for three years before his death, and after his death in 1881 the estate sank into financial ruin and was taken over by the Land Commission. His widow, Belinda, lived as a tenant under the Court and was so successful she was able to keep both Mount Loftus and Richfield. She later got married to Maurice Coates and went to live in England in 1888. John and Belinda had three sons and two daughters.[351] In 1889 Belinda's brother, Symon Creagh, and his wife, came to Mount Loftus as tenants and remained there until Symon died in 1899. Richfield was sold and much of the land and outhouses of Mount Loftus.

John and Belinda's three sons were Francis Cochrane, John Edward Blake and Pierse Creagh. The three assumed the surname Loftus. The eldest son, Captain Francis served in the South African War and was killed in action at the battle of Colenso, Natal in 1899. He was only 26 years old.

His brother, John Edward, bought the House and demesne back from the Land Commission. It was almost derelict. The old house was demolished and a new house was built around the Range which was formerly a granary and a steward's house. It was completed by 1910. He was able to do this because of the generosity of his stepfather, Maurice Coates. John Edward was given Royal licence to take the arms of Loftus quarterly with Murphy in 1910. He was a D.L and a J.P. and a High

---

[350] Old Kilkenny Review – no. 23
[351] Belinda died unmarried and Nora married Robert Alexander Gardiner of Sagtikos Manor, Long Island in 1909 and they had children. According to Bernard Segrave Daly Gardiner's Manor is an island itself of some 3000 acres. It was supposedly the island where Captin Kidd buried his treasure. It is still owned by a descendant of Nora Murphy Loftus.

Sheriff in 1908. He fought in World War I (gaining the rank of Major) but survived to come home to Mount Loftus where he died in 1936. He was married to Paulina Lichtenstadt of London, an heiress, and they had one son who died young in 1930 and three daughters, Bettina, Patricia and Linda.

Major John was politically active and a strong supporter of Home Rule. He gave his covert support to Sinn Fein. His cousin was Maire de Buitleir an active Gaelic revivalist. She gave the name to Sinn Fein via Arthur Griffith. She was also a friend of Bean deValera. Major John and his brother Pierse Loftus offered de Valera the use of their house just off Belgrave Square in London during the negotiations for a truce. The house had been left to the brothers by their aunt Henrietta Sankey widow of Sir Richard Sankey, who died in 1920

The Major had much correspondence with De Valera subsequently and became a friend of William Cosgrave also. He was elected to Kilkenny Co. Council in 1926 and remained a councillor until his death. He was a member of various committees – agriculture, vocational education and the mental hospital. A cultured man the Major was also a member of the RIA and was a fellow of the Royal Society of Antiquaries of Ireland. Being farsighted he was a founder member of the Barrowvale Co Operative Society and Gowran Park Race committees. This is what Fr. McDonnell, Parish Priest of Goresbridge, had to say about the founding of the Co Operative at the launch of the Cois Bearbha Society in 2001.

"Ninety one years ago, on February 19, 1910, about 200 farmers from the surrounding area met in Mount Loftus House (outside Goresbridge). They were called together by Captain John Blake Loftus for the purpose of forming an agricultural co-operative society. Out of that meeting, with the guidance of Sir Horace Plunkett, founder of the co-operative movement and president of the Irish Association of Co-Operative Societies, grew Barrowvale Co-Operative Creamery."

A fire destroyed part of the house in 1934 but most of the family heirlooms were saved and the house was rebuilt.

Bettina and her husband took over Mount Loftus after the death of her father in 1936. Bettina, like her sister Patricia, was a very competent sportswoman and was joint Master of the Mount Loftus Harriers with Patricia from 1930 to 1935. Bettina married Thomas Henry Grattan-Bellew of Mount Bellew Co. Galway. She died in 1995, when Mount Loftus was sold.

Loftus of Mount Loftus

Mount Loftus

Patricia married Captain Temple Bayliss from Staffordshire and they had three children – two sons John and William and a daughter Phillipa Anne who is a professional artist with an international reputation. She was educated at the Byam Shaw School of Painting and has exhibited widely. Her husband is Henry Garner and they have three sons Henry, James and Temple Victor.

Linda (who died in 2003) by her first marriage to Reginald Segrave –Daly had two sons and two daughters. The elder daughter is Rosalind a puppeteer and artist and she married a New Yorker, James Belford and they have a daughter Alicia. The younger daughter is Valerie Mary whose husband is William Newton of Bristol. They have two sons Gerald and Owain and a daughter Teresa.

Linda's sons are Piers and Bernard. Piers is a Dublin based actuary and he is married to Susan Kilkelly. They have a son John and four daughters Louise, Elizabeth, Ruth and Zoe. Bernard became Managing Director of Adnans Brewing company. He was educated at Glenstal and UCD and his wife is Oonagh Hopkirk from Scotland. They have three sons Francis and Dominic and Justin   Francis is married and has two children Kiera and Robert.

John Bayliss (mentioned above) a Judge Advocate, served 35 years in the Royal Navy and qualified as a barrister. His parents Captain Temple Bayliss and Patricia lived for many years in Corries House near Bagenalstown. The Captain died in 1989 and Patricia in 2004. John Bayliss married Annelize Kors from Holland and they have two children Alexander and Ilona both born in the 1980s.

Pierse Creagh was the 3rd son of John Murphy. Pierse adopted the surname Loftus like his brother John, and trained as a brewer in Copenhagen and Munich before working in South Africa, following which he settled in Suffolk and took charge of Adnams brewery. He fought in World War I, attaining the rank of Captain in the 5th Suffolk Regiment, and was mentioned in despatches. He was M.P. for Lowestoft from 1934 to 1945. He was also the High Steward of Southwold from 1945 onwards. He was the author of several books on politics and the economy. His wife was Dorothy Reynolds and they had two sons Murrough and Nicholas. Murrough was a Lieutenant in the Army and fought in World War II. He was married and divorced twice but had no family.

Nicholas was an Army Captain and served in World War II also, before becoming Joining Adnams brewery, where he eventually became Managing Director. He also served on the Suffolk County Council. He married Prudence Montague Wootten and they had three sons and two daughters. The elder daughter Belinda became the Assistant Keeper in the Department of Art in the Imperial War Museum, a post she held from 1970 until 1973. She subsequently married John Kidd and settled in Northern Ireland, where she works as an Arts consultant. She has two daughters. Her younger sister is Rose Therese, who lives in Suffolk and is married to Mark Titchener. They have two daughters and a son.

The sons of Nicholas, who died in 1963 in a motor accident, are Simon Piers, Michael Joseph, and Benedict Nicholas. Simon, who is married to Irène is Chairman of Adnams brewery and author of a number of books. Simon and Irène have a daughter Hana. Michael Joseph and Benedict Nicholas are both married and they have families.

The present Mount Loftus house is the third house on this site. The first was built in 1750s – 60s by the first Viscount Loftus or his son Edward. This was demolished c. 1906 by Major J.E.B. Loftus who built a much larger ornate Edwardian home in its place. The new home was destroyed by fire in 1934, after which the present house was built.

Arms - a black shield with a chevron between three trefoils and crest of a Boar's head - motto Loyal au Mort

McCalmont of Mount Juliet

The McCalmont family came from Abbeylands, White Abbey, County Antrim. Major General Sir Hugh McCalmont leased Mount Juliet house and demesne from the Earl of Carrick in the first decade of the 20th century. They purchased the house and property a short time later in 1914. Even before they purchased the demesne, they continued to maintain and improve the house and the grounds. Sir Hugh was married to Lady Rose Bingham, the third daughter of the Earl of Clanmorris, in 1885[352].

Sir Hugh's brother, Colonel Harry McCalmont was a very wealthy man who had been left an immense fortune. He was left over four million pounds by an uncle in 1888. Harry purchased Cheveley Park Mansion and estate in England. He became Member of Parliament for Newmarket and a J.P. and earned distinction in the South African war. He also earned much respect as a well known local sportsman and benefactor. In 1899 he paid for extensive repairs and improvements to Wood Ditton Church and also made generous contributions to Cheveley Church. He built a number of architecturally attractive houses for his employees which are still known today as 'The McCalmont houses'. He died in 1902 at the young age of forty two and one of his beneficiaries was his nephew Dermot of Mount Juliet.

John Kirwan recorded the event as follows: 'Dermot McCalmont was still at his preparatory school in England, when unexpectedly he was left a large fortune. He was reputed to be the richest commoner in these islands, made so by the death of his uncle, Harry McCalmont. At that time the windfall was said to be worth £100,000 per annum. From then on, Mount Juliet was the centre of every sort of fun and hospitality. The house and grounds were lavishly staffed and maintained well into the 1980s.'[353] John went on to state that 'the family stayed at Mount Juliet until 1987, when escalating costs and taxation forced them to sell the estate. Their hospitality during these years has passed into legend. The upkeep of their amazing establishment for some eight decades meant that the family made a substantial contribution to the local economy'.

Major Dermot McCalmont made a new entrance in what had formerly been the back of the house. In the 1920s he created a ballroom in one of the two, two storey wings which flanks the main block at the rear. Mount Juliet now has a large collection of superb marble mantelpieces in the Adam manner, practically every room having one and one room even having a pair. These were mostly accumulated by Lady Rose, Major Dermot McCalmont's mother.

---

[352] The remarkable Bingham family descended from George Bingham, the military governor of Sligo during the latter years of the reign of Queen Elizabeth. George's descendants went on to become the Earls of Lucan and Clanmorris and were connected through marriage with every titled family in the west of Ireland. George himself was one of the great adventurers of the Elizabethan period of the same ilk as Cosby of Laois, Masterson of Ferns, Hartpole of Carlow, Colclough of Tintern and Wallop of Enniscorthy.

[353] John Kirwan in Old Kilkenny Review

Near the house is a series of gardens which were laid out in the 1930s. These were largely the work of Marguerite Solly-Flood. In her memoirs she states that she was offered a large salary (which in part she refused) a house, a car and the supervision of over twenty men including a greenhouse foreman. With this staff she had a 'free hand' to make any alterations or additions which she thought desirable in the general layout of the demesne, for which she had responsibility i.e., about one mile of avenue with adjacent woods, lawns and rides. She was to keep the house supplied with exotic plants. She also had charge of the kitchen garden of seven acres, which was supposed to produce enough fruit and vegetables to supply the large household and also once a week, enough vegetables for outside employees - in all, over one hundred families. Major Dermot was interested in the gardens, particularly a rose garden, which he had Mrs Solly-Flood design. He inspected them a great deal, while his wife, Lady Helen, who was not a lover of gardening, liked to have lots of blooms in the rooms of the great house[354].

Rose Barton, a leading Irish watercolourist, was a kinswoman of the McCalmonts. She was an occasional visitor to Mount Juliet. During some of these visits, she captured some of the magic of the place in a series of watercolours which she did of the gardens. These were retained by Major Victor McCalmont and his family after he had moved to Norelands. On occasion they have been loaned for exhibition.

During the war for national independence Mount Juliet like many of the great Irish houses received unwelcome callers. The Kilkenny -Journal of the 4 September 1920 carried the following report:

The residence of Major Dermot and Lady Helen McCalmont, Mount Juliet House, was raided by armed and undisguised men on Sunday afternoon. When the raiders, who arrived by motor, entered the dining-room, Major and Lady [Helen] McCalmont with a visitor were at lunch. The latter drew his revolver, but was immediately cornered by the raiders, who relieved him of the weapon. So far as can be learned, the only weapons found were a couple of swords and curios.

While still the property of the McCalmonts, Ballylinch became renowned as a stud, which was established by Major Dermot in 1915. The family still carries on this tradition at nearby Norelands Stud. The most famous sires in the stud's history have been The Tetrach who started his duties here in 1915. His son Tetratema and his grandson Mr. Jinks were also well known stallions. The McCalmonts largely though not entirely patronised the flat, both

---

[354] Marguerite Solly-Flood: *Memories of Six Reigns* printed privately in 1978.

McCalmont of Mount Juliet

here and in England. Lady Helen McCalmont, born a Conyngham of Slane Castle and mother of the late Major Victor McCalmont, preferred the jumps and had many successes under National Hunt Rules - most notably in 1933 when her horse Red Park won both the Irish Grand National and the Galway Plate. The McCalmonts sponsored a number of races at Gowran Park, including the Tetratema Cup which is still a feature at this track. The estate was sold by her son Major Victor, who moved to a smaller property at Norelands, just across the river from Mount Juliet.

A 1920s Kilkenny Point to Point - Lady Helen McCalmont seated

Also included are Baroness Prochazka, Mrs. Newport, the Countess of Desart, Lady Ainsworth and Hon. Rose McCalmont.
(photo courtesy John Kirwan)

In 1920 'Ikey' Bell, who is still remembered in hunting circles, retired as master of the Kilkenny pack. In the following year Major Dermot McCalmont took on the mastership of the Kilkenny Hunt which office he held until his death in 1968.

His mother, Rose, Lady McCalmont, was a noted rider in her day. She was always well mounted on a beautiful thoroughbred horse with a groom, equally well mounted, in attendance. In 1914, Harry Worcester Smith, a visiting 'Master of Foxhounds' wrote about a days hunting in her company. 'For a woman whose son was at least twenty-five' he wrote, 'it was surprising to see her go. Not only was she putting the thoroughbred horse over the narrow banks and ditches, but now and then she would cheer the hounds on, and never in all my sporting experience have I ridden with one who had carried me to such a high degree of enthusiasm as did this descendant of Burton Persse, who hunted the Galway Hounds for thirty-three years'.[37]

This hunting tradition was carried on at Mount Juliet by her descendants. Upon the death of his father in 1968, Major Victor McCalmont became sole master which office he had held jointly with Major Dermot for a number of years. In 1921 when they first assumed the mastership they built the existing kennels at Mount Juliet which are still used by the Kilkenny pack. When the family sold the estate, they, with their customary generosity, passed the kennels to the Kilkenny Hunt on a very long lease. Major Victor McCalmont died in March 1993 and is buried in nearby Ennisnag with other members of his family.

The McCalmont Rolls – 1930s
(Photo courtesy College Books)

Ponsonby of Bessborough

Because of the film 'Waterloo' the vision of General Sir William Ponsonby charging to his doom at the head of his cavalry will be forever etched in the memories of the millions who saw the cinematic images. The General was in fact the grandson of Kilkennyman John Ponsonby, the Speaker of the Irish House of Parliament and contemporary of Henry Grattan. Sir William Ponsonby (MP for Londonderry), who led the Union Brigade's charge on D'Erlon's troops was killed by French lancers. As if he had a premonition of his death he handed his watch and ring to his aide-de-camp, prior to his charge, telling him to give them to his wife.[355]

The ancestor of this remarkable Kilkenny family was Colonel John Ponsonby, originally from Hale Hall in Cumberland. The Colonel raised a regiment

---

[355] Strangely this was also done by an earlier Ponsonby who was killed at Fontenoy.

of cavalry and accompanied Cromwell to Ireland. When the war concluded he was appointed a Commissioner for the taking of depositions concerning atrocities committed against Protestants during the 1641-49 rebellion, and was made Sheriff of Wicklow and Kildare.

Cromwell looked after his faithful officers very well and within a short time he knighted John Ponsonby who became Sir John. In addition Sir John was granted the forfeited estate of Edmund Dalton at Kildalton and lands that formerly belonged to the Walshes[356] particularly in the Fiddown area[357]. It is said that Cromwell accompanied Sir John Ponsonby into the area and as he gazed over the beautiful valley of the Suir he threw up his hands and cried out with a loud voice "Behold the land flowing with milk and honey which the Lord hath delivered into my hands."[358] The Datons or Daltons as they were later called came to Ireland with the first Normans in 1171. They settled originally in Westmeath but later purchased a large estate in South Kilkenny, where they were living when the Cromwellians arrived. After their lands were confiscated some of the Daltons may have moved to Connaught but a number remained behind as tenants to the new landowners, but not necessarily in the Kildalton area. There was a number of Daltons in the Inistioge area in the 18th century farming large holdings[359].

An interesting but sad tale is told about Catherine Dalton, the daughter of Edmund, who lost his lands to Colonel Ponsonby. Catherine sought the affections of Ponsonby. After some time, Catherine, realising that Ponsonby was already married became insane and regularly dressed in the white clothes in which she intended to wed. Within a short time she died and was found on her father's grave. Legend has it that her ghostly shadow may be seen at "Lady's Bridge".[360]

---

[356] A noted Kilkenny family whose ancestors came over to Ireland from Wales with the first Norman invaders in 1169. They got a grant of lands in South Kilkenny which became known as the Walsh Mountain. The displaced Gaelic families were the Ui Faolain and the Mac Giolla Padraigs. The Walsh family ruler was known as The Lord of the Mountain. After the Cromwellian wars they lost most of their lands, which were confiscated and granted to the Cromwellian soldiers and adventurers.
[357] From the Down Survey
[358] *The Ponsonby Family* by Major Gen. Sir John Ponsonby
[359] John Mannion and Fidelma Maddock in *Kilkenny History & Society*
[360] Rev. T. Clohesy writing in the *Old Kilkenny Review* had a slightly different slant on the story. 'Ponsonby allowed Sir John Daton to stay in the family residence with his beautiful daughter Winifred. It was almost a foregone conclusion that Ponsonby would wed the beautiful Winifred but one day he arrived back at Kildaton with his entourage which included his newly wed. When she was introduced to the Datons, Winifred fainted on the spot and became deranged. She used to spend much of her time, dressed in a white satin dress pruning bushes and trees and one of her favourite trees was an old thorn bush where

Ponsonby of Bessborough

Sir John was in fact married twice. His first wife was Dorothy Briscoe from Cumberland and they had a son John, who was the ancestor of the Ponsonbys of Hale. His second wife was a widow twice over. She was Elizabeth, the daughter of Lord Folliott and her first husband was Sir Richard Wingfield of Powerscourt. He had married Elizabeth in 1640. He died in 1644 leaving a son and heir and a daughter. Her second husband was Edward Trevor the brother of Lord Dungannon. After Edward's death in the 1650s she married Sir John. Sir John had two sons by his marriage to Elizabeth. They were Henry and William. In 1662 he was confirmed in two grants of land and he changed the name of the estate from Kildaton to Bessborough in honour of his wife Elizabeth. He is buried in Fiddown where there is a slab with the inscription – 'Here lieth the body of Sir John Ponsonby of Bessborough who departed this life AD1678 in the 60the year of his age.'

Henry succeeded to the title and estates after the death of his father. It is not known how the Ponsonbys fared during the Jacobite period of dominance in 1689-90, but William took part in the siege of Derry on the Williamite side. After the victory of the Boyne they certainly suffered no penalties and were in a position to buy some further lands in Kilkenny that became available due to confiscation. Sir Henry, although married, had no family, so that after his death in the 1690s he was succeeded by his brother William.

Sir William became involved in politics after the victory of the Williamites and represented Kilkenny County as an M.P. from 1692 until 1721. In that year he was created Lord Bessborough and represented the county in the House of Lords. The following year, he was honoured with the title, Viscount Duncannon of Duncannon Fort in Co. Wexford. He died in 1724. It was Sir William who founded Pilltown village. The first building there was the barracks, a strong stone structure, built for defence, which was erected about 1710. He and his successors continued building in Pilltown where the estate workers were housed.

Sir William was married to Mary the sister and heir of Brabazon Moore of Ardee, Co. Louth. They had three sons and six daughters. The three sons were Brabazon, Henry and Folliott, who died unmarried in 1746.

Henry found a career in the Army and rose to the rank of Brigadier General. He was killed at the Battle of Fontenoy in 1745. A notice of the event stated "At the battle of Fontenoy, near Tournai in modern Belgium, the Irish Brigade of the French army under Lieutenant Charles O'Brien repulsed the British and won the day. Those killed included (on the British side) Henry Ponsonby, MP for Inistioge (sic) and

---

she spent much time clipping with her scissors. The tree became known as 'The White Lady's Tree'. The old father died soon afterwards.'

brother of Brabazon Ponsonby, 1st Earl of Bessborough." At the moment of his death, he had ridden to the head of the 1st Foot Guards when he turned to his son and aide-de-camp Chambre Brabazon and as if he had a premonition of his death he handed him his ring and watch with instructions to give them to his wife should he be killed. With that he rode to the crest of a ridge, paused and took a pinch of snuff. In that very act his head was carried off by a round shot.[361]

Henry's wife was Lady Frances the daughter of Chambre Brabazon, the 5th Earl of Meath, by whom he had a son Chambre Brabazon. Chambre was married three times and by his second wife he had Sarah Ponsonby one of the Ladies of Llangollen[362]. His third wife was Mary Barker of Kilcooley and from him descended the Ponsonby Barkers of Kilcooley.[363]

The following story is told of the marriage of Sir William's eldest son, Brabazon Ponsonby, future MP and Earl of Bessborough, which took place around 1703. 'Brabazon soon found himself in pecuniary difficulties from which he attempted to extricate himself by proposing to marry a rich widow then living in Dublin, a Mrs. Colvill, grand-daughter of Archbishop Margetson. Mrs. Colvill would have none of him and refused to listen to his importunities. Brabazon, however, resolved on a plan for making her his wife. She was awakened one morning by a band playing epithalamic airs outside her lodgings (the custom being to serenade newly married couples), and flying to the window, opened it, and beheld a great crowd cheering; at the same moment, the next window was thrown open, and Captain Brabazon Ponsonby appeared in a night-dress, smiling and thanking the people for their congratulations. He had hired a neighbouring apartment and the band, and by this ruse proclaimed that he was married to Mrs. Colvill. In vain she denied the assertion; public opinion, resting on such convincing proofs, was too

---

[361] *The Ponsonby Family* by Major General Sir John Ponsonby.
[362] Sarah ran away with her friend Eleanor Butler the daughter of the Ormonde heir. Sarah was the object of unwanted affection from her godmother's husband, Sir William Fownes. Eleanor, a Protestant was being persecuted by her Catholic stepmother. Sir William Barker of Kilcooley gave Sarah £580 which helped to keep them for a number of years. When Eleanor's father succeeded as the Earl of Ormonde he was persuaded by Sir William Barker to make provision for Eleanor which he did. The two girls never married and stayed together at Llangollen in Wales until their deaths. They became a very celebrated couple and received visits from very distinguished people including Lord Byron, the Duke of Wellington, Sir Walter Scott, De Quincy, Wordsworth, Southey, and many others. The Duke of Wellington, who made his name in battles against Napoleon's forces in Spain, attributed his knowledge of Spanish to a book given to him as a boy, by Lady Eleanor Butler.
[363] For information on this family see *The Tipperary Gentry Vol.1* by Art Kavanagh and Wm. Hayes

strong for her, and she finally gave way and bestowed her hand and fortune on the gallant officer, who left the Army'

Mrs. Colvill must have been a young widow as she bore Brabazon three sons[364] and four daughters. All four ladies married, so the drain on the family coffers must have been significant. Sarah married Edward Moore, the 5th Earl of Drogheda in 1727, Anne married Sir Benjamin Burton of Burton Hall, Carlow a year later, Elizabeth married Sir William Fownes of Woodstock (Sarah Ponsonby's persecutor)[365] and the youngest girl, Letitia married the 1st Viscount Mountmorres in 1742. Mrs. Ponsonby (Colvill) died in 1733 and Brabazon promptly married again. His second wife, too, was twice a widow and an heiress. She was Elizabeth Sankey from Longford. Her husbands had been Sir John King and the 1st Lord Tullamore. She died in 1738 and Brabazon never remarried. He was created the Earl of Bessborough in 1739 and ten years later he was made Baron Ponsonby of Sysonby, Co. Leicester. He enjoyed his honours for a number of years and died in 1758.

During the ten years between his creations he built Bessborough House. The house, designed by Francis Bindon, was first built in 1745. Castlemorres, another Bindon house was built about the same time. These were huge three storey mansions with acres of gardens and built inside demesne walls. The mid eighteenth century was an age of grandeur and the inside décor of the houses complemented the outside architecture. The very best of furnishings and plate were ordered and an army of servants hired to run the establishment. Rental rolls at the time were adequate to support the lifestyle of the Lords and Ladies of the Ponsonby family.

Despite his earlier financial hiccups, Brabazon's canny astuteness, so evident in winning the hand of the wealthy widow, once more came into play when he strode upon the political stage. His decision to latch himself on to the rising star of English politics, the 3rd Duke of Devonshire[366], opened many doors. Brabazon was able to marry two of his sons, William (his heir) and John (the famous Speaker of the House of Commons) to two of Devonshire's daughters. He was made the 1st Commissioner of Revenue, a very highly paid government post and he was given the titles already mentioned. His remunerations and his rent rolls meant that Brabazon became a very wealthy man indeed.

---

[364] Richard the youngest seems to have died very young.
[365] Sir William and Elizabeth had one daughter, Sarah, who married William Tighe of Rosanna, Co. Wicklow in 1765. Sarah conveyed Woodstock to the Tighe Family after the death of her father.
[366] The Duke of Devonshire was Lord Lieutenant in Ireland 1737-44.

Ponsonby of Bessborough

Bessborough House (photo courtesy College Books)

Brabazon's second son, John Ponsonby, was perhaps the most talented and most outstanding man of the family. Born in 1713 he entered Parliament in 1739. Five years later he replaced his father as Commissioner for the Revenue. In the year just prior to that prestigious appointment he married Lady Elizabeth Cavendish, the daughter of the 3rd Duke of Devonshire. In order to reinforce his position as a most reliable government supporter, John raised four companies of horse for service against the Scots rebels in 1745[367]. In 1746 he was appointed a Privy Councillor which carried with it the title of Rt. Honourable. Ten years later he reached the pinnacle of his power when he was appointed as Speaker of the House of Commons (in Ireland).[368] In addition to this he became an 'undertaker' for the government. This meant that he undertook to manage the business of the government in the Irish Parliament, in the absence of the Lord Lieutenant. In return he was given power to appoint people to high offices, acted as Lord Justice, was consulted about policies and given the necessary means to enable him to bring in a majority for the

---

[367] *The Ponsonby Family* by Major General Sir John Ponsonby.
[368] This post carried with it an annual salary of £4,000 – a massive sum in those days.

government when bills needed to be passed. He retained this position until 1770.[369] After this time the practice was discontinued as Lords Lieutenant were obliged to remain in Ireland as residents. The Hon. John died in 1787.

John and his wife, Lady Elizabeth, had five sons and four daughters. Three of his daughters married and it is significant that two of them married political allies, namely, the Earl of Shannon and Lord Lismore[370]. His sons were William, John, George, Richard and Frederick. William and George were M.P.s and were very prominent in their support of the Catholic Emancipation movement, supporting the Catholic Relief Acts according as they were presented in Parliament. George was the more prominent of the two and led the Whig party in the English Parliament after the Union. William tried for the position of Speaker in 1790 but he was defeated by John Foster. George was Chancellor of Ireland in 1806.[371] George's wife was Lady Mary Butler, the daughter of the 2nd Earl of Lanesborough and their only child, a daughter Elizabeth, married the Hon. Francis Prittie of Kilboy, Co. Tipperary, in 1808.[372] George had an illegitimate son, George Connolly Ponsonby, who distinguished himself in the Army. He fought in India and Afghanistan. He attained the rank of Major General. He settled with his family in Germany and there in 1866.[373]

William (d.1806) was created Baron Imokilly[374] and he had five sons John, William (who was killed at Waterloo), Richard who became Bishop of Derry, George and Frederick. John went on to become the 2nd Baron Ponsonby but though married he died without having had children.[375] He was at one time Ambassador to

---

[369] Ponsonby, Lanesborough and Shannon were deprived of their offices. This high handed treatment by Townshend led to riots and Ponsonby had to be reinstated as Speaker. He resigned the following year.

[370] See *The Tipperary Gentry Vol.1* by Art Kavanagh & Wm. Hayes concerning the Lords Lismore

[371] A barrister, he occupied some lucrative posts. He was a keen sportsman and loved hunting.

[372] Ibid. concerning the Pritties.

[373] *The Ponsonby Family* by Major General Sir John Ponsonby.

[374] They had a house and an estate at Bishopscourt, Co. Kildare and it was said that he kept the best hunting establishment in Ireland, where he hunted his pack of hounds and lived in the most hospitable and princely style. *The Ponsonby Family* by Major General Sir John Ponsonby.

[375] Elizabeth the wife of the 1st Marquess Conyngham had an affair in the 1790s with the Honourable John Ponsonby the future 2nd Baron Ponsonby. An extremely handsome man, he was saved from being hanged from a lamppost in Paris during the Revolution by the intervention of women who thought him too attractive to die. More affairs followed for Elizabeth, including one with the future Czar Nicholas I of Russia during a visit to London

Buenos Aires and to the Porte. The baronetcy devolved on his nephew William (son of William killed at Waterloo) but he too died childless in 1861 and the baronetcy went to his cousin, William (eldest son of the Bishop), an Army captain. This man died childless in 1866 when the baronetcy became extinct. The line of the Rt. Hon. John Ponsonby seems to have died out in the male line when the Captain died in 1866. Curiously enough the late Diana, Princess of Wales, was a descendant of the Rt. Hon. John after eight generations.

Lady Elizbeth Conyngham

---

in 1816. She was the Prince Regent's mistress from 1819 to his death in 1830. She was said to have been a beautiful, shrewd, greedy, voluptuous woman. According to reports she received jewels from the king worth in excess of £80,000.

To revert back to the main branch of the family, the Rt. Hon. John's elder brother was William the 2nd Earl of Bessborough (1704- 1793). He succeeded to the estates and titles in 1758. He represented the county of Kilkenny as an M.P. from 1727 until his succession meant he moved to the House of Lords. Like his brother, John, he occupied very important posts in the government, including postmaster general. William was a great connoisseur of Art and collected valuable pictures and antiques for his houses in Pall Mall and Roehampton. Much of this collection was sold by his son, in 1801 at Christies.[376] He was said to have been one of the many lovers of Princess Amelia, the daughter of George II. This lady, who was plumpish, rather deaf and short sighted never married but seemed to enjoy life to the full. On one occasion she rode off from the hunting field with the Duke of Richmond, and retired to a private house in Windsor Forest 'where they remained long enough to afford ground for scandal'.[377] Lord Bessborough had one son, Frederick, and two daughters, Catherine and Charlotte, who married respectively the 5th Duke of St. Albans and the 4th Earl Fitzwilliam.

Like his father, Frederick the 3rd Earl lived to be very old, dying in 1844. He was married to Lady Henrietta Spencer the daughter of the 1st Earl Spencer and they had three sons and a daughter, Caroline, who married Lord Melbourne. Lady Henrietta was in fragile health for much of her life and the young couple may have spent a lot of time in Italy. The children appear to have been raised with their grandmother, the Duchess of Devonshire, in Devonshire House.

The 3rd Earl probably lived most of his life abroad or in Dublin but he maintained the house at Bessborough. He bought a fine mansion, called Belline that had been built by Peter Walsh in Pilltown, in the late 18th century, for his agent. Prior to the agent taking up residence it was made available by the Earl to William Lamb, the son of Lord Melbourne, the husband of the Earl's only daughter, Caroline. He brought her there at the urgings of her frantic family.

Caroline, who was born in 1788, was married to a besotted William Lamb[378] in 1806. Caroline and William had only one son who survived childhood and he was not mentally capable. The marriage became unstable and in 1812 Caroline embarked on a very public affair with Lord Byron, much to the embarrassment of

---

[376] *The Ponsonby Family* by Major General Sir John Ponsonby.
[377] Ibid.
[378] William Lamb was a graduate of Trinity College, Cambridge and became a barrister. He was a member of a group of young radical thinkers that included Shelly and Byron, the poets, as well as Leigh Hunt and Henry Brougham. Brougham and Lamb went into politics and Lamb was elected as an M.P. in 1805. He did not succeed to the title until 1828 when he moved into the House of Lords. He became Home Secretary in 1830 and in 1834 he was Prime Minister.

her family and the annoyance of her husband. Affairs were very much in vogue then but they had to be discreet. Byron was just 24 at the time, three years her junior and on the verge of becoming the darling of society having just published *Childe Harolde's Pilgrimage*. He was feted everywhere. They began a much recognised and indiscreet affair that lasted a tempestuous four months. Byron ended the affair much to Caroline's displeasure.

Lady Caroline Lamb

She then spent the next four years pursuing him. Byron avoided her, seeking refuge for some time with his new mistress, Lady Oxford, and eventually marrying a cousin of Caroline's husband, Annabella Milbanke. As the enforced exile in Belline had no positive effect on Caroline her family frankly told Lamb to divorce her, but this he refused to do. The marriage continued until 1825. During the intervening period Caroline turned to novel writing and the characters of her first novel called *Glenarvon* were easily recognizable as leading society figures of the period, including Byron. She wrote two further novels, *Graham Hamilton*, published in 1822 and *Ada Reiss* published in 1823. She died in 1828.

The 3rd Earl's sons were John William, his heir and successor, Frederick a Major-General in the Army and William Francis the 1st Lord de Mauley. Both Frederick and William Francis became the ancestors of families that continued to expand down to modern times. The descendants of Frederick were high ranking Army officers and trusted members of the Royal Household Staff, and many of their children were sponsored by the Queen (Victoria) and her son King Edward. They all lived in England and many found employment in the Colonial services.

The eldest of the 3rd Earl's sons was John William Ponsonby who succeeded his father as the 4th Earl in 1844 just three years before his own demise. John William occupied important posts and was Lieutenant for the county of Kilkenny.

He was reputed to have been an excellent (and resident) landlord[379]. Like his illustrious forebears he was closely allied to the Whig party and was liberal minded. It was he who first introduced Daniel O'Connell to the House of Commons in 1829 after he had been elected, as the first Catholic, thus gaining Emancipation. It was said of John William that he was 'remarkably calm and unruffled'. When the Whigs swept into power in England, under Lord John Russell, in 1846, he immediately appointed John William the 4th Lord Bessborough, as Lord Lieutenant of Ireland.

His was a poisoned chalice. He occupied the post of Lord Lieutenant during the most calamitous period of Irish History, the Famine. This dreadful disaster was compounded by political unrest which manifested itself in the Young Ireland movement. Ever since 1829, O'Connell had been seeking Repeal of the Union, using all the peaceful means at his disposal, especially mass meetings. But younger, more radical men became more violent in their language and some of their number advocated a peasant led social revolution. These were the Young Irelanders[380]. Lord Bessborough was so alarmed, by these developments that he asked the Whigs to bring in a Coercion Bill, but this was turned down, simply because the Whigs had brought down the Tories a few months previously by refusing to sanction such a Bill for Ireland.

The Lord Lieutenant threw himself whole heartedly and vigorously into the efforts devised by the government to combat the effects of the famine. He urged his fellow landlords and the clergy of all denominations to organize and direct relief committees, public works projects and to become involved in the overseeing of the poorhouses and hospitals. He, himself, gave generously of his time and money in the fight.

Lord Bessborough, in his official capacity as Lord Lieutenant felt obliged to remain most of his time in Dublin. There he resided at the Vice Regal Lodge in the Phoenix Park but he did reside in the castle during the so-called Castle Season, a six week period of entertainment which reached its climax with a Grand Ball on March 17th, St. Patrick's Day. During the famine years the Castle Season went on

---

[379] Prior to the Famine as the population of Ireland swelled to over 8 millions, many people began to emigrate to America and Canada. Some enlightened landlords, including the Bessboroughs, provided paid passage for their tenants who wished to emigrate.

[380] Some of the persons involved were Smith O'Brien, a member of the gentry from Co. Limerick and an M.P. for Ennis, Charles Gavan Duffy, a Monaghan born Catholic journalist and publisher of *The Nation*, Thomas Davis, the Cork born son of an English Army Surgeon and John Blake Dillon a Mayo born Catholic barrister.

as usual.[381] However, in 1847 Lord Bessborough fell ill. He wrote to Lord John Russell and complained that it was the 'balls and drawing rooms' which 'knocked him up' not the responsibilities of his position. His illness proved fatal and he died on the 16th May, the day after Daniel O'Connell died at Genoa.

The Earl was married to Fane, the daughter of the Earl of Westmoreland. They had seven sons and six daughters. One of the daughters married the Earl of Kerry, another married her cousin the 2nd Baron de Mauley and the youngest, Kathleen married Edward Tighe of Woodstock.

Of the seven sons the most prolific was the sixth son who had six sons and five daughters by his wife, Louisa the daughter of Viscount Dillon. He was a member of the Royal Household and all his children and their descendants lived and still live mainly in England.

The eldest of the seven sons was John George who became the 5th Earl of Bessborough in 1847. He occupied some important posts in the Royal Household and although twice married he had no children. He lost the sight of one of his eyes in an accident. It would seem that while on his honeymoon he turned suddenly to embrace his wife who was holding a small Early Victorian parasol. The point of the parasol pierced his eye. He died in 1880 when his title and estates went to his brother, Frederick an unmarried barrister, who became the 6th Earl. He survived fifteen years and died in 1895[382]. The title and estates then passed to his brother, Walter William, a rector, who lived to be an elderly man of 85 before he passed away in 1906. It was during his period as Earl that the Land Acts compelled the sale of the large estates and the Bessborough lands went to the tenants under the terms of the Land Commission regulations.

The Rev. Walter (1821-1906), the 7th Earl, was married and he and his wife Lady Louisa, the daughter of the Earl of St. Germans, had five sons and three daughters[383]. His eldest son Edward became the 8th Earl in 1906. Two of the sons died childless. Cyril the second son was lieutenant of the City of London. He was married and had two sons both of whom were army officers and both of whom were killed in the First World War. The fourth son, Arthur, who was married to Kathleen

---

[381] In the countryside the landlords, in order to keep up morale, entertained as they had always done. At Bessborough 'the guests hunted by day and participated in tableaux vivants at night' – *The Great Hunger* by Cecil Woodham Smith

[382] His one passion was for cricket which he learned at Harrow. He and his brother and some friends founded a club the I Zingari, for cricket enthusiasts. He was also fond of amateur theatricals and hunting. He succeeded his brother as President of the Commission dealing with the Land Question.

[383] Two of the daughters, Ethel and Sara both married and had families. Their husbands were respectively the 3rd Baron Raglan and Major Charles Skinner.

Sillery, had two sons, Guy and Cecil (d.1945 unmarried) and two daughters Iris and Diana, who both married and had families[384]. Guy's wife was Irene Greig and they had one son David and three daughters, Evelyn, Patricia and Judith[385]. Guy was wounded in the First World War but survived. He died in 1960.

Edward, the 8th Earl was a J.P. for Carlow and Kilkenny and was a Deputy Lieutenant for Kilkenny and High Sheriff of Carlow. His father made over the Bessborough property to him in 1895 after Frederick's death. Edward, the first of the family to go into business, was also a very distinguished Civil Servant being Secretary to both the Lord of the Treasury in the early 1880s and to the Speaker of the House until 1895. He was married to Blanche a daughter of Sir John Guest. They had three sons and three daughters Olwen, Helena and Gweneth[386]. Only two of the sons were married. The 3rd son, Bertie a barrister, was wounded in the First World War and although married, had no family. The eldest of the three sons, Vere Brabazon, went on to become the 9th Earl in 1920 when his father died. The second son, Cyril was a highly decorated Army Officer and was ADC to His Royal Highness the Duke of Connaught. He served in both the Boer War and the First World War. He lost his life in that war in 1915. Cyril was married to Rita, the daughter of Lt. Col. Moutifort Longfield and they had one son, Arthur, who became the 11th Earl.

Edward the 8th Earl started a pack of harriers at Bessborough for the amusement of his sons. They hunted all around the area adjoining Bessborough. When the Waterford hunt finished up towards the close of the century the pack was converted to one of fox hounds. Members of the hunt included Captain Congreve, John Power of Mount Richard, Rev. Fr. Murphy, Mr. Stafford and many more.[387]

One night in November of 1920, while staying at Bessborough, the 8th Earl was awakened by raiders searching for arms. The leader of the raiders excused his presence in the bedroom in the middle of the night by saying 'Times have changed'. The Earl, a month later, was addressing a company meeting in Birmingham and had

---

[384] Their husbands were Thomas Mitchell and William Haslam. One of the Haslams – Ralph- married Judith the daughter of the 4th Baron Oranmore and Browne.

[385] The three ladies married David Dekker (U.S. citizen), John Cummins and Kenneth Ungermann (U.S. citizen). All three have families.

[386] Olwen married the 3rd Baron Oranmore and Browne, Helena's husband was John Congreve from Waterford and Gweneth was married twice. Her first husband was the Hon. Windham Baring and her second husband was Colonel Ralph Cavendish. The ladies had families and Gweneth had two.

[387] *The Ponsonby Family* by Major General Sir John Ponsonby.

just used the story of the raider to illustrate the necessity of adapting to changing circumstances when fell down dead.[388] He was succeeded by his eldest son Vere.

Vere Brabazon Ponsonby, the 9th Earl of Bessborough, who was born in 1880 and educated at Cambridge, went on to become a very highly decorated member of the establishment. He held very important posts in the Government, being Governor General of Canada and Commander in Chief of its forces. Among his many decorations he was made a member of the Russian Order of St. Anne, the Order of Leopold of Belgium and the Order of St. Maurice and St. Lazarus of Italy. He was honoured with the Grand Cross of the Legion on Honour. His wife, Roberte, a J.P., was also a highly decorated lady. She was the only daughter of Baron Du Neuflize from Paris. They had three sons and one daughter, Moyra. She married Sir Denis Browne and led a very active life, holding amongst other prestigious posts the Chairmanship of the Victoria League, the Presidency of the Royal College of Nursing and the National Chairmanship of the Support Group Research into Ageing[389]. The two younger sons died prematurely – Desmond when he was only ten and George[390] who died aged twenty as a result of an accident in Germany where he was serving as an Army officer. The eldest son, Frederick Ponsonby, became the 10th Earl in 1956 following the death of his father.

Frederick, the 10th Earl of Bessborough, glittered almost as much as his father and held many prestigious posts. He served in various capacities during the Second World War, in France and North Africa and was involved in the Atlantic Treaty Organization. His wife was an American artist, Mary Munn. They had one daughter, Charlotte who married Yanni Petsopolous[391].

Frederick died in 1993 and was succeeded by his cousin, Arthur Mountifort Ponsonby who became the 11th Earl. Arthur was educated at Harrow and Cambridge and served in the Army during the Second World War as a Captain. He was married three times and had children by his first wife, Patricia Minnigerode from the U.S. and by his third wife, Madeleine Grand the daughter of Major General Grand of Delaford Manor.

Arthur had a son and a daughter by his first marriage. The son of his first marriage is Myles Ponsonby, Viscount Duncannon, who, like his father was educated at Harrow and Cambridge. He is married to Alison Storey and they have

---

[388] *The Ponsonby Family* by Major General Sir John Ponsonby.
[389] She had one son, Desmond and one daughter, Rosemary. Desmond, an Eton and Oxford old boy, became a prominent and successful barrister. He is married to Jennifer Wilmore and they have two daughters Natasha and Harriet. Rosemary married Count Franco Lanza from Italy and they have twin sons Aleramo and Riccardo (born in 1979)
[390] King George V was his baptismal sponsor.
[391] Charlotte and Yanni have two sons Alexis and Eric.

two sons Frederick and Henry and one daughter Chloe. The daughter of the first marriage is Sarah. Lady Sarah is a painter and sculptress.

    By his third wife, Arthur had two sons, Matthew and Charles. Matthew is married to Jamilie Searle and they have a son Douglas.

Power of Kilfane

The story of the Powers of Kilfane is quite extraordinary as the founding father of the Kilfane Powers, John, later knighted as Sir John Power, was what might be described as the Saint Hubert of Kilkenny Hunting, while his brother Richard was the inspirational light that led to the founding of the Kilkenny Theatre. These brothers blazoned a trail in their respective fields, that still to this day, lights the way for many Kilkenny rural and urban dwellers. The traditions they nurtured and to which they devoted a great amount of time may have resulted in the love of Kilkenny people for the sport of hunting and the pastime of amateur dramatics, as evidenced today by the existence in the city of a vibrant theatrical company named Barnstorm and the Watergate Theatre.

This particular Power family is an offshoot of the great family of Le Paor from Waterford[392]. They settled in Tipperary and the first of that family to rise to prominence was John Power of Clonmel, who was the father of Ambrose Power of Barrettstown[393], Co. Tipperary and Richard and John of Tullamine, also in Tipperary. Richard, who never married, became a very important Government official - a Baron of the Exchequer. He died in 1794 and his considerable fortune passed to his nephews. John of Tullamine Castle, as a younger son, joined the Army and served with Clive in India, where he took part in the Battle of Plessy, the most decisive of the campaign. He was A.D.C. to General Clive. His wife was Jane Newman from Co. Cork and they had two sons John and Richard. These were the two men who settled in Co. Kilkenny.

Prior to his arrival in Co. Kilkenny, John Power was a noted sportsman whose passion was hunting. John is reputed to have settled first at Knocktopher 'with horse, hound, horn and hunting gear'. Then he won the hand of the heiress Harriet Bushe and moved into Kilfane. Colonel John Bushe, the first of his family in Kilfane, came to Ireland with Cromwell's Army and was rewarded for his services with a grant of land. The dispossessed owners of Kilfane were the Anglo Norman family of Cantwell, descendants of the famous Cantwell Fada, whose larger than life effigy gave rise to the soubriquet 'the Long Man of Kilfane'.

Colonel John Bushe was the father of Arthur Bushe M.P. and Amyas who was attainted by James II in 1689, but survived in Kilfane. Amyas was the great great grandfather of Charles Kendal Bushe the most famous man of the family[394]. Charles was a talented politician, a gifted orator and his brother-in-law was Henry Grattan. Charles's sister Harriet married John Power who became the first baronet, Sir John Power of Kilfane, when he was knighted in 1836. He was known locally

---

[392] The first Le Paor in Ireland was Robert who was governor of Ireland with Hugh de Lacy in 1171. They acquired a barony in Waterford where they established themselves at Curraghmore.

[393] Ambrose Power was a magistrate. In 1776 he was murdered by Whiteboys. His brother Richard, a Baron of the Exchequer had heard some Whiteboy trials in Clonmel. Ambrose had arrested a William Mackey, a Whiteboy from Fethard. Following the murder over sixty leading figures in Tipperary pledged to suppress the Whiteboys. Two Whiteboys were convicted for that murder and were executed on a temporary Gallows opposite Clonmel gaol.

[394] Another noted man in the family was Gervase Parker Bushe, Charles's father. He was a political ally and friend of Henry Flood. When Flood fought James Agar of Callan in a duel, Gervase acted as Flood's second. Gervase was married to a sister of Henry Grattan, so becoming involved in politics must have been a necessity.

as Captain Power, having been a captain of the yeomanry in Kilkenny prior to and during the rebellion of 1798.

After his wedding in 1797, having taken possession of Kilfane, Captain Power immediately extended and renovated the house. He began many improvements to his demesne and new houses were built for the tenants. In 1800 he was appointed as the first chairman of the Thomastown Farming Society. An annual show was held and prizes were awarded for excellence in all areas of farming. As the rebellion of 1798 scarcely touched Co. Kilkenny (apart from the brief incursion of the Wexford insurgents into Castlecomer) life went on as usual in areas like Kilfane.

According to Sir Hercules Langrishe in 'Records of Kilkenny hunt' it was Sir Wheeler Cuffe who persuaded Power to settle in Kilkenny and to try and hunt it in the Leicestershire fashion. Power did just that, buying the most valuable dogs and having on his doorstep some of the most pleasant land in the world. Miss Muriel Bowen wrote that Power said 'he found the country so unenclosed he could ride from the Walsh mountains to Waterford bridge without having to jump a single fence!' He planted fox coverts and had makeshift kennels in various places so that the dogs had never too far to travel after a day's hunting. His pack was described as a 'superlatively bred pack going back to Merkin, a kind of Master McGrath foxhound, regarded as the fastest in her day.'[395]

Maureen Hegarty in her fine article in the Old Kilkenny Review goes on to say 'He was above all a sportsman and not a butcher. Once in Clara when a vixen rose to the dogs he ordered the opening of all the earths to give her a chance to escape. One run lasted five hours and a half, only four huntsmen being left for the kill. Two of the horses died on the spot. Sir John's 'Barley Corn' was later sold to the Marquis of Waterford and renamed 'Sir John' under which title it came second in the Aintree Grand National of 1841.'

According to Caroline Corballis in her excellent book about Hunting in Co. Kilkenny 'Power's contribution to Kilkenny hunting was enormous and had lasting effects. Coverts he planted are still drawn by the hunt he founded. He supervised their planting and enclosure. He presided over the evolution of the Hunt from being a small pack to becoming an important county institution. So much so that on one occasion Sir John was excused by a grand jury from attendance on the grounds that he had "other business" He was dressed in his hunting Jacket.

In his younger days he hunted over a vast area from Coollattin in Co. Wicklow to Durrow in Co. Laois drawing the last vestiges of the forests. He called the meetings for daybreak and sometimes went there the night before, sheltering

---

[395] Maureen Hegarty in *Old Kilkenny Review* 1974

under the lee of a house until day dawned. As time progressed he confined himself to hunting in the county.[396]

He is remembered in folklore also. The best remembered story is that of the Devil's visit as recounted by a Gowran schoolgirl in 1934. The story is broadly similar to that of the Devil's visit to Loftus Hall in Co.Wexford. A stranger joined the hunt and Power with his customary generosity gave him a warm welcome and invited him back to Kilfane to be entertained with other guests. The stranger proved to be most affable man. After dinner the men sat down to card game and during the course of the game someone dropped a card and on bending down beheld the cloven hoof. With that the stranger, the Devil, vanished up through the roof which was subsequently found to be badly burnt.[397]

Local tradesmen and labourers found welcome employment on the estate. Extensive tree planting and the construction of gorses, earths and fox coverts were undertaken. Captain Power directed that patches of natural gorse in wild places should be used and enclosed. His workmen planted areas such as Castlewarren, Bishopslough, Cloghala, Dunbell and Knockroe. At the close of the 18th century and for some years after, his was the only established pack of county foxhounds in Ireland so he was practically free to hunt where he pleased, going as far as Tullow in County Carlow, Coollattin in County Wicklow, parts of Wexford and as far at Durrow Wood in County Laois[398].

Captain Power established the Club in Rice's Hotel in Kilkenny city and ever since it has been known as The Clubhouse Hotel. In his own inimitable way the Captain brought the hounds to town for the Theatre Festival and ordered that they be cared for with no expenses spared. Jollity and mirth were the order of the day on the biannual excursions to the city. Carousing and socializing characterized the dinners establishing good fellowship among the huntsmen and from time to time reckless wagers were laid. On one occasion Lord Waterford's horse was challenged to jump the dining room table and did so with consummate ease!

Sir John Power was a close friend of Daniel O Connell who complimented him by saying 'no man has seen Ireland who has not seen John Power.'

Between 1802 and 1819 a private theatre, known as The Athenaeum and located in The Parade, enjoyed great success. Founded by Richard and John Power of Kilfane, with the help of Kilkenny neighbours such as the Floods, Langrishes and Bryans, it took its inspiration from the strong 19th century tradition of country house amateur theatricals. There were other motivational factors, too, which moved the

---

[396] Caroline Corballis *Hunting in Co. Kilkenny*.
[397] Ibid.
[398] *Old Kilkenny Review*

Powers and their friends to commence this innovation. After the Act of Union Dublin ceased to be the great social centre that it had been in the halcyon days of the Volunteers. The entire social scene moved to London.

The Club House Hotel

    The Kilkenny gentlemen had other ideas and it was to that end that they started the Private Theatre and initiated their bi-annual seasons of socializing that included the theatre, hunting, balls and parties. Many families travelled from long distances to attend including some of the glitterati from Dublin. Audiences were treated to prologues that on occasion sang the praises of the participants and sometimes the city as in the following example.

> "This town shall still remain our island's boast,
> Nor mourn one glory set, one laurel lost . . .
> Here Berkeley, Congreve, Swift in days of yore
> Lisped the first accents of their classic lore,
> Here Bushe, here Flood were born, here Grattan planned
> In early youth the welfare of the land".

These words, penned by Robert Langrishe, were originally heard by an audience that included no fewer than seventeen peers and peeresses. Mr. and Mrs. Edgeworth and Maria, author of 'The Absentee' and 'Castle Rackrent' were also present. The actors in the plays were mainly young gentlemen from the area while the actresses were brought in from London. Music was supplied by the Theatre Royal Orchestra from Dublin.

One of the visiting actors was Thomas Moore, best known as the composer of Moore's Melodies, and it was he who inspired Kilkenny writer John Banim[399] to embark on his successful literary career. Other well known names in these productions included Rothe, Tighe, Bushe and Butler.

Richard Power was the driving force behind the productions but illness forced him to go to the continent for the sake of his health. During his enforced absence of two years the theatre struggled but on his return he again took up the baton. Thomas Moore paid him a fine compliment in one of his epilogues when he recited as follows:-

"Wits at his request are changed to fools
And dull Jogs learn to jest;
Soldiers for him good trembling cowards make
And beaux turned clowns look ugly for his sake."

Sir John, too, had a flair for the theatrical. One of the visiting actresses, a Miss O'Neill fell in love with Mr. Becher, a local member of the gentry. They decided to get married quietly and made arrangements with a clergyman for a quiet wedding at Kilfane church. The Powers got wind of the wedding and it turned out anything but quiet. Sir John arrived blowing the horn, with all his huntsmen and the theatrical people all arrived wearing the most outlandish costumes they could find. The bride and groom soon got into the spirit of the occasion and their wedding was most memorable.

Sir John Power and Harriet had six sons and two daughters Mary and Frances. Mary and Frances both married suitable matches – Mary's husband was William Burton of Burton Hall, Co. Carlow and Frances married John Power, M.P., of Gurteen, Co. Waterford.

The eldest of the six sons was John who became Sir John Power 2nd baronet of Kilfane in 1844 the year his father died. Four of the other sons all found employment in the service of the Empire in India, and the Windward Isles in the

---

[399] The Banim brothers were early 19th century literary men. John and Michael both wrote plays and novels. Their best known works were *The O'Hara Tales* (a series of novels) and John's play *Damon & Pythias* which was produced in Covent Garden.

case of George, a Government official on St. Vincent[400]. The other three sons in the service were Richard[401], a Captain, Gervase[402] a Lt. Colonel and Henry[403] a Colonel.

The Residency at Lucknow

Ambrose was the son who entered the Church and became Venerable Archdeacon of Lismore. He inherited Barrettstown, in Tipperary, from a cousin. He married Susan Thacker from Co. Laois and they had four sons and three daughters[404]. Three of his sons married and had families. They were Ambrose, George and Robert Henry.

Sir John Power, the 2nd Baronet of Kilfane, who succeeded his father in 1844, was, if anything, even more enthusiastic about hunting than his celebrated father. Unfortunately he was quite short sighted but ingeniously he devised a

---

[400] His only son, William, a Captain in the Army was severely wounded during the siege of the Residency at Lucknow and died later from his wounds. Lucknow was the scene of many dramatic events during the 1857 Indian uprising. British residents were besieged in the Residency for many months before finally being rescued. The ruins of the Residency have been maintained exactly as when the siege ended. George was married twice and had two daughters by his second wife Catherine Prendergast. One of the daughters, Georgina, married Robert Stubber of Co. Laois.
[401] Died unmarried in India.
[402] Gervase was married but both he and his wife died within six years of the marriage. They had children.
[403] Henry's wife was Anne Prendergast and they had two sons and a daughter. Neither of the sons married and the daughter Heidee married a Colonel Fry.
[404] The three daughters were Rebecca, Mary and Susan and their respective husbands were Leeson-Marshall from Co. Kerry, Villiers-Stuart (Co. Waterford) and Bellingham (Co. Louth). Henry Windsor Villiers-Stuart was the author of a number of books including - *Nile Gleanings* 1879, *Egypt after the War* 1883, *Funeral Tent of an Egyptian Queen* 1882, *Adventures amongst the Equatorial Forests* and *Rivers of South America* 1891

hunting cap with a lens attached to the peak so as to enable him to undertake the rigours of the chase. His enthusiasm was legendary. On one occasion he pursued a fox for a distance of over twelve miles as far as the Suir. The fox jumped into the river and swam across. The doughty Sir John, who had far outstripped his companions and was now alone, except for his horse and his dogs, promptly seized a boat which was tied up nearby. He loaded a half dozen or so of the hounds, crossed the river and continued the chase on foot.

Sir John Power (courtesy Lady Langrishe)

The 8th Duke of Beaufort, Henry Somerset, who had been stationed for a time in Kilkenny was quoted as saying that he never had such sport as when he hunted in Kilkenny 'for Johnny Power had a first rate pack of hounds'. Such was Sir John's enthusiasm that it was during his term as Master that ladies were allowed to hunt for the first time. The first three ladies ever to hunt (in Kilkenny at any rate) were Miss Langrishe of Knocktopher, Miss Smithwick of Kilcreene and the Duchess of Beaufort.

During the famine of 1845-47 Sir John was appointed chairman of the Thomastown relief committee and soup kitchens were set up to help feed the poor. While the effects of the famine were generally not bad in Co. Kilkenny, two people from the Kilfane area were said to have died from hunger[405]. Living conditions for the poor were wretched even prior to the famine according to H.D. Inglis[406], an English traveler in the area in 1834. He saw women begging for potatoes and gathering sticks for fuel by the roadside[407]. According to Walter Walsh, a local historian, the Kilfane demesne was off limits to the local people and one Mark Seigne from Stoneen was transported to Van Dieman's Land for killing a hare in the Deerpark. Sir John II resigned his post as master of the Hunt in 1850 but continued as a member and participant until his death in 1873. The famine had a huge impact on the Hunt, which fell into decline for a number of years.

In addition to his passion for hunting Sir John was noted as one of the men who helped save the Irish wolfhound from extinction. In the period after the famine it was Sir John who prompted Captain Graham, his friend to gather all the specimens available and revitalise the breed.

Sir John, the 2nd baronet married Frances Wade of Clonabraney, Co. Meath in 1835 and they had five sons and one daughter, Augusta, who married Sir Willoughby Francis Wade from Birmingham in 1880.

Sir John's sons were, John, who died at the age of six, Richard Crampton, Adam Clayton, George and William le Poer. Richard Crampton was the only one of the sons to have a family as neither Adam Clayton nor George married. While William le Poer did marry he had no family either. Adam Clayton and George survived to become the 6th and 7th baronets respectively.

Sir Richard Crampton Power was a J.P., High Sheriff and Deputy Lieutenant for the county. He was born in 1843. He married an heiress, Florence Elliott in 1869. Four years later his father Sir John died and Sir Richard became the 3rd baronet. Richard and Florence had two sons and two daughters May and Vera.

The eldest son, John Elliott, a J.P. and D.L. for the county and High Sheriff in 1898 was born in 1870. He became an Army officer, rising to the rank of Captain. He succeeded his father as the 4th baronet in 1892. He was killed in action at Lindley in South Africa in 1900. *The Irish Times* of January 25th 1900 reported that 'the

---

[405] Walter Walsh in an article about Kilfane on the Internet.

[406] HD Inglis, a well known 19th century travel writer was regarded as 'a hostile writer' on Ireland.

[407] This was not really an unusual thing as the only means of lighting fires at the time was by using sticks for kindling. As late as 1950 this writer saw women in Co. Wexford gathering 'brosna' for the same purpose. The 'brosna' was a collection of sticks tied with a rope and carried on the back. And there was never a shortage of beggars - even today!

Power of Kilfane

Kilkenny meet was at Kilfane, residence of Sir John Elliott Power 4th Baronet, who was out hunting for the last time before joining his regiment, the Imperial Yeomanry, en route for South Africa. Mrs. Langrishe had made an appeal to the Hunt whose numbers had been greatly reduced by war for funds to equip a bed at the Base hospital'. Sir John was only 23 when he died.

Sir John Elliott's brother, Elliott Derrick succeeded to the estate and title. He became Sir Elliott Derrick Power the 5th baronet. Like his brother he served in the armed forces and became a Captain before he too met his death, not on the battlefields of South Africa, but as a result of a disease he contracted there in 1902.

As Sir Derrick had no brother the title went to his uncles Adam Clayton Power and George who became the 6th and 7th baronets respectively. George was survived by his sister May Beatrice Wilmot who moved out of the mansion and went to live in a cottage on the estate. She was almost a recluse and survived by selling off pictures and items of value. She died in 1966.

May Beatrice was considered to be a kind and generous sponsor of the Kilfane Handball Club and it was her money that paid for the erection of the local alley. When approached by some members of the founding group Miss Power was most enthusiastic and gave her consent to have the alley erected on lands that belonged to her. The ball alley was erected in the very early years of the 20th century and over years prior to her death May Beatrice continued to give her financial and moral support to the venture. When the handball alley was renovated, repaired and extended in 1932 it was Miss Power who contributed most. She was present at the official opening in that year when the ceremony was performed by Canon Drennan P.P. of Tullaherin.

The Power arms consist of a gold shield with two foxes heads and on the second part of the field three escallops. The crest is a Stag's head. The motto is Pro Patria Semper.

Smithwick of Kilcreene

Kilcreene House, the home of the Smithwick family for many generations and now a hospital, in Kilkenny, was first built, according to Peter Smithwick, in 1660. The lands of Kilcreene were originally owned by the Rothe family and then after the Cromwellian War they were acquired by Sir Henry Bayley Meredith[408]. The Smithwick family bought the lands from the Merediths.

Kilcreene Lodge was built on lands in the possession of Richard Cole. He got a lease of the land from the Ormondes - a portion of St. Francis Abbey Brewery. According to Walter Smithwick, Peter's father, the house was a Miller's house as there was a linen bleach there and the remains of a retting pond could still be seen not more than four hundred yards from the property. John Smithwick, the son of Edmond Smithwick (d.1876) was the first of the family to live at Kilcreene Lodge in 1861 after his marriage to Christina Devereux, whose father owned a distillery in Bishopswater in Co. Wexford. They spent considerable money on the house and

---

[408] He was married to one of the Butlers of Lanesborough – *Lodge.s Peerage of Ireland*

grounds. A very fine chandelier was purchased from Baccaret, France and installed in an extension to the house built in 1884. In 1871 a lake with a waterfall and additional features was formed from a stream that ran through the property. These works included installing a system of running water and Kilcreene Lodge was the first house in Kilkenny to have a bathroom with running water.

Kilcreene Lodge (Courtesy College Books)

Walter told a quaint family anecdote concerning John William and Christina. Shortly after their marriage they were invited to dinner at Jenkinstown by George Bryan. However en route the wheels of the carriage gave a lot of trouble and they arrived late. George Bryan was not amused.

According to family tradition the Smithwicks originated in Hertfordshire. Walter Smithwick, who gave a talk to the Kilkenny Archaeological Society, mentioned the fact that he went to the parish church there a few years prior to his talk and found that all references to the Smithwick family ceased there before the end of the 16th century.

In 1572 William Camden, the Clarenceux King of Arms conducted the heraldic visitation of Hertfordshire. He recorded that Robert Smithwick of Abbot's Langley was a great grandson of Richard Smithwick of Cheshire 'a younger son' and confirmed his coat of arms, adding a crest.[409] Robert's father had initially moved to London and Robert himself married a lady from Abbot's Langley and in her right was deemed to be the patron of the living and the Lord of the Manor of Sarat and

---

[409] Peter Smithwick – family historian.

the Hyde[410]. Robert's son, also Robert, moved to Ireland sometime after 1624, following the death of his wife. He became the business agent of Richard Boyle the 1st Earl of Cork. His name is recorded as being present at the funeral of the Earl's daughter, Lady Digby. This was one of the last funerals in Ireland marshalled formally by heralds.

Robert's son, Henry, who was born in 1600 found a career in the Army and fought on the Parliamentary side in the Civil War of 1641-49. He is the Captain Smithwick mentioned in Hore's History of County Wexford as the shadowy emissary sent by Lord Inchiquin, a Royalist, who was leaning towards the Parliamentarians, in an attempt to persuade Lord Esmonde, the governor of the fort of Duncannon to go over to the Parliamentarian also. Captain Henry was sent to the fort on two occasions in 1644 but to no avail. In the event Lord Esmonde,[411] who was quite elderly at the time died two years later. After the Cromwellian wars Captain Henry was rewarded with grants of land in Carlow, Kilkenny and Tipperary and was promoted to the rank of Lt. Colonel.[412] Despite his alignment with the Cromwellians he served in several official posts, after the restoration, such as collector of taxes and commissioner investigating claims.[413] He lived at various times at Shandrome, Co. Cork and at Ballydarton, Co. Carlow. His son, Henry, was an officer in Colonel Coote's regiment in the Williamite wars and removed King James's Royal Arms from the Tholsel in Kilkenny and replaced them with those of King William.

John Smithwick was Henry's son and grandson of Lt. Col. Henry Smithwick. Henry's wife, according to Lodge, was Mary Meredith, the daughter of Sir Faithfull Fortescue of Dromiskyn, Co. Louth (and granddaughter of the 1st Viscount Moore of Drogheda).[414] Lt. Col. Henry also had a brother William of Ardaragh Castle, Castlecomer, Co. Kilkenny a J.P. and High Sheriff in 1691 and Colonel in the Army.

John was married twice. His first wife was Jane Dunphy and his second wife was Mary Grace of Lazybush and it is from Mary that the Smithwick family of Kilkenny descended. It would seem that the Smithwicks became Catholic from that time onwards, though it is not known if John himself ever embraced that faith.

---

[410] Ibid.
[411] Ironically Lord Esmonde's son, Sir Thomas who had been reared as a Catholic in Connaught by his O'Flaherty mother, sided with the Confederates. See the account of the Esmondes in *The Wexford Gentry Vol. 1* by Art Kavanagh and Rory Murphy.
[412] *Notes on the Smithwick family history* by Peter Smithwick.
[413] Ibid.
[414] The Smithwicks later bought lands from the Merediths who owned Kilcreene and other estates near Kilkenny.

He was buried in the churchyard adjacent to St. Canice's Cathedral, thereby starting a tradition that has lasted until modern times.

John had three sons[415] and one of them, the Rev. Edmond Smithwick, Parish Priest of St. Patrick's, Kilkenny, was drowned in 1776[416], in the Nore. The second son, Peter Smithwick married Margaret Murphy and he died three years before the death of the Rev. Edmond. Peter had four children and his eldest son, John, who was only ten years old when his father died was the man who restored the family

---

[415] Burke says he had eight sons of whom Peter of Lazybush was the 7th.
[416] Drowned, in suspicious circumstances, in 1772, according Burke. Peter Smithwick states that the coroner returned a verdict of accidental drowning but the Diocesan archives indicate that he took his own life.

fortunes. He was a very astute businessman and set up a wine importing business and expanded into other luxury goods. In addition to importing he became involved in the export of various foodstuffs. John bought the estate of Lower Grange and other lands near Kilkenny and within his own lifetime became one of the wealthiest men in the county. He had two properties Kilcreene Cottage and Birchfield and was made a freeman of Kilkenny.

John married Catherine Butler of Dangan in 1789. He had six sons and two daughters. John died in 1842 and his widow lived to be 103 years old. The daughters were Margaret who married Harry Devereux, and Mary who married Owen O'Callaghan. Both ladies had families. Three of the sons had no families[417].

One of his younger sons, Paul, married Eleanor Murphy and they had one child, who found a career in the Church also. He was Canon Paul Smithwick, curate of St. Mary's Donnybrook and later Parish Priest of Howth and Baldoyle.

The 3rd son, Peter, a member of the Kilkenny Corporation, was married to Ellen Delaney and they had a daughter Mary. His second wife was Jane Howlett of New Ross but had no other family.

The 6th son, Daniel, of Drakelands House and Kilcreene Cottage[418], was a High Sheriff in 1855. He also, like his brother, was a member of the Kilkenny Corporation. His wife was Ellen Morris and they had three sons, one of whom died unmarried, and three daughters. One of the daughters became a nun, in the Order of the Good Shepherd and another married her cousin Edmond Smithwick.

Daniel's sons were John Francis and Daniel. Both John Francis and Daniel were very active politically in Kilkenny. John Francis was a J.P., Deputy Lieutenant, High Sheriff in 1870 and Mayor of Kilkenny in 1884. He was married to Marian Power the daughter of James Power, J.P., of Eastlands Co. Waterford. Daniel, his brother was High Sheriff of Kilkenny in 1873 and his wife was another Power from Waterford, Frances from Newtown. Both brothers had families. John Francis had three sons but none of them had children. His eldest son was an Army officer and

---

[417] The eldest, Peter, died in infancy, the 4th son, John died when a boy and the 5th son Richard, although married to Margaret Delaney had no family. He was an M.P., a High Sheriff of Kilkenny and a solicitor. As Chairman of the Goresbridge Relief Committee he was very active in supporting the poor during the famine. The Lower Grange Estate was near Goresbridge. Richard was the owner of Birchfield and after his death it passed to John Francis Smithwick.

[418] According to Walter Smithwick John Francis acquired Birchfield after the death of Richard his brother. He left it to his son Richard Hubert who died unmarried in 1924.

served with distinction in both the Boer War and World War I[419]. Daniel had five sons and two daughters[420].

The five sons of Daniel Smithwick were Daniel, Matthew, John, Joseph and William. While some of them were married[421] only Joseph had a family. Joseph's wife was Elizabeth Bowen, a widow, formerly Burden and they had one son Daniel[422] and two daughters, Mary Frances and Marcella, all born after 1940.

The second son of John Smithwick, (died in 1842), was Edmond, who inherited most of the Smithwick fortune and estates and expanded them by buying the St. Francis Abbey Brewery. Edmund, too, was very politically active and was High Sheriff of Kilkenny in 1852 in addition to being appointed a magistrate. He was made a Freeman of the city in 1826 and was one of the first Directors of the National Bank. He was Mayor of the city for a number of years (1843-44 and 1864-65). Like his father before him he was an active supporter of Daniel O'Connell and the family still has the large volume of correspondence from Daniel O'Connell in their possession. In 1847 Edmond and Richard Sullivan[423] set up a soup kitchen at Sullivan's brewery to help relieve the distress being experienced by some country people who flocked to the town for support. Edmund was rebuked by the Dublin Castle officials for overspending on poor relief in his capacity as Chairman of the Board of Guardians.

Edmond was a keen sportsman who often hunted five days a week and ran the Kilcreene Harriers for eight years.[424] He kept the pack of Harriers at his home, Kilcreene House where the gentry and aristocracy of the county were lavishly entertained.

He married an heiress, Ellen Williams of Clonmel and they had three sons and two daughters. Their daughters were Helen and Clare, whose husband was

---

[419] He was James Arnold. His two brothers were Richard Hubert and William.

[420] Neither Frances nor Jane had any families.

[421] Matthew was married to Blanche McNamara from Dublin, John's wife was Mary Byrne from Wicklow and Eileen Fitzgerald from Cappawhite was married to William.

[422] Daniel has two sons Dean and Allan. His wife is Joan Brennan of Newrath.

[423] The Sullivans were a Protestant family who came to Kilkenny about the year 1702, according to Judge Peter Smithwick in his article in the O.K.R. 1964. They were very sympathetic to Catholics and did in fact shield the Bryans of Jenkinstown by assuming ownership of some of their property on a secret trustee basis. The family representative, Daniel Sullivan, fl. 1750-1818, was a Catholic. He was actively involved in the Emancipation movement. The Richard Sullivan mentioned above, his son, was a very influential and wealthy man. He was actively involved in the Repeal movement.

[424] Walter Smithwick in O.K.R. 1960

Michael Kelly a J.P. and D.L from Co. Clare. Edmond's sons were John, Edmond[425] and Daniel O'Connell (born c. 1836) who was the ancestor of a number of modern Smithwicks. The Liberator was god father to Daniel O'Connell Smithwick.

Kilcreene House (courtesy College Books)

Daniel O'Connell Smithwick, of Prospect House, Kilkenny, was married to Louisa Walmesley from Essex and they had two sons and two daughters. Their daughters were Louisa and Florence who married Thomas Levins Moore of Castleknock, Co. Dublin. The two sons were George and Alfred. George (b.1875) was the first of the family to be educated abroad. His alma mater was Downside, a very upmarket public school for Catholics. He married Helen Lowry from Co. Kildare and they had one daughter Georgina[426]. Alfred (b.1879) was also a Downside old boy. He married Emma Warner from the U.S. and they had two sons Patrick[427] and Daniel[428].

The eldest son and heir of John Smithwick, was John William (b.1833). Following the family tradition he was very active in his community. He was a J.P.

---

[425] Edmond, of Kilcreene House, married his cousin Mary. He was a D.L. and a J.P. and High Sheriff of Kilkenny in 1866. They had a son, John Daniel and two daughters, May and Helen. None of the three had a family. Helen was the only one married. Her husband was Augustus Bennett. After John Daniel's death the house reverted back to his cousin.

[426] Georgina's husband is Patrick Sleator from Grangecon, Co. Kildare and they have two daughters Diane and Shirley.

[427] Patrick Smithwick (d. 1973) was educated in the U.S. His wife was Suzanne Whitman and they have one son Alfred and two daughters Susan and Salli. According to Walter, Paddy Smithwick was the leading steeplechase jockey in the U.S. He had a brother Michael, a horse trainer.

[428] Daniel (b.1929) married Dorothy Fred from the U.S. and they have one son Daniel.

a D.L. and High Sheriff of the city in 1860 and the county in 1874. John William as already mentioned carried out extensive works on Kilcreene Lodge where he had a stream dammed to form a lake and a waterfall. Using the waterfall he installed the first electricity generator in Kilkenny. He married Christina Devereux of Bishopswater, Wexford in 1861 and they went to live at Kilcreene Lodge. John died in 1894 while out following the Kilkenny Hunt. They had three sons and one daughter, Mary Teresa[429]. The three sons were Edmond, James and Daniel. Edmond died young and Daniel pursued an Army career. He was a Major in the Worcestershire Regiment and was wounded in World War I. He was mentioned in despatches. He was married to Olive Limerick but had no family. He died in 1942.

James, the second son of John William succeeded as his heir in 1894. James of Kilcreene Lodge was a J.P. and High Sheriff in 1899. He was educated at Beaumont College where he became an adept cricketer. He married Gertrude Boland from Dublin and they had four sons, Francis, Arthur, Harold and Walter. Francis died while only a boy and Arthur although married[430] had no children. Harold who was conferred with an OBE in 1946 served with distinction in World War II. He was later Medical Officer to the Viceroy of India, Lord Irwin and gave medical treatment to Mahatma Gandhi. There is a road named after Harold in Bihar. He subsequently worked in Rhodesia where a road was named after him in Salisbury (now Harare). His wife was Phyllis Pegge from Rhodesia and they had one daughter Marilyn (now deceased). Marilyn's daughter Katharine lives in London.

Walter Smithwick, the youngest son, succeeded as the heir to the family home and the Smithwick empire. He was educated at Weybridge and Trinity College, Dublin and became a solicitor. Walter was the Chairman of Smithwicks in the 1930s and only retired in 1973. His career was most distinguished and he was a member of a number of prestigious clubs. He became a Knight of Malta in 1935. His wife was Eileen Savage from London. They had four sons and two daughters – Ann, a nun in the Order of the Sacred Heart and Judith who lives in Co Meath with her husband G. Donald O'Doherty and her two daughters. The four sons of Walter Smithwick are Peter, Michael, Paul and John all born after 1937.

All four sons were educated at Castleknock College, Dublin, and two of them, Peter and Paul found careers in the legal profession. Michael and John have carved niches for themselves in the commercial sector. Peter, Paul and Michael married.

---

[429] Mary Teresa married Patrick Considine, a J.P and D.L. from Derk, Co. Limerick and had a family.
[430] His wife was Sarah Smithwick from Co.Tipperary.

Paul's wife is Eleanor Donaghy and they have three children.[431] Michael, now a U.S. citizen, married Margaret MacManamy and they have two sons Kevin and Brian and two daughters Maureen and Eileen.

Peter Smithwick admitted a Solicitor in 1958 is now Judge Peter Smithwick, an ex officio Judge of the Circuit Court (1995) and President of the District Court (1990). His has been a most distinguished career. A director of a number of companies and of the family brewery (1964) he was also very active in politics. From 1974 to 1978 he was a Councillor of Kilkenny Borough Council. He was Secretary of the Constituency Executive of Fianna Fail for many years and Director of Elections during that period, while also serving as a member of the National Executive.

Peter became a Knight of Malta in 1962 and is currently Bailiff Grand Cross of Honour and Devotion and President of the Irish Association of that Order since the start of the 2nd Millennium. His wife is Deirdre Cooper from Markree Castle, Co. Sligo. They have two daughters Thalia Mary and Aoife.

The Smithwick arms consist of a gold chevron between 3 laurel leaves and the crest is a bent arm holding a rose.

---

[431] Paul and Eleanor had two other children who died young.

St. George of Freshford

Howard Bligh St. George was a J.P for counties Galway and Dublin and in 1891 he married Evelyn Baker of New York. They lived at Screebe Lodge in Connemara and at Clonsilla Lodge in Dublin. Evelyn St. George was the celebrated Mrs. St. George, who, having become quite friendly with William Orpen, the internationally renowned artist, became his inspiration leading him to paint many portraits of her, which afterwards became quite famous. A full length portrait of Mrs. St. George hung in Straffan House for many years.

Perhaps the most popular and best known man of the St. George family was Shoeshine a member of the Woodsgift branch. He was the man who set up a shoeshine business in Picadilly in 1941 and became a legend in his own lifetime. He continued working the same stand until well into the 1960s when he retired. Shoeshine was married and had a family.

St. George of Freshford

The ancestor of the St. George family, Baldwin, was known as the Companion of the Conqueror and arrived in England in 1066 with William. This man took his name from the town of St. Georges near Limoges in France. He settled at Hatley St. George in Cambridgeshire where the original house is still standing.[432]

The Irish branch of the family descended from Sir Richard of Hatley St. George a direct descendant of Baldwin. Born in the 16th century Sir Richard lived until 1635. He was the Clarenceaux King of Arms.[433] He had five sons. His two eldest sons, William and John were killed fighting against the Irish in the Elizabethan wars. The 3rd son was Sir Henry St.George[434], who held the prestigious post of Garter King of Arms[435] in the court of Charles I. Sir Henry does not appear to have come to Ireland and his descendants, among whom were a number of Garter Kings of Arms, appear to have died out during the 18th century.

Sir George, of Carrickdrumrusk, Co. Leitrim, was the 4th son of Sir Richard St. George. He was also killed in Ireland at Croghan in Co. Offaly. He was married to Catherine the daughter of a Captain Gifford of Castle Jordan in Co. Offaly. Sir George's grandson, also called Sir George, was created a peer in 1715 as Lord St. George. He had no sons and his daughter, Mary, married John Usher an M.P. for Carrick on Shannon. Their son St. George Usher became the owner of the Leitrim/Galway properties and was created a peer in Ireland, in 1763 as *Lord St.George of Hatley St. George in Co. Leitrim*. His daughter married the 2nd Duke of Leinster, a brother of Lord Edward FitzGerald who met his tragic fate in 1798. The St. George family continued in Co. Leitrim until modern times[436].

---

[432] *They came with the Conqueror* – L.G. Pine

[433] The Clarenceux King of Arms was a member of the College of Heraldry and he was responsible for the granting of coats of arms to families who lived south of the river Trent in England. The original application had to be made to the Earl Marshal, and a fee paid. If the Earl Marshal found the application satisfactory (there are no specific criteria), he granted a Warrant authorising the King of Arms to proceed with the designing of arms. After the designing process concluded, the Kings of Arms granted letters patent authorising the grantee to use the arms blazoned therein.

[434] He lived at Hatley St. George where he is buried with members of his family.

[435] The Order of the Garter was open only to those of noble birth or to those whose service to the King so warranted. The Garter King of Arms had specific duties for which he was paid an annual stipend. It was a most prestigious post carrying with it many obligations and responsibilities.

[436] As late as 1872 the local landowners, the St. George family, were granted ownership of the St. George Oyster Fishery in Clarenbridge by the then Inspectors of Irish Fisheries, excluding local people from what they viewed as their heritage. The ensuing 100 years saw many battles including court cases, imprisonments and threatened hunger strikes until BIM,

Hatley St. George, Co. Leitrim

The 5th son was Captain Richard St. George who was born at Hatley St. George in England, in 1590. The Captain was married twice but had no sons with his second wife[437]. His first wife was Anne Pinnock from Co. Roscommon and they had three sons and two daughters. One of the daughters was married to a Major Wood[438]. Major Wood who had no family left his Kilkenny property to his wife's nephew, George, and the estate became known as Woodsgift. The other daughter, Mary, married Thomas Ashe. Mary's son was St. George Ashe the Bishop of Clogher.[439]

---

at the behest of the Government of the day, purchased the fishery in 1981 on behalf of the state.

[437] They had a daughter, Martha who, although married to Joseph Jackson, had no children.
[438] This man might well be the Lieutenant Edward Wood who 'on the certificate of William St. George Esq. J.P. of the county of Cavan, dated 6th November, 1658, (was paid) twenty five pounds for five priests and friars by him apprehended viz. Thomas McKernan, Turlough O'Gowan, Hugh McGeown, and Turlough Fitzsymons, who upon examination confessed themselves to be both priests and friars.' - *Prendergast*
[7] A Topographical Dictionary of Ireland (1837)
[439] He was a Provost of Trinity College and was a Tutor to Dean Swift. He was considered as one of the foremost intellectuals of his day. He went into exile during the Jacobite period of 1689-90 and was attached to Lord Paget who the ambassador of William of Orange in Vienna.

St. George of Freshford

Captain Richard's sons were Captain Arthur of Turrock, Richard who was killed at the siege of Galway in 1652 and Henry St. George of Athlone. Captain Arthur was known as 'The Black Captain' and according to the family historian, Richard St. George, he was something of a wild type. His impetuosity led to his joining the Cromwellians and fighting for that cause during the ensuing wars. Like Captain Arthur his brother, Henry, pursued a career in the Army, but unlike 'the Black Captain' who supported the Parliamentarians Henry sided with the Royalists and got a commission in the Army of Charles II. It is not unlikely that he became quite friendly with the Duke of Ormonde who became the most powerful man in Ireland after the Restoration. In any event Henry was granted the estate of Cloghmantagh, or Clomanto, a parish in the barony of Cranagh, county of Kilkenny. The estate was not far from Freshford, and in the 19th century comprised 3597 statute acres of which 480 acres were mountain and woodland. The whole of Cloghmantagh had been occupied continuously since the 13th century by Anglo Normans. Originally Fitzpatrick or Phelan lands, a family of Fanyn[440] took possession in the early days of the conquest, as vassals of the Marshall overlords. At some time later the Shortalls came into possession of the property. This was an area of significant military importance in ancient times and the Shorthalls built several castles to defend the pass from Munster into Leinster. Thomas Shortall, a Catholic, was partly dispossessed by the Cromwellians[441]. Captain Arthur, 'the Black Captain' was the man who took possession and the lands were later granted to his brother Henry, the Royalist. Captain Arthur forced the removal of the

---

[440] *Kilkenny History & Society* – ed. William Nolan

[441] In 1653, he lost his estate, which consisted of the townlands of Ballylarkin, Adamstown, Kyle [ballynamoe], Kilrush, Killashoolan, Ballykirin (now Frankford), Balleefe, Sart (part of), Ballyroe-Shortall, Ballynolan, Bawnanooagh or Three Castles, Laugh, Ballycarran, Brownstown, and Nicholastown. A certificate for transplantation to Connaught was signed for him on Dec. 23rd, 1653. In the *Gentleman's Magazine* for the year 1762, occurs the following interesting obituary notice: "Aug. 9th - Died at Landrecy in France, Mr. Thomas Shortall, a native of Kilkenny, formerly Lieut. Colonel in the regiment of Clark, Irish, aged 104 years 7 months and 5 days. The day before his death he ate and drank with his friends as usual, and had no ailment but old age. He was a captain of foot at the siege of Limerick in 1691, and from thence went over to France amongst the relicks of the Irish army. After various gradations in the military life, he was made Lieut. Col. the 10th of June, 1745, and withdrew from the service, the 31st Jan., 1747. He was the only survivor of above 30,000 Irish who went over to France after the capitulation of Limerick, and of upwards of 100,000 who have gone thither since. As there was found among the deceased veteran's papers a 'schedule of his estate, on which were several fine seats,' it may be concluded that he belonged to the house of Ballylarkin, which was far the most important branch of the Shortall family in Co. Kilkenny."

Shortalls who went to live in a Castle[442] on part of their old lands and whose descendants still live there today. Captain Arthur died unmarried in 1702.

The early St. Georges probably lived in the tower house adjacent to Kilrush House and in the Tower House at Balief. In later times the principal seats were Woodsgift and Kilrush House, both belonging to the St. George family.

The St. Georges of Kilrush

Henry married Anne Hatfield of Dublin. They had four sons, two of whom had legitimate families. The sons were Richard, Henry, Arthur and George. Richard was an Army officer who rose to the rank of Lieutenant General and appears to have lived mostly in Dublin, where he died in 1755 at his house 8 Henrietta St.[443] He was married to Elizabeth Coote, the daughter of Lord Coote of Colooney, but they had no family. Richard had his portrait painted by Bindon.

Henry who was Sheriff of Roscommon in 1717 died unmarried in 1723. Arthur the 3rd son was the ancestor of the Kilrush St. Georges. Arthur became a parson and was made Dean of Ross. His wife was Lady Jane Molyneaux and they had six sons and one daughter, Catherine, who married Clement Wolseley. It may well have been Arthur who built Kilrush House. William Robertson, who was the pupil of John Nash, was the architect. The six sons of Arthur and Lady Jane were Richard, Thomas, Capel, Arthur, Howard and Henry. Richard was married to Sarah Handcock and they had a son Richard who sold Kilrush to his uncle Howard. Richard senior died c. 1755 and his son Richard junior died unmarried in 1840.

Thomas was an M.P. for Clogher and his wife was the Hon. Lucinda Acheson. Thomas and Lucinda had a large family, one of whom, Acheson St. George, was the ancestor of the St. Georges of Wood Park, Co. Armagh. Another of their sons, William, a Lieutenant in the Royal Navy was killed at the Battle of Trafalgar in 1805. Capel, a Captain in the Army died unmarried. Howard, a Doctor of Divinity who purchased the Kilrush estate from his nephew was married to Mary Lucas and they continued the Kilrush line. Rev. Henry the youngest son of Rev. Arthur St. George had three sons and three daughters but none of the sons had children except the eldest, another Rev. Henry, who had a son Oliver who appears to have died young. Two of the sons went to live in Co. Carlow, Nelson at Altamont and William (d.1871) at Kildavin.

---

[442] This Castle or Tower House is still standing today.
[443] Richard purchased the house from Nathaniel Clements the architect. Richard was reputed to have had an illegitimate daughter.

Richard the son of Henry St.George and Anne Hatfield
(courtesy Richard St. George)

A local historian writing about Altamont said 'the main bulk of the house (Altamont) was considerably altered sometime between 1740 and 1750. At that time, the front of the house faced towards the Slaney River and Wicklow mountains. The road to the estate initially ran from Carrigslaney, behind the lake, and up to Kilbride. Upon construction of a new road from Carrigslaney to Kilbride circa 1740, the St. George family turned the house back-to-front by breaching the hall wall in the (then) back of the house and building on the porch with its decorative fanlight and the bow-ended wing consisting of dining room, smoking room, two bedrooms and a lift room. They also added elegant plaster work, rebuilt the staircase, enlarged the windows and altered the house in other ways. A new front and back avenue was made in a semi-circle enclosing the park and very handsome entrance gates erected. It was about this time that lines of magnificent beech trees were planted along the front avenue, roadside and Nun's Walk, and specimen limes, beeches and chestnuts planted in the park.' It would seem from the above that the St. George family was in possession of the Altamont property for almost one hundred years as Nelson probably went to live there in the early decades of the 19th century.

The Rev. Howard D.D. and his wife Mary Lucas had four sons, Arthur John of Kilrush House (d.1853) Henry Lucas, Rector of Dromore (d. 1872), Thomas Belmore, a Barrister, and Richard Quintus, Vicar of Crossmolina (d.1877). The four men were married and had extended families. Arthur John's son, Howard John, an Army officer, succeeded to the estates in Kilrush as did his son Arthur. Henry Lucas, the Rector of Dromore and Richard Quintus, the Vicar of Crossmolina, married Kilkenny ladies, Elizabeth Warren of Lodge Park and Henrietta Langrishe, the daughters of Mr. Edward Warren and Sir Robert Langrishe, respectively.

Howard John, an Army officer, had two other sons, Howard Cecil and John Edward in addition to Arthur and five daughters. None of the daughters appear to have married. The only son to marry was John Edward. This talented man was a Resident Magistrate from 1908 onwards and was Private Secretary in Ireland to Neville Chamberlain. John Edward's wife was Elizabeth Kinahan the daughter of George Kinahan of Roebuck Park, Dundrum, Co. Dublin. They had two sons, Howard Edward and Arthur John. Arthur John, an Army officer was killed in action in World War II in 1944. Howard Edward who was born in 1900 was married to Margaret Wotherspoon from Canada and they had one son Richard and one daughter Anna, now Mrs. Scott.[444] Richard of Kilrush and his wife Sally (nee Wilmot), the present owners of Kilrush, have two sons Arthur and Henry.

The St. Georges of Woodsgift

George, of Woodsgift, the 4th son of Henry St. George of Athlone, an M.P. was born in 1682. His wife was Elizabeth Bligh from Co. Meath, the sister of the 1st Earl of Darnley. They had three surviving sons and a daughter who never married. The line was continued by Richard St. George, the second son. Henry the eldest son,

---

[444] The Scots have one son William and two daughters Caroline and Victoria.

who predeceased his father, died a single man and the third son, George, an Army Captain married and had a family[445].

Woodsgift (courtesy College Books)

Richard St. George, of Woodsgift, succeeded his father in 1762 and at that time must have been a man of about forty five or fifty. Two years later he married Sarah Persse, an heiress from Co. Galway. The year after the birth of his eldest son, Richard Bligh, he was created a baronet of Ireland as Sir Richard St. George. They had four other sons and a daughter. Three of those sons married and some of them had children but within a generation or two they had died out in the male line[446]. Hercules Langrishe St. George was a grandson of Sir Richard and of Sir Hercules Langrishe. He was a J.P. and High Sheriff of the county in 1848. After his death he was survived by a daughter who does not appear to have married.

After Sir Richard's death in 1789, Sir Richard Bligh the 2nd Baronet of Woodsgift, succeeded. His wife, whom he married in 1799, was Harriet Kelly the daughter of Rt. Hon. Justice Kelly of Kellyville, Co. Laois. They had three daughters, two of whom married. Sarah's husband was John Dillon and Harriet

---

[445] Richard his younger son was drowned in the St. Lawrence and the elder brother Sir Thomas Bligh St. George a Lieutenant General in the Army, although married to Elizabeth Walker from Co. Wexford had no family.

[446] One of those sons was Robert St. George of Balief Castle. Robert died in 1840 and either his daughter or a niece Rebecca was forced to sell all the household goods from the Castle in 1847 (O.K.R. 1990 pg.56).

married Hugh Eccles of Cronroe. After the death of his first wife, sometime prior to 1807, he married again. His second wife was Bridget Blakeney from Co. Galway. Sir Richard and Bridget had six sons and three daughters. The eldest son was Richard who died in infancy, Theophilus who succeeded Sir Richard, Robert who became the ancestor of an extended family of highly talented and well educated people, William (died young), James Cuffe, the ancestor of numerous gifted descendants and John Henry who never married.

The descendants of Robert, William and James Cuffe will be dealt with at the end of the Chapter.

Theophilus succeeded his father, as Sir Theophilus St. George, the 3rd baronet, in 1851. He married Caroline de Lautour from Hertshire in 1836 and they had two sons and one daughter who married Horatio Seftenberg Ross[447], most probably of Rossie Castle in Scotland. The younger of the two sons died young.

Sir Theophilus resided in Port Natal in South Africa where he was a Resident Magistrate. He was the first commanding officer of the Natal Carbineers, a Royal regiment. After the death of his wife he remarried in 1847 and his second wife was Maria Power from Churchtown, Co.Waterford. Sir Theophilus and Maria had four sons and three daughters. It would appear that the family was domiciled in Pietermaritzburg. Only one of the daughters married. She was Maria the second daughter and her husband was Charles Glyn, a first cousin once removed of Sir Richard Glyn, of Dorset. The sons were John, Arthur (a solicitor who married and had three daughters), Theophilus John (a master of the Supreme Court in Natal) and Charles St. George Power who assumed the name Power.

When Sir Theophilus died in Pietermaritzburg in 1857 he was succeeded by his eldest son, Sir Richard de Lautour St. George the 4th baronet. Like his father he pursued a career in the army and while still a young man attained the rank of Captain in the Bengal Artillery. He was only twenty four years old when he died in India in 1861. He was succeeded in his title and estates by his half brother, John.

Sir John St. George was born in 1851 and was only ten years old when he succeeded. Like his father and grand father he was an army officer. He married Rose the daughter of Sir George Berkley in 1894. They had no children so when Sir John died in 1938 he was succeeded by his brother Theophilus then a man of eighty.

Theophilus the 6th baronet, who spent most of his life in Natal, died in 1943. He had a distinguished career at the bar before being appointed Assistant Master of the Supreme Court of Natal. His wife was Florence Vanderplank from Natal. He

---

[447] Horatio Ross of Rossie Castle was a contemporary of Horatio Seftenberg Ross and most likely a cousin. Horatio Ross was a pioneer photographer whose works are highly valued today.

had five sons and five daughters. Three of the daughters, Anne Rose, Florence and Patricia married and all three had families[448].

Richard and John, the two eldest sons of Theophilus served in the war in South Africa and both fought in the First World War in France. Richard was wounded on two occasions and died in 1923 aged only 31. His brother, John, was killed in action at the Battle of the Somme in 1916.

Sir Robert St. George, the 3rd son of Theophilus, succeeded him in 1943. Sir Robert, the 7th Baronet, was born in 1900. He began his army career as a trooper in the South African Armoured Car Regiment and later joined the R.A.F. He fought in World War II and was captured and held as a P.O.W. for a number of years. After the war he joined the Oblate Order as a Lay Brother. He died in 1983. He was succeeded in the title by his brother Denis.

Rev. Sir Denis St. George, the 8th Baronet, became a priest and worked in South Africa. He died in 1989 and was succeeded by his brother George.

Sir George St. George, the 9th Baronet, began his career as a Lieutenant in the Natal army and fought in World War II. After the war he obtained a post as Deputy Director of Administration in Addington Hospital in Durban. His wife was Mary Sutcliffe of Durban and they have two sons John and Peter and three daughters, Elizabeth, Catherine and Angela.[449]

Peter, the second son, is an investment banker, now living in London. He married Elizabeth Williams of Newport and they have one son William and two daughters Caroline and Alice.

Sir George the 9th Baronet died in 1995 and was succeeded by his eldest son, Sir John St. George the 10th Baronet, a company director, now living in London, who has been married twice. His first wife is Margaret Carter of Mayes Park House, Sussex and they have two daughters, Elinor[450] and Catherine. His second wife is Linda Perry from Glasgow and they have two sons Robert and Benjamin.

---

[448] Anne Rose married William Ogilvie and had a son John Alexander (m. Pamela Brown of Pietermaritzburg) who is father of Marion, Helen, Alison and Clare. Florence's husband was Rudlolph du Preez from the Transvaal and they have two sons Rev. Fr. Christopher and Rev. Fr. David. Patricia's husband was Michael Power and they have two sons and a daughter, Jane (married Gerald Stewart) who has a son Simon and a daughter Kim. One of Patricia's sons Richard, married, and he and his wife Susan Peiser have a son Richard and a daughter Catherine.

[449] Elizabeth's husband was Peter Bailie and they have two sons David and Derek and two daughters Fiona and Linda. Catherine married John Walker and they have one son John and two daughters Jane and Felicity.

[450] Elinor (Mrs. Richard Newbold) is married and has a son Cameron and a daughter Georgia.

The descendants of Robert St. George son of Sir Richard Bligh St. George 2nd Baronet.

Robert St. George the second surviving son of Sir Richard Bligh St. George the 2nd Baronet married Sophia Mahon the daughter of the Dean of Dromore, in 1841 and they had two sons and six daughters. Only two of the daughters had children – Elizabeth who married Charles O'Hara Trench of Clonfert, Co. Galway and Henrietta the youngest, who married Arthur Burdett of Coolfinn in Co. Offaly. Robert's two sons were **Robert James** and **Howard Bligh**.

Robert James, a Trinity College, Dublin graduate, married his cousin Katherine St. George from Tyrone, Co. Galway. They had three sons and three daughters. None of those ladies had any families. Two of the sons, **Richard** the eldest and **Robert Charles** the youngest, married and had families. Richard had only one child, a daughter, Catherine, who was born in 1917. Robert Charles whose wife was Lillian Talmadge from New York had one son also called Robert Charles who was born in 1920. He too married a U.S. citizen, Priscilla Tillerton and they have one son Christopher, born in 1946.

Howard Bligh St. George was a J.P for counties Galway and Dublin and in 1891 he married Evelyn Baker of New York. They lived at Screebe Lodge in Connemara and at Clonsilla Lodge in Dublin. Evelyn was the famous Mrs. St. George, who, having had an affair with Orpen the internationally renowned artist became his inspiration leading him to paint many portraits of her, which afterwards became quite famous. Howard Bligh and Evelyn had three sons and two daughters – Evelyn (b.1897) who married Major Gunsten and had a family, and Vivien (b.1912) who was married three times. Vivien's husbands were Alexander Clarke (with whom she had a family), Dr. William Winch and Charles Graves who was the nephew of Robert Graves the author. Howard Bligh's three sons were George Baker Bligh, Howard Avenal Bligh and Frederick Ferris Bligh. **George Baker Bligh St. George** was educated at Eton and Cambridge and in 1917 he married a U.S. Congresswoman, Katherine Delano from New York. They had a daughter, Priscilla, who married Angier Duke, with whom she has a son Angier St. George. Angier who was born in 1938 married Jeanne Farmer with whom he has two sons George and Benjamin both born in the 1960s. **Howard Avenal Bligh St. George**, an Eton old boy, joined the Army and fought in World War I. He was killed in action in 1914. He was only 20 years old. **Frederick Ferris Bligh St. George**, like his brothers, was educated at Eton and joined the Army where he rose to the rank of Colonel in the Life Guards. He was High Sheriff for Gloucester in 1959. He married Meriel Radcliffe from Hantshire and they had three daughters, Meriel, Diana and Sally.

Meriel had no family but Sally and Diana both had children. Sally's husband is John Alford from Gloucester and Diana is married to Sir George Algernon Earle.

Mrs. Evelyn St. George – nee Baker

The descendants of William Oliver the son of Sir Richard Bligh St. George 2nd Baronet.

William Oliver St. George was born in 1813. He married Sarah Quirk of Woodsgift, Co. Kilkenny. They had eight sons and three daughters. Only the eldest of the daughters, Fanny had a family. Her husband was James Burn of Ottawa. The eight sons were Richard, William Henry, George, Robert, Theophilus, James, Hercules and John. They were all born between 1847 and 1867. Five of the sons married and had children. They were George, Robert, James, Hercules and John. **George** married Henrietta Simms of Ottawa and they had one son Leslie and one daughter Jane who married John Mallen of New York. Jane and John had three sons John Leslie, Richard and Thomas. John Leslie, a major in the U.S. airforce was killed in a mid air collision in 1964 and left a widow, Shirley (nee Winnick) and a family (John, Leslie Ann and Sharyl Jean). Richard and Thomas both have children. Richard and his wife, Lois Taylor have a daughter, Michelle and Thomas and his wife, Sharon Douthwaite have two sons Thomas and Joseph. **Robert St. George** married Elizabeth Tovey of Ontario and they had three sons and three daughters – Lily, Daisy and Margaret. Only Lily had a family. Her husband was Edgar Coleman. Robert's youngest son George Edgar was the only son to have a family. He married Ruth Richardson of Ottawa and they had four sons, George Edgar, Richard, Michael and Tovey and one daughter Ruth. None of the children had any family except George Edgar who married Lise Lamothe and had two sons, Eddie and Richard and two daughters Suzanne and Julie. **James Howard St. George**, who was born in 1864, married Catherine Burns of Ottawa and they had two sons and two daughters, Violet and Hazel, neither of whom appear to have had a family. The two sons were James Howard II and William Oliver who died in his youth in 1914. James Howard II married Elizabeth Belch of Ottawa and they had one daughter Constance who after her marriage to Dr. Robert Bocieck had two sons Robert and James and two daughters Virginia and Beverley. **Hercules St. George** married Rosaline Dunn from Quebec in 1895 and they had two sons, Hercules and Richard, neither of whom had a family. **John St. George** was the youngest son of Robert and he married Lily Magladry in 1900. They had one son and four daughters but none of them appear to have had children. They were William John, Gladys, Marjorie, Fanny and Sarah.

The descendants of James Cuffe the son of Sir Richard Bligh St. George the 2nd Baronet.

James Cuffe, a J.P. was born in 1814. He married Jane the only daughter of Captain Arthur Loftus (a relative of the Marquess of Ely) and they had one son Loftus and one daughter Florence. **Loftus St. George** was the only son and he joined the armed forces. He rose to the rank of Lieutenant in the Surrey Militia. He was decorated for bravery in life saving activities in Australia. His wife was Marguerite Borrer from Sussex and they had one son, **Clifford** and three daughters, Aline, Kathleen and Violet. Aline was married twice and by her second husband Michael Pakenham she had a family. Kathleen, married to Colonel Clarke from

St. George of Freshford

Sussex and Violet whose husband was Sir Hugh Jackson both had families. **Clifford St. George**, an Oxford graduate, after a short career in the army during World War I became a Clerk in the House of Lords. His wife was Gwen Dalton from Sussex and they had one son John and one daughter Mary who died in infancy. **John St. George**, a gentleman farmer, was born in 1942. He was married in 1965 and had a son, William and two daughters Lucy and Marina. John's second wife is Elizabeth Westgate from Sussex.

Wandesforde of Castlecomer

In 1842 a commission set up by the British government to investigate the employment of children issued a report on children working in mines in the United Kingdom. Frederick Roper, one of the commissioners, visited mines in the south of Ireland. Writing about the Castlecomer coal field on the borders of Kilkenny and Laois, or Queen's County as it was then called, he said: "I inspected about a dozen of the different shafts, worked by contractors and found none but men employed. Indeed, I was informed that none but strong, able young men would be of any use in the pits, the labour being severe. I did not see any under eighteen years of age".

He goes on to say that he went down into the pit and saw the people at their work and even the "hurriers" who draw the coals to the foot of the shaft, were mostly strong young men. Elsewhere, Roper stated that no female of any age was employed in mining. It was not necessary to employ child labour as there was a surplus of adult workers. He described the "hurriers" in the collieries of Kilkenny – Queen's County going along the narrow low passages of seldom more than three feet high and often down on their hands and feet, the body stretched out. 'They drew the sledge, on which wooden boxes containing the coal are placed, by a girdle round the loins and a long chain fastened to the sledge going down between the legs. It was a matter of wonderment to me how these hurriers many of whom were stout men upwards of six feet high, could manage to get along these very narrow low passages at such a rate as they do.'[451]

The Wandesfordes owned, and except for brief periods of leasing, ran the mines. In the late 1880s Captain R.H. Prior-Wandesforde inherited the family estate. He inherited a position of great power in the area.[452] The family had amassed a substantial fortune from mining and owned thousands of acres of woodland and farmland as well as the game and fishing rights of this land.

Just before the outbreak of the First World War another seam was discovered at Skehana. This was first worked at a pit in West Skehana and then at the Deerpark, which opened in 1924. This coal proved to be of a high quality and compared with the best anthracite found anywhere in the world, being practically free of sulphur, and of good heating power. By the early nineteen thirties there were five major pits in the Castlecomer coalfield, The Jarrow, The Deerpark, The Rock Bog, The Monteen and The Vera, named after the Wandesforde's eldest daughter.[453]

At one time – between the two World Wars- almost 1,000 men were directly and indirectly employed. Later, as pits closed, this number was reduced to about

---

[451] R.C. Prior Wandesforde *History of Coal Mining in Ireland*
[452] According to Seamus Walsh who wrote *In the Shadow of the Comer Mines* 'Captain Wandesforde was withdrawn and reserved and regarded by the men as stern and hard. Most of the miners in the 1920's saw him as their lord and master determining salaries and conditions. Instead the Wandesforde family boasted of not yielding to pressure, strikes, or conflict of any type. But in the late 1920s and early thirties there was a lot of unrest about housing, looking for better conditions in the pit and somewhere to wash because at that time there were no baths at the mine.' Seamus recounts in his book how the miners eventually founded a union, against management's wishes, by covertly sending one of their number, Nixie Boran to Russia! After his return the miners came into conflict with the P.P. of the parish who denounced communism from the altar.
[453] R.C. Prior Wandesforde *History of Coal Mining in Ireland*

Wandesforde of Castlecomer

400 and at the end even less. The mines were closed in 1969 with the loss of 180 jobs.[454]

The Wandesfordes were a very old Yorkshire gentry family with an estate at Kirklington. Christopher Wandesforde was the first Wandesforde to come to Ireland. He came in 1633 with his friend[455] Thomas Wentworth (later Lord Strafford) who was Governor of Ireland. He appears to have brought over some of his relatives also, as his brother Nicholas was an M.P. for Thomastown and his eldest son, George, was an M.P. for Clogher in 1639[456]. Within a short space of time he was made Master of the Rolls- a legal appointment – and became a very powerful man in the administration.

Christopher bought the lease of Kildare castle and Manor from Sir Charles Coote shortly after his arrival in Ireland and intended living there. He did in fact live in the castle for a year with his family, but the Earl Wentworth (Strafford) took a fancy to the place and two years later it was sold on to him.

In July 1637 he bought Castlecomer Castle and an estate of some 20,000 acres. These lands were formerly owned by the famous Gaelic Brennan clan from the barony of Odough, of which Castlecomer is the focal point.

The Brennans, in common with other old Gaelic families of Leinster, such as the O'Moores in Co. Laois, the Kavanaghs in Carlow and Wexford, the O'Byrnes of Wicklow and the Fitzpatricks of Ossory, saw their lands pilfered from them under the governments of Henry VIII and Elizabeth I. Ruthless adventurers, from both new English and Anglo Norman stock, exploited the turmoil of the times to their advantage leaving the old Gaels with little more than their pride and a hateful resentment of their conquerors. In Odough the main beneficiaries were the Earl of Ormonde and Robert Ridgeway[457].

An inquisition held in Kilkenny in 1635 found that the Brennans had no title in the area as they were 'mere Irish' and only held the territory by force of arms. In 1636 Christopher Wandesforde commenced negotiations to buy the Brennan lands from Ormonde and Ridgeway. The sale included the castle of Castlecomer which was in the possession of Richard Butler, the 3rd Viscount Mountgarret. The

---

[454] Many of the Managers were "characters"- the best being "tough" men, but just. Many men in the district will still have memories of such managers as Mr. Whittaker, Mr. Hargreaves and of course the last manager Mr. Jim Bambling. – Ibid.

[455] In Burke's Landed Gentry it is stated that 'Christopher Wandesforde, Esq. of Kirklington, being upon close habits of intimacy and friendship with Sir Thomas Wentworth, Earl of Strafford, accompanied that eminent and ill fated nobleman into Ireland'.

[456] Burke's *Landed Gentry of Ireland.*

[457] J. Prendergast *Ireland from the Restoration to the Revolution 1660-1690*

Brennans sought to remedy their position by getting Lord Mountgarret to plead their case in England.

By 1638 Wandesforde had still not succeeded in obtaining possession so Strafford send a body of soldiers to Castlecomer where they seized the parents of about one hundred families of Brennans, took them to Dublin and imprisoned them.[458] They also took possession of the castle.

Christopher's conscience must have been causing him some trouble, as in his will made in 1640, he made provision for the payment of money to some of the Brennan families to the value of a 21 year lease on whatever lands they occupied at the time. In another gesture of good will he managed to secure the release of one of the Brennans who had been convicted and sentenced to death for sheep stealing from his lands[459]. He installed his half-brother William as his agent. William and his wife took up residence in the castle. The year before, in 1637, Christopher, in making meticulous preparations for his estate, granted £20 per annum to William and his heirs out of the Manor of Castlecomer, 'payable upon Strongbow's tomb in Christ Church'.[460]

During the next three years he built the old Castlecomer House (burnt in 1798) and built and endowed a church. He also built the town and a Deerpark and planted woods. The town was modelled on Alsinore in Italy[461]. He introduced the manufacture of cotton and earthenware and founded both collieries and a forge at which were produced all sorts of ironwork, even ordnance. He was granted a weekly market at Castlecomer on Tuesdays with three fairs on Ascension Day, the Feast of

---

[458] Burtchaell & Dowling in *Kilkenny History & Society* ed. by Wm. Nolan

[459] In this case the steward of the property was instructed by William Wandesforde to visit all the Brennans in the Castlecomer area to try and establish who was stealing the Wandesforde sheep. The steward and his assistant had a bad day but the last person they called to see was O'Brennan, the chief of the Brennans. He, too, knew nothing about the sheep stealing but as it was evening he invited the steward and his assistant to stay for supper. A fine dish of mutton was served. As the visitors left the house, having thanked O'Brennan for his hospitality a fleece was thrown out the door after them and struck the steward on the shoulder. When he examined it he could see the Wandesforde brand on the hide. O'Brennan was arrested and brought to Dublin where he met with Christopher. As a result of the parley O'Brennan was allowed to go home, but he promised Wandesforde that he would not regret his generosity in dropping the sheep stealing charge. The sheep stealing ceased and when in 1641 William Wandesforde and his wife had to fly from Castlecomer dressed as Irish people it was said that the clothes were provided by O'Brennan

[460] Burke's *Landed Gentry of Ireland*.

[461] According to McCall the town of Alsinore is in Italy but I have been unable to locate a town of that name there. There is an Alsinore north of Copenhagen where Arab Israeli talks were held recently.

St. Lawrence and the 14th September each year. Courts of Pie Powder[462] could be held on the fair days. In addition he was granted liberty to hold courts baron dealing with all cases of felony in the district. The grant named all the townlands and Christopher was given leave to impark 4,000 acres for 'keeping horses, deer, rabbits, partridges and pheasants and for hunting. No one save the said Christopher his heirs or assigns or those authorised by their special licence to hunt, hawk etc. in the same.'

Castlecomer House

It was he and his grandson – another Christopher Wandesforde – who started the mining project in Castlecomer that lasted right down to the 20th century. At various times the mines were leased by the Wandesfordes to others- the last long lease being to the Dobbs family and it was during their lease that most of the Jarrow seam was worked. When Capt. R.H.Prior-Wandesforde succeeded to the property at the end of the 19th century he took over all the mining and extended it very considerably, supplementing capital from the sale of certain lands in Yorkshire[463].

Wentworth was given further promotion in Ireland and was made Lord Lieutenant. When he was recalled to England in the spring of 1640 he made Christopher his Lord Deputy. This was a very turbulent time in England with rumblings of war in Ireland too. During the period Christopher applied himself to his task with his usual zest. One curious affair in which he was involved was an

---

[462] The Courts of Pied Powder were groups of travelling lawyers and judges who adjudicated on breaches of agreement made between merchants. These Courts of Pied Poudre (dusty feet) travelled from one market to the other ruling on disputes.
[463] R. C. Prior-Wandesforde- last Managing Director of Castlecomer Collieries Ltd

inquiry into witchcraft. In one of his many letters he wrote to Bishop Bramhill in September of 1640 asking him to assist Sir. William Coote and Mr. A. Hill in examining certain persons in Co. Antrim, accused of bewitching the Duchess of Buckingham (sic).[464]

Wentworth was having a torrid time in England and in late November of 1640 he was arrested and imprisoned. The news, when it arrived in Ireland, had a devastating effect on Christopher Wandesforde. According to Sir J. Coke in a letter to his father 'the Lord Deputy Wandesforde, upon the first word he received of Wentworth's accusation and imprisonment swooned and died within a very few days.'[465]

Strafford (awaiting trial) said of him ' I attest the eternal God that the death of my cousin Wandesforde more affects me that the prospect of my own, for in him is lost the richest magazine of learning, wisdom and piety that these times can boast.'

Christopher had his portrait painted by Vandyke and that picture was in the possession of the Comber family of Winchfield, Hants in the early 1900s.

At his funeral in Dublin it was said that he was lamented by some of the native Irish who began their traditional keening[466]. He was buried in Christ Church in front of the Lord Deputy's Chair, but the writing on the flagstone has been obliterated by the passage of time.

In his will he left the bulk of his estate to his eldest son and decreed that his widow (Alice[467] nee Osbourne of Derby county) was to get £300 per annum. He left money for (memorial) rings to be given to various dear friends such as the Earl of Strafford who was to get one valued at £20. The other rings were to cost £5 and his brother John was to get one of them. Other £5 ring recipients were the Bishop of Derry, Sir George Ratcliffe, the Earl of Ormonde, Lord Dillon of Kilkenny West, Sir Edward Osborne and his cousin William Wandesforde. He left numerous other

---

[464] Hastings Mss in NLI
[465] Cowper Mss in NLI
[466] McCall in *Wandesforde of Castlecomer*.
[467] When Alice died she left to her daughter Alice Thornton 'the use of my plate, jewels etc. for her life. Also to her all wearing linen and apparel, books and writings, my lute and vyoll and my late husband's picture, also harpsicall virginals for her life; afterwards to my grandchild Alice Thornton for her life; afterwards to my grandchild Katherine Thornton for her life; and afterwards to the eldest daughter of Alice Thornton successively for their lives'. Alice was nothing if not thrifty as she left to her son Christopher 'all the iron ranges in my house at Hipswell and the locks and keys of the doors there; all which I bought since coming thither except five old locks and keys I found there; also the Irish tables in the kitchen…'

bequests to charity and to his staff and 'to my sister Mary Wandesforde[468] the £100 in which I am indebted to her and £200 more'. He left £5 yearly to his servant Sara Moffet.

After his death his widow stayed a number of months at Damask Street, Dublin with three younger children, Alice, Christopher and John and two grandsons Thomas and Chris Danby. George the eldest son who had studied at Trinity College was travelling in France with his tutor Mr. Anderson from Scotland. The family fled to Chester at the outbreak of the 1641 rebellion. They were royalists and after some difficult times managed to reach Kirklington where they took up residence in the Hall. The eldest son George returned from France and was hounded by the Parliamentarians and requested to subscribe to the Solemn League and Covenant. He did not do this and his lands were declared forfeit. The family was compelled to leave Kirlkington and settle at Hipswell[469]. Soldiers were quartered upon the lands there and the family was reduced almost to penury, as no rents were forthcoming from Ireland.

George's sister Catherine, Lady Danby, died in 1645 on the birth of her sixteenth child. She was aged 30. The Dowager Lady Wandesforde died in 1659 at Hipswell. George was drowned crossing a river in March1651. The youngest son, John, after attending Cambridge became an M.P. for Richmond. He died unmarried, aged 32 in London. Their other sister, Alice, was married to William Thorneton in November 1651 and she was the mother of Alice who married Rev. Thomas Comber, dean of Durham.

The year after the death of Christopher senior the Great Rebellion broke out and William and his wife, having been forewarned about a possible pogrom escaped from Castlecomer wearing Irish clothes[470]. The castle was retaken by a contingent of the army of Viscount Mountgarret, consisting mainly of Brennans. The manor remained in the hands of Mountgarret and the Brennans until after the Cromwellian war. Castlecomer was placed in the hands of William Wandesforde, a cousin of

---

[468] Mary was an unusual person who left a picture of Our Blessed Saviour and the Virgin Mary to Lord Castlecomer to be kept in the mansion house of Kirklington. She also left £2400 for the foundation of a house 'where ten poor gentlewomen who were never married shall retire from the hurry and noise of the world where they shall be obliged to continue there for life'. She also left a codicil in her will 'I desire that there be no state nor trouble in my funeral, but six of the poorest unmarried women in Kirklington may have white veils from head to foot prepared for them and white gloves and carry my corpse into the church at what place I happen to be buried in. Let the white veils be of such cloth as will do them service hereafter.'
[469] This family estate had coal and copper mines.
[470] Burtchaell & Dowling in *Kilkenny History & Society* ed. by Wm. Nolan

Christopher the elder, who acted as trustee. He regained possession of Castlecomer, after much difficulty in 1654 and placed his son-in-law, Captain Preston there to manage the property. Later after the Restoration of Charles II the Brennans made an application to the courts to have the terms of the will of Christopher I implemented. The chancellor of the period found in their favour but the death of Sir Christopher II in 1687 meant further delays. The outbreak of the Williamite wars finally put paid to their chances of success and after that the matter was never again pursued by the Brennans.[471]

Christopher, the second son and now heir to the estates of Castlecomer and Kirlkington married his brother's fiancée, as was expected of him. She was Eleanor the daughter of Sir John Lowther[472]. They married in Sept. of 1651. Lowther paid a dowry of £2,000 which was most welcome at the time. Christopher settled his estates on himself and his wife and their descendants.

Upon the restoration he was created Sir Christopher Wandesforde because of the suffering of the family in the royal cause. He was elected in the Parliament of 1679 as an M.P. for Ripon. He seems to have visited Ireland occasionally as he was robbed there of £307 and a gold ring. He died in 1686 and was buried at Kirklington. His wife died in 1714 aged 80.

They had thee sons and six daughters. The eldest girl, Mary and the fourth daughter Alice died unmarried and the second girl, Eleanor married Amyas Bushe of Kilfane. The other girls married gentlemen from England, including the youngest, Christiana who married her cousin Richard Lowther. The three sons were Christopher, George and Charles (who died unmarried).

George, the second son married Elizabeth Foulkes the widow of Garret Foulkes. Elizabeth Foulk (Wandesforde) and her daughter Elizabeth Foulk made a petition to the government concerning Garret Foulk's lands. Garret was imprisoned and condemned in Galway and Dublin and lost his estate for serving King William. He was killed at the battle of Aughrim. Elizabeth got a grant under the Privy Seal of £200 a year of forfeited lands in 1697 in lieu of a pension of the like sum which

---

[471] Ibid.
[472] Eleanor was alive in 1694 when she appointed Christopher Phillipson of Grey's Inn as her attorney 'to call John Bradley of the coal pits in the Co. of Kilkenny to account for all arrears of debts, rents and colliery produce due and owning to me and to give acquittances and discharges of the same.' She was still alive in 1707 when she appointed John Buck of Dublin as her attorney 'for receiving a certain sum on money due to her' She died in 1713 and in her will she left to her grandson Lord Viscount Castlecomer 'for life, my wrought bed and damask bed, my gold and silver quilt, my best diamond ring and my great silver looking glass, to go to the heirs male of the family of my dear husband.'

had been promised to her by Queen Mary in 1692. George and Elizabeth left a son Osborne Sydney Wandesforde.

After his death in 1687 Sir Christopher was succeeded by his eldest son, Christopher. Christopher III was a committed Protestant and fought on the side of King William during the disturbances of that period. He was attainted by King James's parliament in 1689 and his estates were officially confiscated. However following the victory of the Williamites he was restored to his estates and in the first decade of the new century he was given further honours being created Baron Wandesforde and Viscount Castlecomer. A Cambridge graduate, he was High Sheriff of Yorkshire in 1690. Shortly after this Castlecomer became the principal residence of the family.

In 1694 he successfully appealed against the terms of his grandfather's will, in so far as it favoured the Brennans, citing the wrongs suffered by both his father and himself at their hands in the 1641 wars when the property was burnt, improvements destroyed and livestock killed.[473] In addition he claimed that they had killed many of his English tenants and prevented him from enjoying the use of his property for the ten years of the war.[474] In his petition he stated that 'the said sept of the Brennans are still very numerous, are a great terror to the English inhabitants of that country and frequently commit many great robberyes and murthers and were in armes for the late King James' He was given a grant of Idough 'in consideration of the manifold great and good services done unto us and our crown by our well-beloved subject, and for the better strengthening and supporting of the English Protestant interest within the country of Idough'.

In 1692 he was admitted a burgess of the Irishtown of Kilkenny and the same freedom was taken up by his eldest son in 1706. In the same year, 1706 he was created Viscount Castlecomer. He died in London in 1707 aged 54. He was buried in Kirklington. He had his portrait painted by a disciple of Sir Peter Lely, if not by Lely himself, although Lely died in 1680 before Sir Christopher had succeeded. His widow, Lady Elizabeth Montagu survived until 1731 and in her will left £10 to the poor of the parish of Kirklington and desired to be buried with in her own family (Montagu) plot in London. The will also stipulated that the funeral was to be private 'one mourning coach only; wherein her domestic servants shall go to see her body laid in the grave.' She also left the servants one year's wages each.

Sir Christopher and Elizabeth had four sons and one daughter Henrietta, who married William Maynard of Curryglas, an M.P. for Tallaght and collector of

---

[473] Burtchaell & Dowling in *Kilkenny History & Society* ed. by Wm. Nolan
[474] It was at this stage that some of the Brennans became tories and raparees. For the extraordinary and full story of the Brennan raparees see *Kilkenny History & Society*.

customs for the port of Cork. The four sons were Christopher, George, John and Richard. John was a churchman, rector of Kirklington and Catterick until his death in 1747. Richard died unmarried in 1719. Christopher succeeded his father and after Christopher's death he in turn was succeeded by his brother George. Christopher the 2nd Baron was only 24 when he succeeded to the title and estates.

The second Baron seems to have spent much of his time in England where he was politically active, being an M.P. for Morpeth and for Ripon on different occasions. He died in 1719. His wife of four years was Lady Frances Pelham. They had one son Christopher, the 3rd Baron, who died of smallpox in 1736 aged 19. He was only two at the time of his father's death

Christopher was succeeded by his uncle George who became the 4th Baron. He had pursued a career in the Army in which he was a Captain of foot in the regiment of Brigadier-General, Sir Charles Hotham. His wife was Susannah Griffith the daughter of the Venerable John Griffith, Archdeacon of Killaloe. He lived in the Ripon area until his succession and after that event the family lived between Castlecomer and Dublin where he had a residence on St. Stephen's Green. George died in 1751, after an illness, and was buried at the Church of St. Anne. He and Susannah had one son John, and two daughters, Susannah and Elizabeth who died unmarried in 1806. Susannah married Thomas Newenham an M.P. for Cork city. His wife, who inherited his lands in Cork died five years later than he in 1756.

John, the 5th Baron, was 26 when he succeeded to the title and estates in 1751. Seven years later he was elevated to the dignity of Earl of Wandesforde in the county of Kilkenny. He married Agnes Southwell an heiress, of Enniscough, Co. Limerick in 1750. Her father had estates in Limerick and Clare. This lady died in 1781 having had a son who died young and a daughter, Anne, who became the sole heir of the Wandesfordes. The Earl survived his wife for three years and was buried with her in Castlecomer. He had his portrait painted by Sir Joshua Reynolds at some time in his middle life.

The Lady Anne Wandesforde, the heir to the estates, was married to John Butler of Garryricken in 1754 when she was 15 years of age. John Butler, in 1791 assumed the title of the Earl of Ormonde and so Lady Ormonde was the last of the Wandesfordes[475]. Her youngest son Charles-Harward[476] was the second surviving

---

[475] She had her portrait painted by Comerford.
[476] This was the Charles Butler who at the age of seventeen, in 1798, took part in the defence of Castlecomer against the Wexford Rebels (led by Fr. John Murphy and Miles Byrne) who were seeking to get support from the miners for their failing rebellion. The defenders abandoned Castlecomer House and concentrated their efforts on defending a house near the Bridge. This was held for several hours until the arrival of General Sir Charles Asgill. Much of the town was destroyed in this battle and the church and its registers were burnt.

son when the Countess died in 1830. Prior to that he had been left estates by his brother Walter, the Marquess of Ormonde. These estates had come to the Marquess from his wife Anne Clarke of Sutton Hall in Derby. Because of this Charles-Harward took the name Clarke. When he succeeded to the Kirklington and Castlecomer estates he took the additional names of Southwell and Wandesforde.

The Hunt at Castlecomer (courtesy College Books)

His wife was Lady Sarah, the youngest daughter of the Earl of Carrick, whom he married in 1812. When Lady Sarah died in 1838 he married the Dowager Countess of Carrick, Lucy Butler, Lady Sarah's sister-in-law. By his first marriage he had three sons and two daughters. One of his daughters survived him. This was Sarah, the wife of Rev. John Prior of Mount Dillon Co. Dublin, the Rector of Kirklington. Charles Haward died in 1860 and was buried at Kirklington.

He was succeeded by his grandson Charles, High Sheriff of Kilkenny in 1879. He died of fever in London in 1881 aged 29. He was buried at Castlecomer where there is a tablet to his memory, placed there by the parishioners as a mark of their esteem and in his memory.

Mrs. Prior now became the heir of the family fortunes and titles, and, in accordance with the will of her father assumed the name and arms of Wandesforde, in addition to Prior, for herself and her descendants. Rev. Prior died at Kirklington

---

Castlecomer House was rebuilt in 1802 (for a full account of this battle see *Ireland 1798 the Battles* by Art Kavanagh).

and was buried there in 1867. His widow, The Hon. Lady Prior Wandesforde survived until 1892 and after her death in Castlecomer was buried at Mount Juliet.

They had two sons and a daughter Sophia Elizabeth who married Major General Henry Ely of Copse Dale, Co. Tipperary. The two sons were Charles Butler Prior of Crossogue House, Co. Tipperary, a J.P. and D.L and Henry Wallis Prior Wandesforde of Castlecomer, Co. Kilkenny, a career Army officer and a J.P.

Index

Abbot's Langley, 194
Abercorn, 107
Acheson, 206
Adams
   John, 155
Agar, 1, 2, 3, 4, 5, 6, 7, 9, 10, 11, 12, 14, 99, 100, 126, 130, 184
   Henry Welbore, 12
   James, 1
Alcock, 45
Alford, 213
Alsinore, 219
Altamont, 102, 103, 206, 207
Alyward, 137
Anderson, 222
Andrews, 65
Annaghmakerrig, 58
Annaly, 13, 14
Annesley, 132
Anson, 91
Ardee, 170
Arklow, 78, 81
Armagh, 140, 148, 206
Armstrong, 21, 122
Arran Quay, 7
Artukovich, 51
Ascherson, 52
Ascot, 111
Ashbrook, 12
Ashe, 204
Athenry
   Lord, 6
Athlone, 40, 103, 142, 205, 208
Aughatubrid, 30
Australia, 23, 144, 215
Austria, 30, 52
Aylmer, 30, 31
Badham, 99
Bagenalstown, 21, 23, 150
Bagot
   Lord, 12
Baker, 96, 202, 212
Baldwin, 120, 203
Balief, 206, 209
Ball, 71
Ballcummin, 140
Ballingarry, 38
Ballinvegga, 40, 66, 68, 85
Ballycarney, 152
Ballyconra, 72
Ballydarton, 195
Ballyduff, 20
Ballylarkin, 205
Ballylinch, 41, 42, 165
Ballymagir, 63, 154, 159
Ballynaslaney, 132
Ballyrafton, 32
Ballyragget, 11, 25, 67, 68
Ballysax, 64, 82
Bambling, 218
Banim, 188
Baring, 180
Barker, v, 171
Barmeath, 33, 34, 36, 37
Barrachore, 122
Barrettstown, 184, 189
Barrington, 71, 88, 116, 132, 138, 152
Barrow, 5, 52, 154
Barrowmount, 4, 117, 118, 147
Barton, v, 165
Bassett, 13
Bath, 40, 107
Bawnmore, 27, 28, 30, 41
Bayliss, 161
Bayly, 5
Beaufort
   Duke of, 190
Becher, 21, 59, 188
Bedford, 107, 135
Befordshire, 48

Index

Belford, 161
Bellew, 34, 36, 37, 146, 147, 154, 155, 156, 161
Belline, 176, 177
Bellingham, 107, 189
Belmore
    Earl of, 43
Bence Jones, 75, 134, 135
Bence-Jones, 19, 97
Bennetsbridge, 6, 50, 57
Bennett, 199
Berenson, 114
Beresford, 97, 103, 129
Bergh, 73
Berkeley, 97, 187
Berkley, 210
Bertie, 122
Berwick, 87
Bessborough, 94, 115, 120, 151, 168, 170, 171, 172, 176, 178, 179, 180, 181
Bihar, 200
Bindon, 19, 120, 172, 206
Bingham, 164
Birch, 137
Birchfield, 137, 197
Bischoffsheim, 109, 111
Bishopscourt, 174
Blackstairs, 53
Blackwater, 33
Blanchville, 3
Blaney, 136
Blayney, 150
Bligh, 202, 208, 209, 212, 214, 215
Blood, 68, 86
Blount, 150
Blundell, 69, 70
Blunden, 15, 96, 97, 99
    Overington, 16
Bocieck, 214
Boer War, 120, 122, 180, 198
Boleyn, 79
Bolton, 17

Bookey, 122
Boran, 217
Borrer, 215
Bowen, 185, 198
Boyle, 10, 43, 99, 140, 195
Bradley, 223
Bradstreet, 4
Brandon
    Countess, 2
Brecon, 56
Breens, 26, 27
Breffni, 80
Brennan, 26, 27, 28, 30, 136, 198, 218, 219, 224
Brereton, 17
Bridgewater, 107
Briscoe, 170
Bristol, 161
Brodsky, 52
Brougham, 176
Brownes, 102
Bryan, 25, 26, 27, 28, 29, 30, 32, 33, 34, 35, 36, 37, 41, 48, 139, 159, 194
    Elizabeth, 26
    George Leopold, 34
Buccleuch, 105, 107
Buck, 223
    Frederick, 57
Buckingham, 86, 221
Buckinghamshire, 65
Bunbury, 59
Burden, 198
Burdett, 212
Burghley, 149
Burke
    Edmund, 139
Burma, 48, 122
Burn, 214
Burnchurch, 2, 55, 56, 57, 125, 127, 128, 129, 130
Burns, 214
Burrowes, 71

Index

Burtchaell, 3, 4, 11, 44, 219, 223, 224
Burton, 100, 172, 188
Bury, 122
Bushe, 3, 8, 42, 70, 130, 184, 187, 188, 223
   Gervase, 3
Bussher, 65
Butler
   1st Duke, 84
   Black Tom, 82
   Brian 9th Earl of Carrick, 49
   Captain James, 45
   Catherine, 197
   Charles, 226
   Charles, Earl of Arran, 87, 99
   Edmund 1st Baron Dunboyne, 54
   Ellen, 41
   Florence, 57
   George of Maidenhall, 57
   Gilbert, 58
   Harriet, 57
   Hubert, 50, 52, 56, 58
   James 19th Earl of Ormonde, 89
   James 2nd Duke, 86
   John, 225
   Major Charles, 47
   Piers Roe, 79
   Piers Roe 8th Earl, 61
   Rev. Richard, 56
   Sir Edmund, 68
   Sir Richard 3rd Viscount Mountgarret, 65
   Walter 11th Earl, 84
Byrne, 26, 30, 31, 32, 71, 198, 226
Byron
   Lord, 171
Caherconlish, 78
Cahir, 78
Callan, 1, 2, 6, 7, 8, 11, 99, 100, 102, 122, 127, 128, 129, 130, 184
Cambridgeshire, 203
Camden, 194
Cameron, 109, 212
Camoys
   Lady, 13
Campbell, 104, 107, 109
Canada, 56, 108, 118, 178, 181, 208
Candler, 129
Cantwell, 184
Cappawhite, 198
Carew, 64, 82, 91
Carey, 154, 158
Carlisle, 12, 107
Carlow, 21, 27, 32, 61, 63, 64, 65, 66, 68, 75, 81, 82, 89, 100, 118, 125, 150, 154, 156, 164, 172, 180, 186, 188, 195, 206, 218
Carnelly House, 19
Carrick
   Lord, 38, 43, 44, 46, 47, 48, 49, 70, 75, 78, 82, 86, 147, 163, 203, 226
Carrickdrumrusk, 203
Carrigslaney, 207
Carroll, 157
Carson, 20
Carter, 211
Cartland
   Barbara, 143
Castle Morres, 117, 120, 124
Castlecomer, 4, 30, 36, 65, 89, 118, 185, 195, 216, 217, 218, 219, 220, 221, 222, 223, 224, 225, 226, 227
Castleinch, 94, 97, 99
Castleknock, 158, 199, 200
Caulfield, 129
Cavan, 80, 118, 121, 141, 204

230

Index

Cavendish, 132, 173, 180
Cawdor, 107
Ceylon, 59
Chaigneau, 5
Chaine, 142
Charles II, 41, 42, 68, 85, 86, 94, 135, 205, 223
Charlton, 48, 74
Chatsworth, 112
Cheshire, 194
Chester, 222
Chetham, 150
Chichester, 105
China, 23, 45
Christian
   Wm., 137
Christie, 74
Churchtown, 210
Clancarty, 46
Clanmorris, 164
Clanricarde, 106
Clare, 3, 19, 21, 40, 120, 159, 198, 211, 225
Clarenbridge, 203
Clarke, 58, 92, 212, 215, 226
Clements, 206
Clifden, 1, 7, 8, 10, 12, 13, 14, 130
Cliffe, 150
Clogh, 30
Clogher, 142, 204, 206, 218
Cloghgrennan, 64, 82
Clohesy, 169
Clohosey
   Rev. T.J., 77
Clonabraney, 191
Clonakenny, 38
Cloney
   Sean, 151
Clonfert, 212
Clonmacnoise, 55, 56, 57
Clonmel, 81, 82, 184, 198
Clonmell, 70
Clonmullen, 66

Cloughinche, 82
Cluer, 74
Coalbrook, 41
Coates, 159, 160
Cobh, 55
Coke, 221
Colclough, 3, 63, 150, 164
Cole, 193
Colles, 57
Colley, 150
Colooney, 206
Colvill, 171, 172
Comber, 221, 222
Comerford, 94, 117, 226
Conahy, 36
Congreve, 122, 180, 187
Connellan, 141
Connemara, 122, 202, 212
Connolly, 174
Conyers, 68
Conyngham, 35, 59, 166, 174
Cooke, 54, 100
Coolcullen, 118
Coolfinn, 212
Coolnaheen, 65
Coolnamuck, 30, 120
Cooper, 201
Coote, 94, 195, 206, 218, 221
Copenhagen, 162, 219
Corballis, 185, 186
Cork, 21, 55, 57, 96, 99, 100, 178, 184, 195, 225
Corkagh, 59
Cornwall, 14, 104
Cosby, 164
Cosgrave, 160
Cottingham, 141
Courtmacsherry, 21
Cowes, 66, 90, 108
Cox
   Watty, 9
Crampton, 58
Cranagh, 205

Index

Crawford, 5
Creagh, 159
Creaghe, 22
Crimea, 10
Crimean War, 44, 46
Croatia, 52
Croghan, 203
Cromwell, 3, 14, 29, 40, 42, 54, 67, 85, 94, 105, 117, 121, 127, 150, 169, 184
Cronyn, 45
Crossmolina, 208
Cuddihy
   Paul, 54
Cuffe, 15, 17, 57, 94, 95, 96, 97, 98, 99, 100, 101, 102, 103, 104, 105, 107, 108, 109, 111, 112, 113, 114, 128, 185, 210, 215
Cuffe., 15, 94, 99, 101
Cumberland, 128, 169, 170
Curraghmore, 97, 111, 184
Curryglas, 225
Curtis, 22
Cutting
   Wm., 114
Czar Nicholas I, 175
Dalton, 169, 215
Damagh, 27
Danesfort, 6, 18, 104
Dangan, 197
Darnley, 208
Daton, 169
Davidstown, 62
Davis, 42
de Bermingham, 54
de Burgh, 105
de Burgo, 78
de Fine Sucht, 72
de Lautour, 210
de Marisco, 78
de Mauley
   Lord, 177, 179
de Montmorency, 115, 118, 120, 121, 122, 124, 125

De Quincy, 171
de Rutant, 31
de Walden, 74
Deerelegh, 117
Delaney, 197
Delano, 212
Delgany, 7, 122
Denison, 35
Denn
   Foulks, 62
Derby, 35, 221, 226
Derry, 43, 70, 170, 174, 222
Desart, 1, 57, 93, 94, 95, 97, 98, 99, 100, 102, 103, 104, 105, 106, 107, 108, 109, 110, 111, 112, 113, 128
Desmond
   Earl of, 27, 63, 64, 78, 81, 82, 119, 181
deValera, 160
Devereux, 63, 149, 154, 193, 197, 200
Devonshire, 31, 105, 107, 172, 173, 176
Di Biasio, 143
Diana
   late Princess of Wales, 10, 180, 213
   Princess, 48
Diana, Princess of Wales, 175
Digby
   Lady, 195
Dillon, 77, 89, 178, 179, 209, 222
Dingwall
   Baron, 83
Dinin (River), 28
Disraeli, 106, 109
Dockrell
   Judith, 154
Dodd, 36
Donaghy, 201
Donegal, 154
Doninga, 122
Donnybrook, 115, 197

Index

Donoghue, 49
Dorset, 210
Doudney, 59
Douthwaite, 214
Dover
    Baron, 12
Doyle
    Rev. Martin, 156
Drake, 104, 147
Drennan
    Canon, 192
Drogheda, 135, 172, 195
Dromore, 208, 212
Drummond, 91
Drumroe, 147
Drury, 144
du Preez, 211
Dublin, iii, 5, 7, 10, 19, 21, 23, 31, 32, 33, 46, 47, 53, 55, 57, 59, 63, 66, 67, 68, 69, 70, 77, 84, 85, 86, 89, 90, 95, 96, 99, 100, 104, 107, 109, 115, 117, 118, 120, 132, 136, 138, 140, 143, 148, 149, 150, 151, 154, 158, 171, 176, 178, 187, 188, 198, 199, 200, 202, 206, 208, 212, 219, 221, 222, 223, 224, 225, 227
Duffin, 125
Duffry, 26, 27
Duffy, 88, 178
Dunbell, 11, 186
Dunboyne
    Lord, 39, 40, 42, 54, 55, 61, 71, 75, 81, 82, 84, 86, 89, 91
Dundas, 138
Dundrum, 208
Dungannon, 170
Dungarvan, 44
Dungulph Castle, 151
Dunkerrin, 78
Dunmore, 3, 30, 77, 86
Dunphy, 195
Dunsany, 145

Dunton, 77
Durban, 211
Durrow, 185, 186
Dyke, 25
Dysart, 97
Earle, 213
Eaton, 108, 146, 147, 148, 154
Edgeworth, 56, 57, 188
Edinburgh, 21, 58, 72
Edward Longshanks, 61, 78
Egan, 21, 132
Ellesmere, 107
Elliott, 191, 192
Ellis
    Anne, 7
    Welbore, 7, 10
Ellis Quay, 7
Ely
    General, 227
Enniscorthy, 26, 27, 42, 64, 66, 68, 164
Ennisnag, 167
Esmonde, 84, 195
Eton, 73, 74, 89, 104, 107, 143, 144, 181, 212
Eustace, 31, 34
Evans, 48, 117, 118
Falmouth, 111
Fannings, 39
Farmer, 213
Farmley, 126, 129, 131, 132, 133
Farnham, 44
Farrell, 66, 72, 154
Fassadinin, 4
Fawcett, 13
Fermanagh, 151
Ferns, 62, 63, 124, 142, 149, 164
Fethard, 54, 55, 151, 154, 184
Feuilherade, 48
Fiddown, 169, 170
Fingall, 105
Finley, 10
Fitzgerald, 61, 63, 96, 109, 110, 127, 198

Index

Michael, 41
FitzGerald
   Lord Edward, 203
Fitzgibbon, 64
Fitzhenry, 66
Fitzmaurice, 63
FitzMaurice, 64, 125
FitzPatrick, 42
Fitzpatricks, 61, 63, 127, 218
Fitzsymons, 204
Fitzwilliam, 90, 118, 176
Fleming, 31, 122
Flood, 2, 3, 8, 10, 126, 127, 128, 129, 130, 131, 132, 133, 165, 184, 187
   Henry, 1, 126
   Warden, 2
Florida, 48
Fortescue, 195
Foster, 52, 174
Foulk, 223
Foulkes, 223
Fowler, 70
Fownes, 88, 171, 172
France, 30, 32, 52, 68, 75, 77, 79, 85, 87, 104, 142, 153, 181, 194, 203, 205, 211, 222
Frankfort, 118, 119
Fratini
   Gina, 48
Frazscher, 72
French
   Lucy, 45
French Park, 45
Freney, 44, 147
Freshford, 67, 118, 202, 205
Frewen, 122
Fry, 189
Galloway, 107
Galmoy, 4, 30, 118, 147
Galway, 6, 24, 40, 67, 105, 120, 122, 142, 144, 161, 166, 167, 202, 203, 205, 209, 210, 212, 224

Gandhi, 200
Gardiner, 154, 159
Garner, 161
Garryricken, 88, 225
Gibbs, 47, 48
Gifford, 203
Gilbey, 36
Glanmore, 16
Glasgow, 24, 48, 212
Glasnevin, 47
Glencairne, 70
Glendalough, 139
Glin, 6, 96
Gloucester, 78, 213
Glyn, 210
Glynn, 62
Golden, 22
Gooch, 143
Gore, 4, 45, 118, 147
Goresbridge, 4, 122, 147, 159, 160, 197
Gorges, 96, 97
Gortnamona, 105
Goslingtown, 17
Gowran, 1, 3, 4, 5, 6, 9, 10, 11, 12, 13, 14, 78, 88, 126, 128, 160, 166, 186
Grace, 42, 77, 90, 96, 102, 123, 136, 195
Gragara, 32, 34, 35
Granard, 139
Grand
   Major Gen., 181
Grangecon, 199
Grantstown, 82
Grattan, 70, 130, 131, 146, 147, 154, 155, 156, 161, 168, 184, 187
Graves, 108, 212
Greene, 137
Greeneville, 137
Greig, 180
Griffith, 50, 51, 160, 225
Grigg, 143
Grosvenor Taunton, 123
Groves, 72
Guillamore, 122

Index

Guinness
    Dick, 71
Guthrie, 58
Haigh, 48
Hakansson, 73
Hale, 169, 170
Hamilton, 43, 70, 97, 99, 104, 108, 109, 123, 177
Handcock, 206
Handford, 133
Hannen, 48
Hanning-Lee, 74
Hantshire, 49, 213
Harewood, 107, 113
Hargreaves, 218
Harristown, 105, 108
Harrowden, 69
Hartpole, 164
Harvey
    Bagenal, 154
    Mrs. M., 133
Haslam, 180
Haslebrook, 45
Hatfield, 206
Hatley St. George, 203, 204
Haughey
    Charles, 75
Haydock, 118
Hayes, 7, 41, 68, 79, 89, 171, 174
Hegarty, 185
Helsham, 20
Henchy, 118
Herbert, 15, 18, 19, 23, 36, 59, 96, 97, 99, 100, 103
    Dorothea, 15
Herberts, 15, 18, 100
Herefordshire, 73
Hernon
    Mary, 151
Hertfordshire, 194
Hertshire, 47, 210
Hill, 23, 52, 86, 221

Hipswell, 221, 222
Hoban
    James, architect, 100
Hobson, 48
Holborn, 82
Hollow Blades, 4
Hone, 21
Hook Peninsula, 26
Hopkirk, 161
Horley, 143
Hotham, 225
Howard
    Lady, 12
Howe, 102
Howlett, 197
Hudson
    Rock, 145
Huguenots, 2
Hume, 134, 143, 149, 151
Hume Dick
    Helen, 134
Hutchinson, v, 115
Inchiquin, 85, 195
Inglis, 191
Isle of Skye, 23
Italy, 34, 113, 114, 142, 176, 181, 219
Ivory, 102
Jackson, 204, 215
Jefferson, 155
Jeffreys, 122
Jenkinstown, 25, 26, 27, 28, 29, 30, 31, 32, 33, 34, 36, 37, 194, 198
Jerpoint, 42, 61, 81
Jesse, 41
Jessfield, 41
Kauffman, 149
Kavanagh, i, iii, 7, 33, 41, 61, 63, 65, 66, 68, 79, 80, 81, 82, 89, 139, 154, 171, 174, 195, 226
    Art Bui, 61
    Donal Reagh, 80
Kearney, 122

Index

Kelly, 41, 102, 198, 209
Kendall, 42
Kensington, 90
Kenyon, 22
Keogh, 2, 130
Kidd, 162
   Captain, 159
Kilbehenny, 64
Kilbline, 53
Kilbride, 140, 207
Kilcash, 66, 82, 83, 85, 87
Kilcloggan, 150
Kilcooley, 171
Kilcoran, 122
Kilcreene, 37, 117, 191, 193, 195, 197, 198, 199, 200
Kildalton, 169
Kildare, 30, 31, 40, 42, 61, 66, 78, 79, 81, 85, 104, 105, 169, 174, 199, 218
Kildavin, 206
Kilfane, 25, 32, 53, 70, 130, 140, 183, 184, 185, 186, 188, 190, 191, 192, 223
Kilkelly, 161
Kilkenny Castle, 39, 61, 71, 75, 76, 77, 78, 86, 90, 91
Killaloe, 94, 225
Killarney, 42, 99, 139
Killyon, 150
Kilmainham, 54, 84, 141
Kilmallock, 64
Kilmoganny, 122
Kilmurry, 8
Kilrush, 40, 42, 66, 68, 85, 205, 206, 208
Kiltynan, 54
Kinahan, 208
King
   Sophia, 99
King Edward VII, 10, 22, 135
King George IV, 106
King George V, 181
King James II, 70, 87

King William, 4, 29, 86, 195, 224
Kingston, 57, 99
Kinsale, 39, 65
Kirklington, 89, 218, 222, 223, 224, 225, 226, 227
Kirwan
   John, 38, 42, 44, 46, 164
Knapp, 2, 130
Knaresborough, 9, 11
Knocktopher, 68, 117, 134, 135, 136, 137, 138, 140, 142, 184, 191
Knox, 13
La Touche, 105, 110
Lamb
   Caroline, 177
   Wm., 176
Lamothe, 214
Lancashire, 73
Landen, 87
Landrecy, 205
Lanesborough, 174, 193
Langley, 41
Langrishe, 91, 134, 135, 136, 137, 138, 139, 140, 141, 142, 143, 144, 145, 185, 188, 191, 192, 208, 209
   Lady, 145
Lanza, 181
Laois, 16, 17, 20, 31, 122, 150, 164, 185, 186, 189, 209, 216, 218
Lascelles, 113
Lavistown, 57
Lazybush, 195, 196
Leach, 36
Lecky, 131
Lee
   Captain, 150
Leeson-Marshall, 189
Leggetsrath, 20
Leicester, 172
Leigh Hunt, 176
Leitrim, 203
Lichtenstadt, 160

Index

Liege, 31
Limerick, 19, 46, 64, 178, 200, 205, 225
Lindley, 192
Lindsay, 47, 49
Lisburn, 72
Lismolin, 38, 39, 41, 42
Lismore, 89, 91, 174, 189
Listerlin, 27, 28
Liverpool, 49, 69, 107
Llangollen', 88
Llewelyn-Jones, 48
Lloyd, 14, 17, 36, 46, 74, 113, 133, 143
Lloyd-Verney, 113
Lockeen, 141
Lodge Joseph, 119
Loftus
   Adam, 140, 148
   Lt. Gen Wm., 140
   Mary Murphy, 157
   Rt. Hon. Nicholas, 146
   Sir Dudley, 150
   Sir Edward, 148, 154
   Sir Francis, 147
   Sir Nicholas, 150, 156
Loftus Hall, 90, 149, 151, 186
London, 2, 4, 8, 13, 21, 30, 31, 32, 33, 37, 47, 86, 93, 103, 104, 105, 108, 109, 111, 116, 120, 126, 129, 138, 160, 175, 179, 187, 188, 194, 200, 211, 222, 224, 227
Long Island, 159
Longford, 28, 172
Lovatt Pierce, 120
Lovett Pearce, 95, 97
Lowry, 43, 199
Lowther, 223
Lubbock, 93, 114
Lucas, 206, 208
Lucknow, 189
Lushington, 122
Lygon, 143
Lyons, 30

MacCoitir, 145
Macdonald, 23
Mackey, 184
MacManamy, 201
Maddoxtown, 11
Madigan, 46
Magee, 21
Magladry, 214
Mahon, 155, 212
Maidenhall, 50, 51, 52, 54, 55, 56, 57, 58
Malcomson, 1, 3, 4, 5, 6, 7, 8, 9, 10, 11
Mallen, 214
Marble Hill, 105
March
   Anne, 72
Margetson, 171
Marino, 129
Markes, 144
Marlborough
   Duke of, 12
Massy
   Lord, 46
Masterson, 149, 164
Mathew, v, 7, 68, 84
Matthews, 18
Mauger, 123
Maxwell, 23, 44, 49
May
   Sir Algernon, 137
Mayfield, 137
Maynard, 225
Mayo, 6, 40, 178
McCall, 219, 221
McCalmont, 47, 163, 164, 165, 166, 167
McClintock, 89
McDonnell
   Fr., 160
McGeown, 204
McGovern, 23
McKernan, 204
McNamara, 198

Index

Meath, 7, 54, 55, 56, 97, 121, 139, 145, 149, 150, 171, 191, 200, 208
Melbourne
    Lord, 176
Mendip, 7, 12
    Lord, 10
Meredith, 193, 195
Milbanke, 177
Minnigerode, 181
Mitchell, 180
Mitchelstown, 64
Molteno, 120
Molyneaux, 206
Monaghan, 58, 178
Mongolia, 23
Montagu, 224
Montague Wootten, 162
Moore, 23, 25, 26, 142, 170, 172, 188, 195, 199
Moran, 4, 6, 14
Morpeth, 225
Morres, 115, 117, 118, 120, 121, 122, 124
Morris, 105, 122, 197
Mossom, 118
Mostyn, 68
Mount Leinster, 23, 53
Mount Richard, 180
Mountgarret, 4, 5, 27, 40, 43, 60, 61, 62, 63, 64, 65, 66, 67, 68, 69, 70, 71, 73, 74, 75, 81, 85, 219, 223
Moutifort Longfield, 180
Mullingar, 54
Munich, 31, 162
Munn, 181
Munster, 79
Murphy
    Fr. John, 226
    John, 162
    Margaret, 196
    Rev. Fr., 180
Nasmyth, 45

Natal, 159, 210, 211
Neigham, 63
Nenagh, 77
New Ross, 5, 27, 44, 52, 61, 62, 65, 66, 85, 147, 156, 197
New York, 74, 202, 212, 214
Newcastle on Tyne, 10
Newenham, 225
Newfoundland, 139
Newly
    Anthony, 48
Newmarket, 164
Newport, 137, 211
Newrath, 198
Newton, 161
Nicholson, 137
Nidd Hall, 72
Norelands, 165
Normanton, 7, 9, 10
Nowlan, 53
O'Brien, 23, 55, 124, 171, 178
O'Byrne, 26, 65
    Feagh McHugh, 149
O'Byrnes, 64, 218
O'Cahan, 100
O'Callaghan, v, viii, 89, 91, 197
O'Connell, 32, 178, 179, 198, 199
O'Connor, 105, 107, 108, 111
O'Daly, 145
O'Doherty, 200
O'Flaherty, 195
O'Flahertys, 6
O'Gowan, 204
O'Grady, 122
O'Hara Trench, 212
O'Meaghers, 38
O'Neill, 65, 67, 85, 188
O'Nolans, 64, 81
O'Reilly, 80
O'Toole, 33, 89
Offaly, 96, 105, 141, 203, 212
Old Leighlin, 6
Oldgrange, 137

Index

Oldtown, 140
Omdurman, 119
Ontario, 214
Oporto, 31, 32
Oranmore and Browne, 180
Orleans
    Duke of, 109
Ormonde, 3, 4, 6, 17, 27, 28, 29, 38, 39, 40, 41, 42, 43, 44, 45, 54, 55, 61, 63, 64, 65, 66, 67, 68, 69, 70, 75, 76, 77, 78, 79, 80, 81, 82, 83, 84, 85, 86, 87, 88, 89, 92, 94, 130, 132, 135, 148, 171, 205, 218, 222, 225
Ormondes, 1, 8, 63, 79, 81, 88, 90, 116, 130, 193
Orpen, 202, 212
Osbourne, 221
Ossory, 28, 55, 56, 62, 63, 80, 81, 91, 122, 124, 129, 142, 218
Ottawa, 214
Otway, 41, 57, 99, 101, 102, 103, 104, 105, 107, 108, 111, 112, 128
Owen, 53
Oxford
    Lady, 177
Paget, 90
    Lord, 204
Pakenham, 215
Parsonstown, 139
Paulstown, 129
Peel, 104
Pegge, 200
Pelham, 63, 225
Penshurst, 106
Percy, 72, 106, 107, 114
Perry, 212
Persse, 167, 209
Perth, 91
Petit, 54
Petsopolous, 181
Petty, 94
Phelan, 57, 205
Philadelphia, 49

Phillipson, 223
Picadilly, 143, 202
Pietermaritzburg, 210
Pilltown, 170, 176
Pinnock, 204
Plowden, 26, 137
Plunkett, 159, 160
Plymouth, 47
Polestown, 61, 78, 80
Pollerton, 100
Pollock, 145
Polmonty, 63, 65
Pomeroy, 59
Ponsonby, 88, 94, 115, 151, 168, 169, 170, 171, 172, 173, 174, 176, 177, 180, 181
Pope
    Harriet, 20
Popesfield, 20
Portlaw, 137
Poulett, 65
Power, 5, 12, 32, 35, 58, 81, 180, 183, 184, 185, 186, 188, 190, 191, 192, 197, 210, 211
Powerscourt, 144, 170
Powerstown, 147, 154, 156
Poyntz, 84
Pratt, 121, 122, 124
Prendergast, 128, 135, 189, 204, 218
Preston, 7, 66, 83, 109, 113, 223
Priestown, 55
Prims, 54
Princess Amelia, 176
Prior, 4, 47, 54, 89, 129, 143, 157, 176, 178, 184, 217, 220, 226, 227
Prittie, 174
Proctor, 118
Prosser, 45
Purdon, 150
Purser, 23
Pym, 124
Queen Alexandra, 22, 91, 135

Index

Queen Elizabeth, 27, 28, 39, 63, 80, 82, 96, 106, 150, 164
Queenstown, 36
Quirk, 214
Radcliffe, 213
Raglan
  Baron, 179
  Lord, 45
Rangoon, 48
Ratcliffe, 222
Rathdonnell, 59, 89
Rathdrum, 149
Rathfarnham, 149, 150
Rathgarvan, 3, 10
Rathmines, 85
Rawson, 72, 73
Raynar, 74
Read
  Anne, 153
Reade, 122
Redman, 41, 42
Redmond, 117, 118, 151
Redondella, 87
Repton, 22
Reynolds, 162, 225
Rhodesia, 200
Richards, 17
Richardson, 21, 22, 214
Richfield, 154, 159
Richmond, 86, 222
  Duke of, 176
Ridgeway, 218
Ringwood, 7, 8, 12, 99, 130
Rinuccini, 67, 85, 94
Ripon, 223, 225
Robartes, 12, 13
  Lord, 12
Robbins, 20
Robertson, 47, 147, 206
Robinson, 139
Rockett's Castle, 137
Rockfield, 55, 99
Roehampton, 176
Romilly, 106
Roper, 216, 217
Rossenara, 122
Rothe, 3, 19, 28, 29, 30, 36, 117, 130, 188, 193
  Richard, 3
Rothwell, 55, 56
Rourke, 11
Rower, 5, 7, 8, 11, 81
Rubens, 9
Rush
  Barbara, 145
Russborough, 19, 120
Russell
  Lord John, 179
Russi, 48
Rutland, 107, 112
Ryves, 118
Salisbury, 200
Samuelson, 72
Sandford, 135, 136
Sankey, 160, 172
Saurin, 133
Savage, 8, 44, 141, 200
Saxe Coburg, 90
Scotland, 138, 162, 210, 222
Scott, 114, 171, 208
Searle, 182
Sebastopol, 10, 46
Seftenberg Ross, 210
Segrave Daly, 159
Segrave –Daly, 161
Seigne, 191
Sellers, 66
Seymour, 13
Shanbally, 91
Shandrome, 195
Shannon
  Lord, 174
Shaw, 53
Shee, 16, 28, 44, 69

Index

Sheffield, 82
Shelly, 176
Shillelogher, 94
Shinrone, 141
Short
   James, 48
Shortall, 205
Shortalls, 39, 53, 205
Shrewsbury, 33, 78
Shuttleworth, 22
Sil Brain, 26
Sillery, 180
Simms, 214
Skehana, 217
Skinner, 179
Slane, 31, 166
Sleator, 199
Sligo, 45, 103, 106, 164, 201
Smith, 70, 90, 167, 178, 179
Smithwick, 191, 193, 194, 195, 196, 197, 198, 199, 200
   Edmond, 198
   Peter, 197, 201
Smyth, 7
Smythe, 106
Solly, 132, 165
Somerset, 14
South Africa, 36, 74, 122, 192, 210, 211
Southey, 171
Southwark, 17
Southwell, 225, 226
Southwold, 162
Spencer, 12, 65, 107, 176
   Earl, 176
Springfield, 17, 18
Sri Lanka, 59
St. Canice's Cathedral, 21, 63, 85, 90, 142, 196
St. George, 139, 202, 203, 204, 205, 206, 207, 208, 209, 210, 211, 212, 214, 215
St. Lawrence, 97, 209, 220

Stafford, 180
Staffordstown, 55
Staines, 28
Steele, 55
Stewart, 118, 119, 211
Stoneen, 191
Storey, 182
Strancally Castle, 46
Strangford, 106
Stuart, 48, 155
Stubber, 189
Suffolk, 162
Sugden, 109
Sullivan, 198
Summerhill, 53
Surrey, 14, 17, 48, 141, 215
Sussex, 48, 148, 212, 215
Sutcliffe, 211
Sutherland, 111, 125
Swift, 96, 120, 187, 204
Switzerland, 114
Sysonby, 172
Talbot, 33, 34, 78, 111
Tallaght, 225
Tallow, 23
Talmadge, 212
Tancred, 74
Taylor, 44, 214
Templederry, 41
Tennypark House, 122
Thomastown, 4, 8, 11, 12, 61, 68, 95, 97, 136, 137, 141, 185, 191, 218
Thomond, 55, 81
Thorneton, 221, 222
Thornhill, 99
Thurles, 41, 78, 84
Tichborne, 106
Tighe, 154, 172, 179, 188
Tillerton, 212
Tinnehinch, 65
Tintern, 3, 63, 150, 164
Tipperary, 7, 11, 22, 38, 39, 40, 41, 54, 55, 58, 63, 68, 77, 78, 79, 82, 83, 84,

241

Index

85, 87, 88, 89, 90, 91, 103, 110, 116, 117, 118, 137, 171, 174, 184, 189, 195, 200, 227
Titchener, 162
Toronto, 118
Torrington, 107
Tottenham, 139, 149, 152
Touchet, 68
Tovey, 214
Townshend, 44, 138, 174
Towton, 79
Trafalgar, 206
Transvaal, 211
Troyswood, 37
Tullaherin, 14, 53, 192
Tullamine, 184
Tullamore, 172
Tullow, 65, 78, 149, 186
Tullowphelim, 82, 83
Turrock, 205
Tyndall, 118
Tyquin, 141
Tyrone, 43, 58, 65, 97, 122, 153, 154, 212
Uppercourt, 118
Urlingford, 28, 67
Usher, 137, 203
Van Dyck, 9
Vanden-Bempde-Johnstone, 13
Vanderplank, 211
Vaux
  Baron, 68
Vevey, 114
Vienna, 31, 52, 204
Villiers-Stuart, 189
Voltaire, 50
von Buttlar-Elderberg, 75
Wade, 191
Walker, 209, 211
Wall
  family, 94
  William, 30
Wallace, 144

Wallop, 164
Wallstein, 26
Walmesley, 199
Walsh, 28, 30, 169, 176, 185, 191, 217
Walshe, 28
Walsingham, 10
Wandesforde, 44, 45, 88, 89, 216, 217, 218, 219, 220, 221, 222, 223, 224, 225, 227
Warden
  Anne, 128
  Colonel, 128
Waring, 17, 18
Warner, 199
Warren, 67, 150, 208
Washington
  George, 155
Waterford, 5, 7, 16, 17, 23, 46, 70, 103, 111, 120, 125, 129, 137, 150, 180, 184, 185, 186, 188, 189, 197, 210
Waterloo, 55, 109, 168, 174
Waterville, 55
Weldon, 100
Wellington, 104, 171
Wemyss, 6, 9, 18, 104
Wentworth, 65, 218, 221
Westcourt, 8
Westgate, 215
Westmeath, 54, 169
Westmerland', 117
Westminster, 7, 31, 86, 87, 91, 103, 104
Westmoreland
  Earl of, 179
Wexford, iii, 4, 18, 26, 33, 34, 40, 54, 61, 62, 63, 65, 66, 68, 73, 85, 90, 116, 122, 132, 139, 149, 150, 151, 152, 153, 154, 159, 170, 185, 186, 191, 193, 195, 200, 209, 218, 226
Weymouth, 107
Wharton, 149, 150
Whitby, 137
White, 18, 27, 64, 79, 100, 170

242

Index

White Abbey, 163
White-Baker, 18
Whiteside, 126
Whiteswall, 27
Whittaker, 218
Whittys, 151
Whitwell, 55
Wicklow, 7, 27, 120, 122, 149, 150, 151, 169, 172, 185, 186, 198, 207, 218
William
   Laura, 74
William of Orange, 87, 94, 127, 204
Williams, 14, 19, 141, 198, 211
Wilmar, 137
Wilmore, 181
Wilson, 74, 139
Wilton, 66
Winch, 212

Winchilsea
   Earl of, 36
Windward Isles, 189
Wingfield, 144, 170
Wolseley, 206
Wood, 164, 186, 204
Wood Ditton, 164
Woodsgift, 139, 202, 204, 206, 208, 209, 214
Wordsworth, 171
Wright, 46, 96, 120, 121, 125
Wyatt, 102
Wynne, 45
Yeats, 112
Yeomanstown, 31
Yorkshire, 3, 60, 72, 73, 218, 220, 224
Yugoslavia, 52
Zoffany, 103

Picture Gallery

Inlaid Writing Desk at Desart

Second writing desk – Desart

The Marquess and Marchioness of Antrim
(The Marquess was married to Laetitia De Montmorency)

St. George Townhouse in Carrig on Shannon